BoatWorks™

BoatWorks

Sailboat Maintenance, Repair, and Improvement Advice You Can't Get Anywhere Else

McGraw Hill

International Marine / McGraw-Hill

Camden, Maine • New York • Chicago • San Francisco • Lisbon • London • Madrid
• Mexico City • Milan • New Delhi • San Juan • Seoul • Singapore • Sydney • Toronto

1 2 3 4 5 6 7 8 9 RRD SHEN 9 8 7

© 2008 by *SAIL* Magazine

Library of Congress Control Number: 2007936352

ISBN 978-0-07-149707-7
MHID 0-07-149707-2

Questions regarding the content of this book should be addressed to
International Marine
P.O. Box 220
Camden, ME 04843
www.internationalmarine.com

Questions regarding the ordering of this book should be addressed to
The McGraw-Hill Companies
Customer Service Department
P.O. Box 547
Blacklick, OH 43004
Retail customers: 1-800-262-4729
Bookstores: 1-800-722-4726

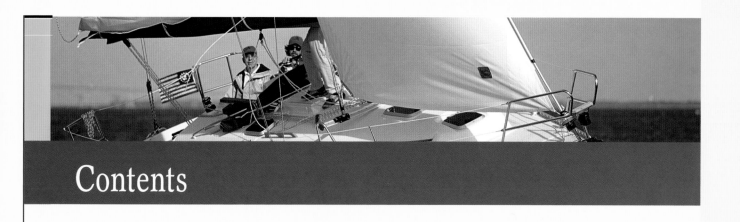

Contents

CONTENTS

Contents

vii

Introduction

BoatWorks started, as so many grand schemes do, over a beer. *SAIL*'s then publisher, Eric Cressy, and I were bemoaning the fact that we weren't able to devote as many pages as we would like to our common passion—working on older fiberglass boats. The solution, I suggested, would be to start up a magazine devoted to just that.

We already knew who our readers would be. They are all those sailors who love communing with their boats as much as sailing them. Some enjoy the process of maintaining, repairing, and upgrading their beloved vessels. Others simply cannot afford to pay up to $80 an hour to have professionals do what any weekend warrior with a little time, inspiration, and the proper instruction can do as well. And still others may not do the work themselves but nevertheless want to know what's involved. In short, our readership is the entire spectrum of boatowners and sailors. After all, a boat starts to need maintenance the moment it is commissioned for the first time.

We knew we had the in-house expertise to put such a magazine together. Our then senior editor, Charles J. Doane, was in the middle of a comprehensive refit of a classic fiberglass sailboat. I had spent 4 years gutting and re-furbishing a big wooden boat, replacing every system within its beautiful mahogany hull. We had such savvy contributors as Don Casey, Nigel Calder, Aussie Bray, and Mark Corke to call on. Between us all, we had an unmatched depth of knowledge just waiting to be plumbed.

We determined right away that *Boat-Works*—named after a long-running technical feature in *SAIL*—would be different from all other boating magazines. I had long envied the ability of do-it-yourself magazines for homeowners, gardeners, and others to illustrate projects with detailed, full-color, step-by-step photography. This was something that the space constraints of a monthly magazine devoted to *all* aspects of boating—not just to DIY projects—rendered impossible. But why should the boatowner not have the benefit of this approach to technical writing? We decided to make clearly photographed, easily followed, step-by-step explanations of both simple and complex projects the cornerstone of our new magazine. All photography would be in color. It was something no other boating magazine did at the time, and we still do it better than anyone else.

When Mark Corke brought his considerable photographic and technical expertise to the magazine after the first is-sue was published, our path was made clear. A good many of the how-to and step-by-step articles in the magazine are written and photographed by our editorial staff, based on work we carry out on our own boats, and no other boating magazine can match that. Others might write about it, but we go out and do it.

We are also fortunate to have an informed and vocal readership, many of whom have taken up pen and camera and contributed their own articles to *BoatWorks*; you'll find some great examples in this book. Our readers have also given us great suggestions for topics to cover.

All of which helps account for the eclectic brew of topics in this book. We have made no attempt to cover every aspect of every subject, because that would be impossible, as we've found over the last 3 years. Rather, we've cast our net widely to come up with a mix of hard information, step-by-step improvements, uncommon solutions to common problems, and the odd project that's just wacky enough to keep life interesting. We hope you have as much fun reading it as we have putting it all together.

Peter Nielsen
Editor, *BoatWorks* and *SAIL* magazines
June 2007

Meet Your Boat

ere's a chicken-and-egg question for you: Does a good knowledge of boat design and construction help you plan and carry out work on your boat, or does working on the boat improve your knowledge of boat design and construction?

Whichever angle you approach this from, the answer is yes. The more you play with your boat, take things apart, replace odd bits and pieces, and make cosmetic and even structural repairs and improvements, the more you learn about how your boat was designed and built. Similarly, if you study the elements of design and construction—the way a hull, appendages, systems, rig, and sails work together, and how different construction techniques and philosophies affect strength and longevity—you will soon acquire a growing appreciation of the kind of maintenance and the sorts of problems that lie ahead of you.

No one is better at explaining these relationships than Nigel Calder, so it's not surprising that he figures so prominently in this section. He takes an in-depth look at hull design that will be of great value to those of us looking to change our boats or just better understand why they behave as they do. He also provides some great hints and tips about how to avoid trouble with older boats.

Things to Watch for When Buying an Older Boat

Even if well maintained, older boats are apt to need some special attention.

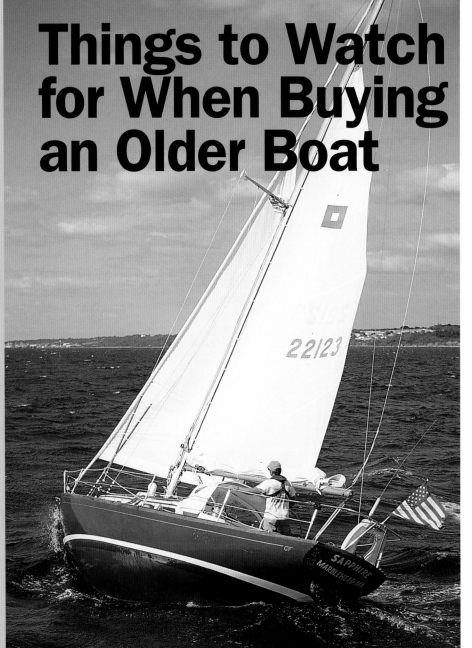

this case, the crew had to struggle with rigging, mechanical, and electronic issues—all common problems on older boats.

Old rigs

Sailing rigs, like anything else, get old and wear out. The principal culprits are flexing and a steady increase in the number of "fatigue cycles" the rig is subjected to. If a rig is set up properly, toggles and similar fixtures absorb much of the flexing and the rig lasts a long time. But often the aging process is accelerated by improper installations that result in "hard" spots. Other issues include the wear on moving parts, notably clevis pins and the holes through which they pass, and, above all else, corrosion.

Most corrosion results from the nearly universal use of stainless steel in end fittings and the hardware to which they are attached (chainplates, tangs, and the fasteners holding these in place). Wherever this stainless steel is in contact with stagnant water, corrosion is a possibility. The warmer the climate, the more likely it is to occur, and the faster the rate at which it will continue. The two most common trouble spots are the lower terminals on wire rigging (moisture wicks down the wire into the terminal) and the chainplates or fasteners where they pass through decks, especially cored decks (moisture gets trapped in the deck). With terminals, the corrosion is generally self-evident (you'll see rust stains and hairline cracks); with chainplates and through-deck fasteners, it generally is not.

Some things on a 10-year-old rig should obviously be checked. All clevis pins should be withdrawn, and both the pins and the holes through which they pass should be checked for wear and deformation. Look for hairline cracks around the holes, for cracking and other signs of damage to the rigging terminals, and for any loose strands where wire exits rigging terminals (this is the most likely place for a wire failure). In particular, look for signs of corrosion.

The points where tangs contact the mast are also potential trouble spots.

recently heard about what should have been a routine delivery up the eastern seabord on a newly purchased secondhand sailboat. Before setting sail, the crew noticed that the rig had no cotter pins, which could easily have brought the mast down. They replaced the pins. Also missing was the hardware for the staysail-sheet leads, so they jury-rigged them. Once out at sea the boat got caught in nasty weather. The crew dropped the staysail while cranking the engine, and the sheet got loose and wrapped around the propeller. Smoke began to pour out of the engine room. The skipper got thrown across the boat and was injured. The VHF radio, it turned out, did not transmit properly. Luckily, the boat was close enough to the New Jersey coast that the crew was able to call for assistance on a cell phone.

It's amazing how, in the wrong conditions, a number of relatively minor problems can cascade into a major crisis. In

The rig should be checked very carefully. Discolored wire (left) is an early warning sign. Through-deck chainplates (below) always warrant a thorough inspection. Make sure that all turnbuckles and clevis pins (right) are well pinned—split rings can work themselves loose.

Photos this page by Peter Nielsen

All bolts should be withdrawn and the bolt and mast wall carefully inspected. Also spin the sheaves at the masthead to make sure they are running freely and that the bushings are not worn. If the mast is keel-stepped, check for corrosion of the mast heel. If the mast track is external, inspect every one of its fasteners to ensure they are tight (a single loose fastener can cause the whole sail to hang up). Spend some time on the gooseneck fitting—look especially for excessive play, signs of deformation, cracking, and damaged welds.

The hard questions on old boats are whether the through-deck chainplates and fasteners should be pulled and whether the standing rigging should be be replaced regardless of its apparent condition. The safe answer is always yes, but it depends somewhat on where the boat has been kept (corrosion is far less likely in a cold climate than in a hot one) and on how catastrophic suddenly losing the rig over the side might be. For a weekend cruiser on a limited budget who never strays far from support services, it is strictly a judgment call.

Furling gear can give you plenty of grief if it's not maintained properly.

Old machinery

Modern diesel engines are incredibly reliable. An engine that has been properly cared for should be good for anywhere from 5,000 to 10,000 hours of running time. So always look first for evidence of consistent maintenance—a log of some kind and, in particular, regular oil and fuel-filter changes.

Assuming good maintenance, the principal concern is that the engine has aged prematurely as a result of being repeatedly run for short periods of time, so that it never warms up properly. Or it may often have been run for long hours at low loads, such as when charging batteries at anchor. Both practices may foul valves and pistons with carbon, resulting in a loss of compression. If an engine is hard to start when cold, this often indicates compression problems. When inspecting an older boat, try to get to it on a cold day before the owner has cranked the engine and warmed it up. If it is slow to start, remove the exhaust from the water-lift muffler and look for carbon accumulation. There should be no more than a light film. This is the easiest way to get some idea of whether there is carbon fouling elsewhere.

You might also pump a sample of diesel from the very bottom of the fuel tank (I carry a small pump just for this purpose when inspecting boats). The fuel system is the single most expensive component of a diesel engine, and if it has been receiving dirty fuel there is some risk of damage. The sample will give a good idea of the state of things. If it is filthy, check both the primary and secondary fuel filters. If the secondary filter is really dirty, you should be concerned. On your own boat, it is a good idea to sample the bottom of the fuel tank at least once a year and remove any water and sediment that you find.

and whether or not the cutless bearing is in good shape (the boat needs to be out of the water to check this—pulling sideways on the propeller, you should find not more than $\frac{1}{16}''$ of play in the shaft). Also check the steering gear (look for excessive play, worn sheaves and cables, undue flexing of mounting brackets, and damaged or missing rudder stops); various pumps (bilge and freshwater); the seacocks (very often they are frozen open); and all hose clamps (which often have corroded screws and need replacing).

quate or moisture-saturated insulation. Correcting this may require rebuilding the box, which is labor-intensive.

Finally, if a boat has metal tanks—fuel or water—you should check them carefully, especially if the tanks can get splashed with bilgewater. While some tanks last decades, the incidence of failure after 10 years or so is high.

Old electrical systems

I've left the worst for last. It's a sad fact that many boats come from their builders with marginal wiring harnesses. Considering the substantial electrical loads most people now take for granted, the harness on an older boat is rarely up to the task. A significant amount of rewiring is almost always a good idea; in the worst case this may amount to pretty much ripping out the old harness and starting over again.

This, of course, depends on what you intend to do with the boat. If you want to add a large battery bank, a high-output alternator and multi-step voltage regulator, an inverter, a mass of navigation electronics, plus sprinkle halogen lights throughout the interior, you're in for a lot of relatively expensive work. However, if you are one of the dying breed who prefer to keep it simple, what you've got may do just fine.

If you're keeping the existing harness, look for corrosion (especially at terminals, fuses, and fuse blocks) and overcurrent protection (fuses and circuit breakers should have the correct amp rating). Many older boats have a mass of added-on circuits that were untidily installed with inadequate (or nonexistent)

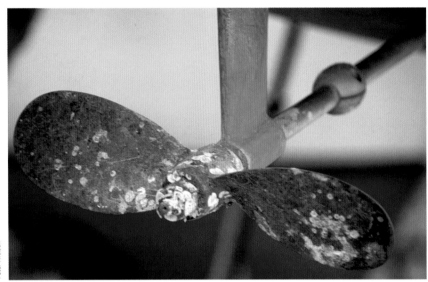

Peter Nielsen

Check for play in the cutless bearing—and a clean propeller is more efficient.

Often the engine itself is in good shape, but the peripheral systems—the cooling system, the exhaust, and the mounts—may be showing their age. The expensive items here are the heat exchanger and, to some extent, the mounts. If the heat exchanger has a zinc anode (not all do), pull it and take a look at it. If the zinc is more than half gone—or worse, all gone—this indicates the heat exchanger may have corrosion problems. Check the mounts to see if they are excessively soft. Unfortunately, it's hard to define "excessive," as it varies quite a bit, but if the mounts are spongy and the engine can be jiggled around, they are likely to need replacement. This is moderately expensive, especially if you have to pay for the labor, as it can be time-consuming.

You should also look for excessive play in the throttle and transmission controls, the state of the shaft seal,

If a boat has refrigeration that is more than 10 years old, there is a good chance it is not in good shape. In all likelihood, the icebox also has inade-

It pays you to check the engine and its ancillaries very carefully.

overcurrent protection. These unprotected circuits can start a serious fire in a matter of seconds if there is a short. What is best on an older boat is to spend a couple of days tracing all the wiring, creating a wiring diagram and noting cable sizes and the location (and amp rating) of all overcurrent-protection devices to make sure they are in the correct place and properly rated (for more on this, see my *Boatowner's Mechanical and Electrical Manual* and similar books). This is the best way to get to know any electrical system.

Also see if the wiring in the boat is tinned, as opposed to untinned. The only places to check this are where there are terminals with strands of the wire in the cable showing. Straight copper wire will be tarnished; tinned wire has a silvery look. Tinned wiring is far better than untinned, which sometimes wicks moisture up its strands, creating corrosion and resistance. Most American boatbuilders now use tinned wiring, but some European builders are behind in this respect, in which case the harness even on a relatively new boat may

be in poor shape. If you add new wiring, always make sure it is tinned. The best general-purpose marine cabling has written somewhere on its insulation "BC5W2" and/or "Boat Cable." Ideally, it is also labeled "Oil Resistant."

Is it worth the trouble?

This is a rather depressing catalog of potential failure points—quite an expensive one as well. The point is not to scare you, but to make you more alert. Some older boats have been immaculately maintained and are ready to head to sea as is, but most have at least one or two significant problems waiting to be discovered. In many respects, regardless of the level of maintenance, the more complicated and sophisticated the systems aboard, the greater the likelihood of problems.

This leads me to a couple of general conclusions about buying older boats. The first is that you should look for one that is structurally sound, but be willing to accept systems that are clearly a mess, recognizing that they will be

Sometimes signs of trouble are obvious, sometimes they are less so.

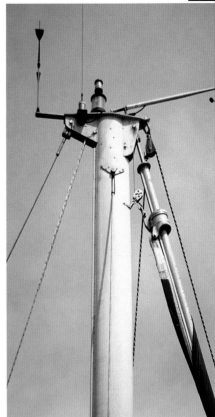

This mast has old-fashioned, reliable tangs, but they still need inspecting. Right: The furling genoa halyard is correctly led through a block so it doesn't wrap around the headstay when the sail is furled, but the spinnaker halyard is badly chafed. Below: Early signs of corrosion on the mast heel. This bears watching.

ripped out and a fresh start made. The purchase price should, of course, reflect this. At the end of the day, you'll end up with mostly new systems, but it will likely take months of work and maybe tens of thousands of dollars to get there.

The second thought is to look for a sound boat with minimal systems and keep it that way. A fair amount of what is spent these days on retrofits, notably on electrical systems, electronics, and cosmetics, results from a desire to have all the latest gadgets and gizmos and to have the boat look smart. Much of it is simply not necessary. I have inspected 40-year-old boats with all-bronze fittings and minimal systems that are still in excellent shape and providing their owners with more fun than boats with ten times the systems. Even today I still meet people in far-flung anchorages on lovely older boats with minimal systems that cost maybe $10,000 to $20,000.

Finally, if you already have an older boat and intend to keep it, you should occasionally give it a detailed inspection, zealously noting its faults and deciding whether or not they need urgent attention. It is easy to get used to working around problems until you no longer see them. In almost all dismasting

cases, for example, subsequent inspections reveal telltale rust stains that should have alerted the owner to the potential for failure, but were consistently ignored. This is why the majority of dismastings occur in less than 15 knots of wind.

Another example is the delivery crew I mentioned earlier. They were aware of a number of problems on their boat. Once they replaced the missing cotter

pins, none of the other problems seemed important enough to postpone the voyage. Individually, they were not. As a somewhat impatient person, I suspect I would also have pressed on were I in their situation. But the sea, unfortunately, has a nasty way of compounding small problems until they became a big problem considerably greater than the sum of its parts. It always pays to err on the side of caution.

Conducting a Mini-Survey

Photos by Peter Nielsen

As the old saying goes, you have to kiss a lot of frogs before you find your prince. Or princess, if you're talking about a boat. It's all too easy to be swept off your feet by a sweet sheerline and a curvaceous transom, but what ugly flaws lie concealed under that shiny skin? Once you've made the final decision to buy a boat, you will, if it is worth anything at all, have it surveyed. Apart from anything else, the insurance company will insist on it, and you'll almost certainly be able to knock the asking price down enough to cover the surveyor's fees. But even before you go as far as phoning a surveyor, a few simple checks can give you a good idea of whether the relationship is worth pursu-

ing—or whether the object of your affections will empty your bank account and break your heart. There are many obvious trouble spots on a sailboat, and if you know what to look for, you'll be able to work out for yourself whether to walk away quietly or make another date.

We asked surveyor Norm LeBlanc of Beverly, Massachusetts, to walk us

Dream boats or nightmare scenarios? Keep your eyes open. Inset: Norm LeBlanc.

around a few boats and point out some signs of neglect and wear and tear that'll take more than some polish to cover up.

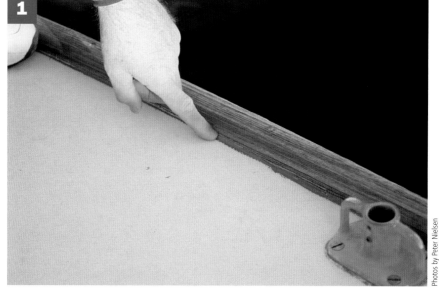

1. A wood toerail bedded onto a fiberglass deck. Over the years the wood has decayed where it meets the deck, and an attempt has been made to fill the growing gap with mastic. The toerail will have to come off, and who knows what horrors lie beneath? Corroded fastenings, at the least, and maybe water in the deck core.

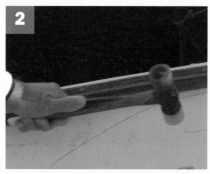

2. "Soft-deck syndrome"—deck delamination—is common on older boats. Water leaks through fastener holes and rots the core material, usually plywood or balsa. By sounding with a wood or plastic hammer, you'll be able to ascertain if the deck is in good condition. It's like tapping on drywall to find a stud—the note changes unmistakably when you go from hollow to solid.

3. Here the deck felt spongy under foot and showed the telltale signs of stress cracking, so we didn't even bother with the hammer. Repairing a delaminated deck is a time-consuming job, and you had better be sure the boat is worth the labor and expense.

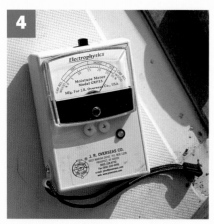

4. Moisture meters can give misleading information in the wrong hands, but they can save a lot of tapping. The plywood core in this cabintop is soaked where water has seeped in from around deck fittings. Many builders used plywood backing plates for deck hardware, and if water gets to them they will eventually rot and swell.

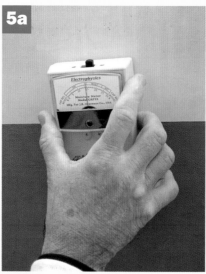

5. When a cored hull is good, it is very good. When it goes bad, it is very bad, to the point where repairs can be prohibitively expensive. On this 15-year-old boat the meter shows different moisture content just a few inches apart, above (a) and below (b) the waterline.

6. Over the years, water has soaked the foam core inside this rudder. The water expands when it freezes and forces the fiberglass skin away from the core. Here, the laminate has begun to split along the leading edge. This will be an expensive fix.

7. Chainplates are another potential source of worry. This one is not secured to a bulkhead or to the hull and has begun to pull up through the deck. The core is likely to be wet around the chainplate, and this shows signs of being an awkward repair job.

8. It looks as though the owner of this boat has had problems with his through-deck chainplates. He fabricated these from stainless steel and bolted them to the outside of the hull. Modifications like this can affect the boat's resale value.

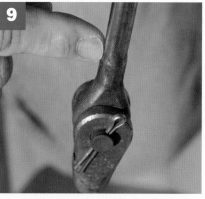

9. Sometimes, cracks in rigging terminals and turnbuckles are hard to detect, requiring much anointing with crack-testing dyes. Other times, like in this photo, they are all too obvious. The remainder of the standing rigging must automatically be suspect.

10. A rusty cast-iron keel—unsightly, but easily fixed at the expense of a weekend's work. Don't let this put you off.

11. Impact damage to the leading edge of an encapsulated lead ballast keel. There may be more to this than meets the eye; the impact may have caused invisible cracks in the laminate, or the laminates may have begun to separate. On the other hand, the damage might be restricted to what you see here. An expert should look at it.

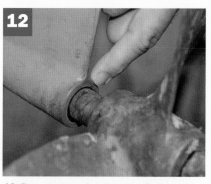

12. Prop struts and cutless bearings are prime suspects for wear and tear. Give the propeller a good wiggle; there should be virtually no play in the cutless bearing and no signs of movement in the strut.

13. If you look down the companionway and see this, walk away and don't look back. This is not to say such a boat can't be resurrected, but you could pour hundred of hours into it and it will still be worth only a couple of thousand dollars.

14. There are signs of water leaking out of this keel-to-hull joint—not a good omen. It may have come from inside, if water has been left standing in the bilge for a long time. If water has been getting to the keelbolts, they may have corroded and should be inspected.

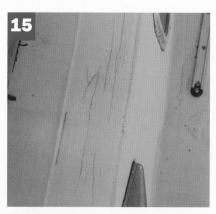

15. Gelcoat cracks are common in older boats. They're caused by movement in the laminate, usually in highly stressed or trafficked areas—for instance, you often see them radiating out from spreader bases or around the edges of a deck or cockpit sole. It is possible to open them out slightly and fill them with new gelcoat before painting the affected area, but this is usually only a short-term solution.

16. Gelcoat crazing is not necessarily a sign of structural weakness—often quite the opposite. Usually it happens because the builder applied too thick a layer of gelcoat, which is why you'll often see crazing even on boats from highly reputable builders. It's usually not structurally significant, but it is unsightly. If you can't live with it, the only answer is to paint the boat.

Thanks to **Norm LeBlanc**, tel. 978-774-5060.

Hull Shape and Boat Performance

Nigel Calder

A generation ago, many boats, especially cruising boats, had long keels and attached rudders. The propeller was in an aperture in the rudder. The boat's cross section had a wineglass shape. There were long overhangs fore and aft. Such traditional full-keel designs were popular for many years.

During the 1970s, '80s, and '90s, the keel's forefoot was progressively cut away. A separate skeg supported the rudder, and the space between the keel and the skeg grew larger as they each grew smaller. The skeg was first re-duced to a partial skeg and then was eliminated altogether to leave a free-standing (spade) rudder. During the process the boat's overhangs were trimmed and became quite short, if not eliminated altogether. The result of these changes is a "contemporary boat."

In its most extreme form, the con-temporary boat has a deep, narrow, ver-tical fin keel and a spade rudder, both of which are suspended beneath a hull with an almost flat bottom and with a plumb (vertical) stem. The propeller is supported by a strut or incorporated in a saildrive leg. The contemporary boat is much lighter than its forebears and looks nothing like them, especially be-low the waterline.

For a given displacement, the evolu-tion from a long keel and attached rud-der to a fin keel and spade rudder has dramatically reduced the wetted surface area. Given that the wetted surface area creates the primary resistance that must be overcome in light winds (the predominant condition experienced by most sailors), any reduction results in an improvement in performance. The re-sulting reduction in lateral surface area,

This racer shows all the attributes of a modern performance boat—narrow waterline beam, high flared topsides, minimal wetted surface, and a deep fin keel carrying most of its ballast in a bulb.

The opposite extreme. The Folkboat exemplifies traditional thinking in cruising-boat design—pretty overhangs, low topsides, a full keel and protected rudder.

Photos by Peter Nielsen

TRADITIONAL HULL

wineglass hull shape
gives a gentle ride at sea

long
overhangs
add length
when heeled

greater
wetted surface
area affects speed

rudder is
well protected

long keel gives good course stability

CONTEMPORARY HULL

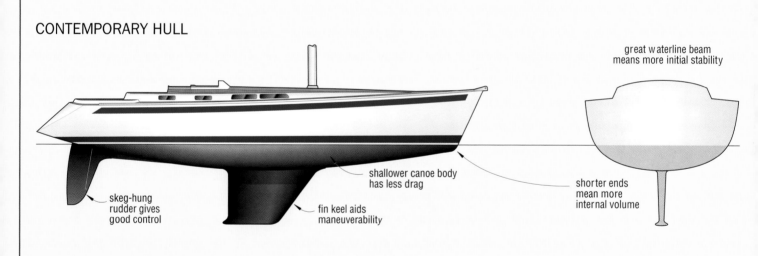

great waterline beam
means more initial stability

shallower canoe body
has less drag

shorter ends
mean more
internal volume

skeg-hung
rudder gives
good control

fin keel aids
maneuverability

PERFORMANCE HULL

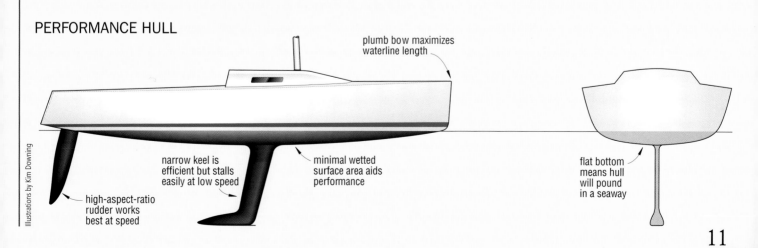

plumb bow maximizes
waterline length

narrow keel is
efficient but stalls
easily at low speed

minimal wetted
surface area aids
performance

flat bottom
means hull
will pound
in a seaway

high-aspect-ratio
rudder works
best at speed

This cruising boat's full underbody indicates a moderate to heavy displacement, which gives it the ability to carry stores for extended voyaging. The hull shape will give a comfortable ride at sea.

The longer the passage, the more unpleasant the conditions encountered, and the smaller the crew, the more likely it is that a sacrifice of nominal performance will not, in fact, result in any loss of actual performance: There are plenty of examples of traditional boats making better passage times in heavy conditions than nominally faster, lighter boats when lightweight boats become too uncomfortable or too much work to sail to their full potential. The crew of the more traditional boat is also likely to arrive less bruised and better rested.

Gunkholing

Aside from comfort and security, several considerations related to draft and running aground may lead to a willingness to sacrifice performance. Performance to windward can always be enhanced by lowering the ballast and increasing the draft. However, my family enjoys exploring regions with relatively restricted depths. Some of our favorites include the northern waters of Belize and the Rio Dulce in Guatemala (both limited to 6-foot draft), parts of the Bahamas, and our home waters in Maine. Thus I prefer boats with a draft of 6 feet or less, regardless of the impact on performance.

Groundings

What about the keel shape? The most efficient shape for upwind work is a nar-

which creates resistance to turning, also improves responsiveness and maneuverability.

If you add a fine entry for upwind work and a flat bottom aft for off-the-wind speed, much of the time a contemporary boat will outperform a more traditional boat on all points of sail. And yet slower underbodies are still popular with many sailors, especially those who go offshore. Is this simply nostalgia?

Theory versus practice

A contemporary boat has a less comfortable motion than a traditional boat in many sea states. If its limited load-carrying capability is exceeded, its performance suffers disproportionately. It generally has poorer directional stability than a traditional boat. This makes steering tiring, increases an autopilot's energy consumption, and may make using a windvane difficult or impossible. The contemporary boat will likely not heave-to quietly in nasty weather and will need to be helmed continuously. With a shorthanded crew this can be a safety hazard. In survival conditions, the contemporary boat is inherently more likely to capsize than the traditional boat.

In declining order of suitability, the contemporary boat is best for racing, for sailing in relatively protected waters, for coastal cruising, and for offshore cruising. In some respects, the farther offshore a boat is intended to sail and the

more shorthanded the crew, the stronger the argument for sacrificing performance in favor of comfort, directional stability, ease of handling, and security.

Right: This rudder is protected by a full-depth skeg. Its lack of balance (area ahead of the rudderstock) may mean the boat is heavy on the helm.

Center: Semibalanced spade rudders like this one provide excellent control at speed but are vulnerable to damage.

Far right: A typical long-keeler's rudder—no balance, but well sheltered behind the keel. The prop is also protected from stray lines or nets.

row, vertical, foil-shaped fin similar to an airplane wing. In terms of the way I use a boat, this is a terrible design. The corollary to my desire to explore relatively thin waters is that I run aground a great deal. If you hit something hard with a vertical fin, you stop dead. People get thrown across the boat and may be hurt. Tremendous shock loads are transmitted to the keel root (the point at which it attaches to the hull) and its supporting structures within the boat. Damage is likely. Even if you don't run aground, if a fishing net or lobster-pot warp gets wrapped around a vertical fin, especially one with a torpedo-type bulb at its base, disentangling it can be a devil of a job.

So I require that the leading edge of a keel must curve back from the underside of the hull in a way that will reduce the shock of a grounding and shed nets and lines. This results in a longer keel (good for directional stability) with a substantially larger root (which spreads shock loads over a larger area of the hull). If the keel stub is designed with a step or an angled face, shock loads will be transmitted to the hull rather than just the keelbolts.

At different times in boats with fuller keels we have run over floating telephone poles and hit rocks at up to 8 knots with nothing more than cosmetic damage. In a contemporary boat the same incidents would almost certainly cause damage requiring an immediate haulout.

I also like to have a longer keel designed so that, if necessary, we can lay the boat up against a dock at high tide and let it dry out without the risk of it toppling over on its ends.

Finally, because of my propensity to run aground, I have a strong antipathy to wings on keels. They make it extremely hard to refloat a boat (if you heel the boat, which is the traditional way of reducing draft, the wings dig in).

Every one of my requirements for the keel has some negative impact on performance. Clearly, they are somewhat idiosyncratic, but my point is that there can be all kinds of good reasons for compromising performance. Each individual boatowner must determine his own priorities.

Rudder balance versus damage control

When it comes to rudders, there is nothing quite like the thrill of sailing a fast boat with a balanced spade rudder that has fingertip response and control. I love it on other people's boats but have always done without it on my own.

Again, because I like to nose around in shallow water, my overriding concern is the difficulty of building a spade rudder strong enough to withstand a serious impact. This is because of the shock loading that occurs at the point where the rudderstock enters the hull. Any kind of a skeg, partial or full, introduces at least one and sometimes two more shock- and load-absorbing points of support.

With a full skeg, you get the most potential support for and protection of the rudder. Unfortunately, a full skeg requires all of the rudder to be located aft of its turning axis, resulting in an unbalanced rudder. Such a rudder is heavy on the helm when a boat is loaded up, or if it is prone to weather helm.

A partial skeg is a compromise that provides a second bearing for the rudder midway down its forward face and also allows the lower part of the rudder to project forward of its turning axis. This results in a semi-balanced rudder that is much lighter on the helm. Unfortunately, the lower bearing can attract fishing nets and pot warps (as can the gap between the forward edge of a spade rudder and the hull), which are then extremely difficult to disentangle. Ideally, this bearing will be protected by some kind of a line deflector. With a partial-skeg arrangement my preference is to make the lower part of the rudder sacrificial. In the event of serious impact, it will break away, leaving the remainder of the rudder functional.

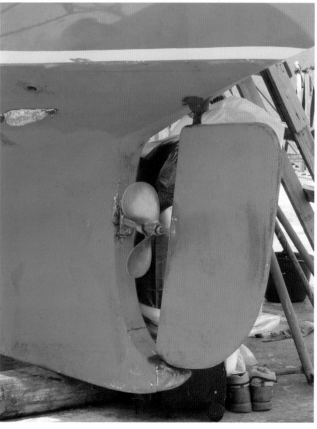

Right: Long-keeled boats are much less likely to be damaged in a grounding than fin-keeled boats.

Center: Long, shallow-draft fins like this offer the advantages of a long keel without some of the disadvantages.

Far right: This keel design is fairly typical and offers good all-round performance.

The deeper the rudder, the more effective it tends to be. Once in a while you will see a boat whose rudder has a deeper draft than the keel. From my perspective, this is absurd. In a grounding, the rudder, the most vulnerable part of the underbody, will hit the bottom first.

Keeping bilge water in the bilges

I am willing to make further compromises in terms of hull shape. One of the most significant of these is driven by the need to remove bilge water from the boat, a subject rarely considered by boatbuyers.

Sooner or later every boat gets water down below. Many a traditional boat with wineglass sections will retain water in its bilges even when heeled 30 degrees or more. In contrast, some contemporary boats won't do this at any heel angle (especially if, as is sometimes the case, there is no keel sump). On all contemporary flat-bottomed boats, whenever the boat heels more than a few degrees, even a small amount of bilge water has a tendency to run all over the boat, soaking goods in lockers and, in some cases, submerging equipment and wiring harnesses. Aside from the inconvenience and the damage that may

be done, submerging of the wiring harness can lead to rampant stray-current corrosion.

Somewhere between a traditional hull and a contemporary hull is a happy

medium. This will vary depending on the perspective of the owner. Given that most modern boats sail at their best heeled no more than 20 degrees and that once this angle is reached, the

If a deep, narrow-rooted fin keel like this one hits bottom with any force, the stresses will be transmitted to the hull floor; major damage can result.

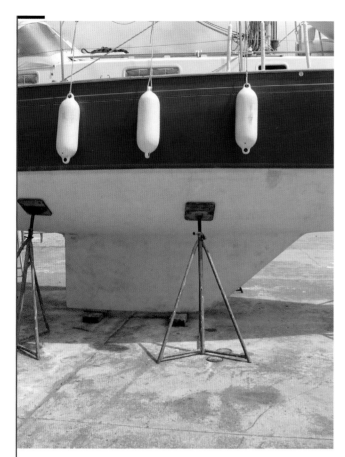

boat should be reefed down, on my boats I look for cross sections and a bilge sump that will retain bilge water at heel angles up to 20 degrees. The necessary curves result in a softer motion in unpleasant conditions, which agrees well with my other priorities for long-distance shorthanded offshore cruising.

If a boat has a structural grid (as many do nowadays), it is important for the grid to have limber holes that allow bilge water to drain at all angles of heel. This is frequently not the case.

Compromise, compromise

Just as there are excellent reasons for the popularity of fin keels, spade rudders, and flat-bottomed boats among racer/cruiser and coastal-cruising aficionados, so there are excellent reasons for the retention of longer keels,

skegs, and more rounded sections on offshore boats. In terms of the design continuum, there are no right and wrong answers about where to draw the line. The decision is a complex one that can only be made on the basis of carefully articulated individual needs.

If these needs change, a different underbody is called for. Recently Lyman Morse, the builder of the relatively traditional Seguin 44, had a client whose focus had shifted more toward performance. They cut the full skeg off his boat and replaced the unbalanced skeg-mounted rudder with a balanced spade rudder. They also cut the lead keel off and remolded it with a more modern foil shape and a small endplate. The result is a dramatically lighter and more responsive helm and an improvement in performance, especially upwind—but at the price of a somewhat less protected

rudder. With its relatively narrow beam and rounded sections, the boat remains an extremely comfortable sea boat that is now optimized more for performance.

At a boat show last year I met with a designer who is famous for his fast, relatively lightweight contemporary cruising boats. At one point in our conversation, he remarked, "You know, Nigel, if you want comfort offshore, you need weight." He has recently poured his heart and soul into a cruising design that looks nothing like most modern boats (or many of his other designs), demonstrating how there can be good reasons for breaking with the contemporary mold. These reasons have nothing to do with nostalgia. They are all about getting the boat best suited to individual sailing plans and dreams.

Repairs and Maintenance

A boat is like a house: as soon as it's built, it starts deteriorating. If you keep on top of the routine maintenance you'll often be able to defer the time when you have to make cosmetic or structural repairs or replace faulty equipment, but sooner or later, time and wear will catch up with you.

Almost every older (10-years-plus) boat is in need some kind of repair work, and all boats require maintenance from the time you take delivery. In this section we cover a cross section of the maintenance and repair work you can reasonably expect to have to do to a boat that's getting a bit long in the tooth.

The need to replace one or more

bulkheads arises more often than you might think, especially in older boats that have had standing water in them or have suffered persistent chainplate leaks that have never been fixed. The prospect fills anyone with trepidation, but James Phyfe's account of how he carried out the project may just make you feel like giving it a try yourself.

Leaking portlights are, alas, an all-too-common problem, and not just on older boats. Leaks from around poorly installed deck hardware are equally ubiquitous. We offer some tried and tested solutions to these issues.

Fixing a hole in a hull turned out to be easier than I thought, and so did fairing a keel (it's all about the elbow grease).

James D. Phyfe

New Bulkheads

When I started searching for a boat to buy, I was only a year out of college, had nowhere to live, and thought a sailboat would make the perfect home. I wanted a fast, strong, offshore-capable boat, but I'd just started working and had less than $30,000 to spend. I reasoned that if I found a boat that needed work I could do myself, I could spend less and make it up with sweat equity. I looked at over 20 boats before settling on the type I wanted and saw several of those before I found one I could afford that needed work I thought I could handle.

The initial survey of my chosen project boat, a 1974 sloop-rigged Contessa 35, turned up some rot in the bulkheads where they were tabbed to the hull. But the hull itself and the deck appeared strong and, more important, free of moisture. The boat in other respects was well maintained, and the rig and sails seemed in good condition. After handing over what small savings I had, I had the boat hauled and, with the

help of several people more knowledgeable than I, began to take it apart.

The most serious problem was the bulkhead rot. The fore-and-aft main saloon bulkheads were so rotten over most of their bottom thirds that I could stick my fist right through them (Photo A1). The partial bulkheads separating the settees from the nav station and galley on either side of the saloon were also fairly soft. I soon realized that these bulkheads would have to be entirely replaced. The same was true of the small athwartship bulkhead in the bow, but the minor rotting in other isolated areas could probably be addressed by replacing sections locally.

The bow bulkhead

After removing everything not permanently attached to the hull—trim, linings, overhead, cabin sole, and so on— I was ready to attack the rotten bulkheads. I decided to start at the bow and work my way aft. I drilled small

holes into the heavy tabbing in various locations around the bow bulkhead and found soggy wood everywhere. Because this is a structural bulkhead, I knew I had to replace it.

The builder had tabbed all bulkheads to the hull on both their forward and aft sides. Using a 4″ angle-grinder and a cutting wheel, I cut through the tabbing on the aft side of the bulkhead as close to the hull as possible (Photo A2). It was then not difficult to pull the rotten wood away from the tabbing on the forward side, thereby removing the entire bulkhead. I ground away the aft tabbing and left the forward tabbing intact so I would know exactly where to position the new bulkhead (Photo A3).

The old bulkhead was ³⁄₈″ teak plywood, and I decided that ½″ MDO (medium density overlay) plywood would be at least as rigid. Because this bulkhead would be painted, there was no need to use expensive teak marine plywood. MDO is exterior-grade plywood finished with a layer of fibrous paper impregnated with phenolic resin. A water-

My glorious new interior. I replaced part or all of the bow and main bulkheads (opposite page), the transverse partial bulkheads at the galley and nav station (left), plus the fore-and-aft bulkheads on both sides (below).

outside. The new tabbing would be more than sufficient to carry the loads over this gap.

Once I had cut and fit the new bulkhead sections, I sealed the paper surfaces and edges of the plywood with West System epoxy, allowing plenty of time for it to set up. I then ground away all traces of wood and paint from the remaining forward tabbing and made it smooth. Because I would be glassing directly over this old tabbing, it was important to taper it to a fine edge where it would contact the new bulkhead. This would create a fair surface for the new tabbing to adhere to as it passed over the old tabbing and onto the new bulkhead. Once everything was in order and I had an ample number of clamps at the ready, it was time to glass the new bulkhead in place.

I completed the glassing in steps over a period of several days. All the new tabbing was done with polyester resin using a woven biaxial cloth with a mat backing. Under the strict supervision of an accomplished boatbuilder, I cut several strips of cloth the approximate width of the remaining tabbing and saturated them with resin. I then laid them in two layers along the inside surface of the old tabbing, where they would be sandwiched between the old tabbing and the new bulkhead. When that was done, I pressed the new bulkhead against the cloth, clamped it securely in place, and allowed it to dry overnight (Photo A4).

proof glue bonds the plies, and the paper surface creates a smooth face, free of knots and blemishes, for easy finishing. It can be found at most lumberyards and mills.

Because the old bulkhead came out more or less in one piece, I was able to use it as a template for the new one. However, the new bulkhead was a little larger than any of the hatches in the boat and therefore had to be constructed in two pieces and joined in place. I routed a ¼″ groove into each of the two halves 4″ in from where they would join. These would later be filled with fiberglass.

After I finished cutting the rough shape of the new bulkhead, there followed several trips between the saw and the bow of the boat as I whittled the new bulkhead to exactly the correct form. The final two pieces fit snugly against the forward tabbing and conformed to the shape of the hull. I left a small ¼″ gap between the new bulk-

head and the hull all the way around so that future expansion or shifting would not create a hard spot visible from the

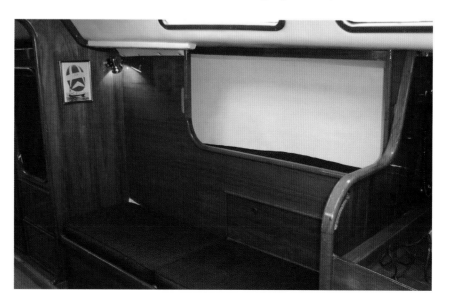

The following morning the glass had set up and the clamps could be removed. Because some of the glass sandwiched between the bulkhead and the old tabbing stuck out in places, I

but did not need to be replaced entirely. The most significant of these was the athwartships structural bulkhead in the main saloon at the mast partners. After removing a ¼″ teak plywood veneer, I

head entirely would most likely cause the hull to change shape, I decided to cut out only the rotten wood and scarf in a new piece. Using a Sawzall, cutting wheel, and jigsaw in various places, I

A1. Bad rot at the bottom of the fore-and-aft saloon bulkheads.

B1. The rot is evident in the lower part of the main bulkhead.

again ground everything fair on the forward side of the bulkhead. I then cut four layers of cloth, each slightly larger than the next, as new tabbing and glassed it over the old tabbing with 3″ margins on the hull and new bulkhead.

I tabbed the aft side of the bulkhead in a similar manner. The next day a light grinding removed any rough spots in the tabbing. Using 8″ pieces of glass cloth, I systematically filled the routed groove at the interface of the two bulkhead sections until the thickness of the original wood had been restored. This was now as strong as, if not stronger than, a solid piece of wood and could later be faired for painting (Photos A5, A6, A7).

Main structural bulkhead

Elsewhere in the boat, I discovered several bulkheads that were partially rotten

discovered that the bottom two feet or so of this bulkhead also required replacement. Because removing this bulk-

cut a clean line across the bulkhead where the wood was still sound (Photo B1). Then, using the same method as

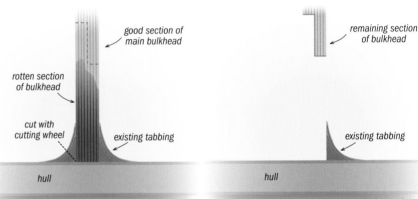

good section of main bulkhead

rotten section of bulkhead

cut with cutting wheel

existing tabbing

hull

remaining section of bulkhead

existing tabbing

hull

First I cut away the tabbing on one side and removed the rotten section of the bulkhead.

I cut a shelf in the upper part and cleaned the existing tabbing.

A2. The bow bulkhead is removed.

A3. The forward tabbing was left as a guide.

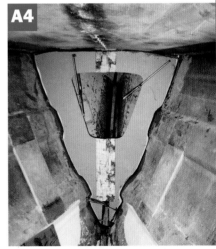

A4. The new two-piece bulkhead fit well.

B2. I cut away the aft tabbing and pulled the rotten wood off the forward tabbing.

B3. The new bottom section is offered up.

before, I cut away the aft tabbing and pulled the rotten wood off the forward tabbing (Photo B2). Much of the remaining tabbing could not be accessed from forward, as it was hidden under the

modular head compartment, so I had to settle for sandwiching new glass between the old forward tabbing and the bulkhead. The aft side could be retabbed entirely.

I cleaned the exposed side of the old forward tabbing as best I could with an angle grinder and ground away what remained of the old aft tabbing. Across the bulkhead where I had cut out the rotten wood, I routed out a 3/4" shelf exactly half as deep as the thickness of the bulkhead. Then, using rolls of light-yellow tracing paper, I made a template of the new piece to be scarfed in and added 3/4" to the top where the new wood would overlap the old. Again I used MDO plywood. Once the new piece was cut (again I left space for a thin gap between it and the hull), I routed out a coordinate 3/4" shelf to form the seam between the new and old sections of bulkhead. These would fit together in the final installation like pieces in a jigsaw puzzle (Photo B3). The figures on pages 20 and 21 show how this was done.

I sandwiched two layers of biaxial glass cloth saturated in resin between the new wood and the old tabbing. The

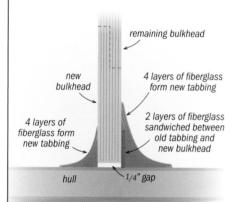

I bonded the new section of bulkhead into place under the old.

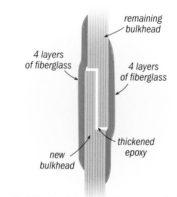

Detail of the joint between the new and old sections of the bulkhead.

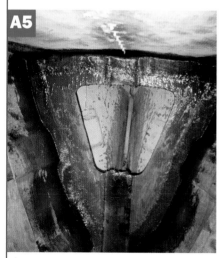

A5. New tabbing is glassed over the old.

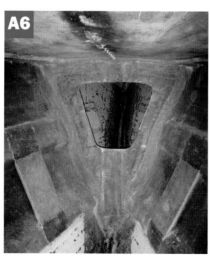

A6. The joint is covered with glass tape.

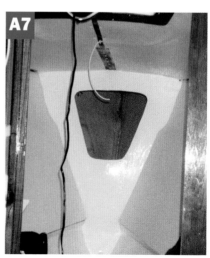

A7. Faired and painted, good as new.

B4. The new piece has been bonded to the old, and new tabbing is being applied.

B5. A thin veneer has been glued over the repaired bulkhead.

overlapping shelves of the seam were then "glued" together with an ample amount of West System epoxy thickened with adhesive filler. Once that had set up, I ground the joint smooth and covered it with two layers of glass cloth approximately 5″ wide. Then I applied four layers of new tabbing to the aft side of the new section where it joined the hull (Photo B4). Once everything had set up, I faired the entire bulkhead

from hull to overhead with automotive filler and finished it with an attractive teak veneer (Photo B5). Today it is nearly impossible to tell that any work has been done.

Partial saloon bulkheads

The last significant job was the fore-and-aft and transverse partial bulkheads in the main saloon. Although re-

moving and replacing these bulkheads was a much larger task than replacing the small bulkhead in the bow, I used essentially the same process. First, I removed all the joinery forming the settees and storage lockers on both sides of the main saloon (Photo C1). I left the nav station on the starboard side untouched, and I had already disassembled the galley to port for other reasons. I decided the best way to tackle

C1. I had to remove the joinery and half-bulkhead on each side. **C2.** The nav station was left intact. **C3.** I used the same method employed for the bow bulkhead.

these four bulkheads was to do one side at a time, thereby reducing the overall impact on the shape of the boat.

Starting on the starboard side, I cut away the inboard tabbing on the fore-and-aft structural bulkhead as I had done the bow bulkhead. When the entire piece was released on that side, I placed an automotive jack on the bilge stringers and lifted the deck enough to release the bulkhead. Then, using a sledgehammer, axe, and Sawzall, I removed the bulkhead, much of which was still sound wood. I removed the small transverse bulkhead forward of the nav station similarly.

With both bulkheads out and the deck and hull held in place by the jack (Photo C2), I ground the remaining tabbing to a fine edge as I had at the bow. Then I made templates with tracing paper for both bulkheads. Because these would both be finished teak in the end, I used the same sort of ½″ teak marine plywood that had originally been used.

Marine ply, although more expensive, is superior to standard plywood because of the waterproof resorcinol glue used and the lack of voids in the inner layers of standard exterior-grade wood. To ensure a strong bond, however, the waxy teak veneer must be completely removed with a coarse grinding disk from the areas that will be tabbed.

One of these bulkheads was larger than a standard 4′ × 8′ sheet of plywood, so it, too, had to be constructed in two pieces that were later joined inside the boat. In joining the pieces, I used the same overlapping joint employed on the bottom of the forward bulkhead in the main saloon. And, again, I left a small gap around the periphery of these bulkheads to avoid creating hard spots.

Installation was no different than in the bow (Photo C3). After treating the edges of the new bulkhead with epoxy, I sandwiched two layers of glass between the existing tabbing and bulkheads. I

then covered all the existing tabbing with four layers of fresh glass and retabbed the other side entirely. After everything set up, I removed the jack and went to work on the other side.

I have often heard it said that a "project boat" always becomes more of a project than you initially bargain for. In many cases, however, this can be a benefit, as the owner becomes intimately acquainted with the ins and outs of his new boat. Similarly, the more work you do to a boat, the more you feel a sense of ownership and accomplishment. While I have sworn to many people that I would never again tackle such a project, I now have a boat worth much more than any I could have afforded with my meager savings. More important, I have a new home.

The author would like to thank **Glen Gordon** of The **Boat Works, Inc.,** in Clinton, Connecticut, for his guidance and assistance.

Peter Nielsen

Holes Below the Waterline

There is nothing quite so discouraging to a sailor as a gaping hole in the bottom of his boat. We wanted to remove the useless old OMC saildrive engine from *Jabberwock,* the *BoatWorks* project O'Day 25, a process that involved much skinning of knuckles, banging of heads, and ricking of backs in the coffinlike space below her cockpit. Once we'd dismantled the tired two-cycle rustheap and heaved it over the side, we were left with a nice big hole in the bottom that had to be fixed. Here's what we did about it.

TIP

Acetone cleans up leftover epoxy resin, but it's nasty stuff and you need to be careful when using it. Plain old white vinegar is surprisingly effective at cleaning up small amounts of resin before it cures.

Photos by Peter Nielsen

1. First we have to remove the fiberglass fairing skirt in which the saildrive leg nested in a bed of goop. We try hacking it off with a hammer and chisel, but it is too stubborn. Inside the hull, it had been puttied in with a 2"-thick layer of resin and chopped-strand mat that formed the engine bed (1a).

2. The fastest way to get the skirt out proves to be by using this Fein cutter with a vibrating head—and a $50 blade—to gouge out the glass. It takes a good half-hour (those O'Day guys were serious about their glass work). Then we are left with an 8" × 10" oval hole.

3. We think about cutting a piece of foam or Coremat to fit the hole and glassing it in place, but ace fiberglass man Greg Dolan has a better idea. We drive to the nearest sail loft and scrounge a piece of ultra-shiny pattern-making Mylar. Greg cuts out a rectangle and duct-tapes it over the outside of the hole, after first cleaning the surrounding area with acetone. We could use Peel Ply for this, but the Mylar is easier to work with. It conforms nicely to the shape of the hull, and the epoxy won't stick to it.

4. Next we cut two pieces of biaxial woven fiberglass mat. Laid on top of each other, these are equivalent to eight sheets of unidirectional glass.

5

5. We match the patch to the hole to make sure it's the right size, then remove it.

6. Greg mixes up a pot of West System 105 epoxy resin and hardener. After wetting-out the surrounds of the hole with the resin, he blends in enough colloidal silica filler to make a putty the consistency of mayonnaise.

6

7. Inside the hull, Greg smoothes the putty into the hole, working it well in around the edges of the patch. Because the hole is below the waterline and the patch will be covered by anti-fouling, there is no need to worry about matching colors. The putty will set very hard, and he has ground the outside edges of the hole to make a better key for the resin.

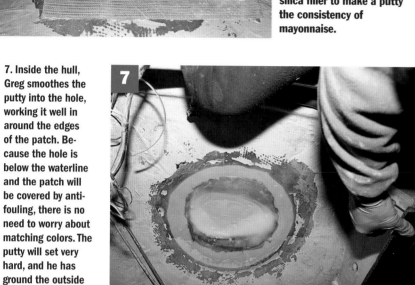
7

8

8. Another pot of epoxy gets mixed up, and Greg wets out the biaxial patch with a disposable brush. He puts plenty of epoxy on the patch.

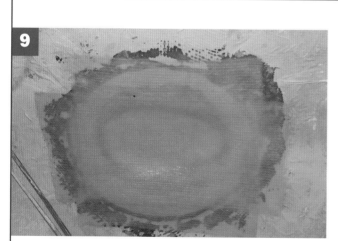
9

9. Inside the hull, Greg lays the patch down over the hole, smoothes it out with his gloved hands to get rid of air bubbles, then uses a small roller to make sure the resin is well worked into the thick mat.

10. Next day, the patch has set rock-hard and is ready for a little filling around the edges with epoxy and microballoons, followed by a thorough sanding.

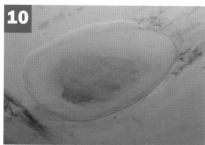
10

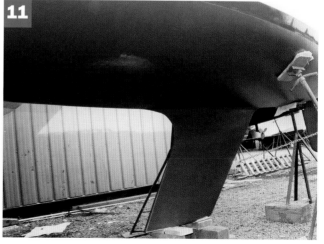
11

11. You'd never know the hole had been there.

Fixed-Port Repair

Mark Corke

On many boats fixed ports or windows are prone to cracking, hazing, and leaking. Leaks are the most serious, as I discovered aboard our Columbia 35; the inner paneling was delaminating, and the core in the coachroof had started to rot.

There are many different types of fixed ports—surface-mounted, surface-mounted with trim rings, flush-mounted, and metal-framed. The process presented here won't be suitable for all of these, but it can be adapted for most boats. The project requires basic competence and a minimum of tools.

First steps

In most boats the ports are installed in simple cutouts in the cabin sides. Usually the inner core, often plywood or end-grain balsa, is not sealed. All is well until water gets into the core and goes unnoticed for months or even years.

Thus, the first step in replacing ports is to make sure the core is sound and well sealed. On my boat the wood core on the starboard side was rotted and wet for a few inches back from the edges of the port. This required digging out the old core and replacing it with a mixture of epoxy and high-density filler. Getting the epoxy/filler in place, with no voids or spills, can be a challenge.

First I coated the exposed core with unfilled epoxy and allowed it to soak in.

TIP

The worst thing you can do when using sealant of any kind is to tighten down the fasteners and squeeze all the sealant out. To prevent this, I used small rubber washers on the back side of the ports. The fasteners are tightened down on these washers and leave a healthy amount of sealant in place. These washers can be found in the specialty hardware section of most home-improvement stores.

I applied a thick paste around the sides and bottom of the port opening and sealed off the upper edge with tape. Then I injected the epoxy mixture into this space with a syringe. This epoxy/filler around the edges of the opening will seal off the core from any future leaks.

The other side of the boat was in much worse shape. There were inner and outer fiberglass skins around the port, but the core between them was mostly gone. I cut the inner fiberglass skin back to sound core, cleaned out the rotted material, and then troweled a thick epoxy/filler mixture in place, equal to the thickness of the original core. After the epoxy cured, I tapered the edges of the original inner skin with sandpaper and then, using fiberglass cloth and

epoxy, I laminated a new inner skin in place. Finally, I painted it to match the rest of the cabin interior.

Pattern making

I taped together pieces of poster board to create a piece large enough for the pattern. I traced around the opening from the inside while a helper held the board in place from the outside.

Since I had decided to overlap the new ports on the cabin sides by 1¼″, drawing this line on the board gave me the port's outside dimensions and allowed me to try a couple of different treatments for the rounded corners until I found one I liked.

Glazing material

The two main choices for replacing port windows are polycarbonate (Lexan) and acrylic (Plexiglas). Each has its pros and cons. Polycarbonate is stronger but scratches more easily. Acrylic is not as tough but is more scratch resistant. I chose ⅜″ smoked Plexiglas.

Suppliers can sell you sheet stock or cut the ports to size from your patterns. I had the supplier cut the first two for me, and I cut the second two myself.

Both materials come with protective paper on both sides. *Leave this on until the last moment.* You don't want to scratch the new ports before they're even installed.

Cutting and drilling

Both Lexan and Plexiglas require care when being cut and drilled. I used a medium fine-toothed blade in my saber saw. Go slowly so as not to overheat the plastic, and cut a little outside the line. Cutting can leave microscopic cracks in the material, and you need a little margin for sanding and polishing these away.

I used a rounding bit on my router to round over the outside edge of the port. Mark the outside and inside faces of the ports on the protective covering so you don't inadvertently round over the wrong edge; most ports are handed left and right.

I sanded the edges of the ports with progressively finer sandpaper, ending up with 600-grit wet-and-dry paper. The final polishing was done with Tripoli Compound, a form of jeweler's rouge. If you don't have this, ordinary toothpaste will work. With the mild abrasive, the edges of the port will be as shiny as the flat surfaces and the microscopic cracks will be gone.

The next job was to drill the holes for the fasteners. I transferred the line for the inner port opening to the protective paper on what would be the inside surface of the port. Then I drew another line, halfway between the inner opening line and the outer edge of the port. This was the centerline for the fasteners. I spaced the fastener holes 2½" apart, adjusting the spacing so that it was uniform around the port. I drilled ⅛" pilot holes at the fastener locations.

A word about drilling these plastics: An ordinary drill bit will immediately grab and crack the plastic when you try to drill it. You can buy special plastic drill bits with modified cutting edges, or you can make your own. I dulled the edge of a regular drill bit on a grinder. Practice on scrap plastic to make sure you have the bit right. It also helps to drill the right size hole the first time as enlarging a previously drilled hole is asking for the plastic to crack.

Fixed-port fastenings

I taped the port in place so that the line marking the opening on the protective paper was lined up with the actual opening and then drilled holes through the cabin side using the pilot holes in the port for guidance.

There are many ways of fastening ports in place. You can through-bolt them, with nuts or fancy cap nuts on the inside; the nuts can then be hidden with a custom-milled piece of wood

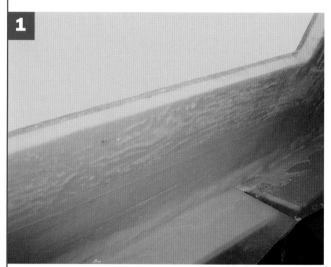

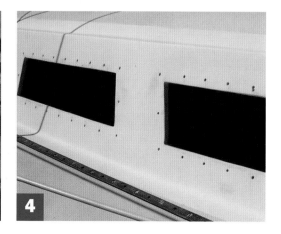

1. Laying the edges of the fixed ports.

2. Counterboring holes for tee-nuts inside the cabin.

3. Installing the tee-nuts prior to covering them with epoxy filler.

4. The exterior of the cabin with all the fastener holes drilled.

Photos this page by Paul Esterle

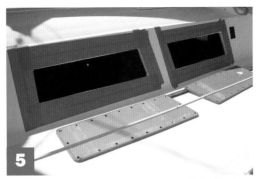

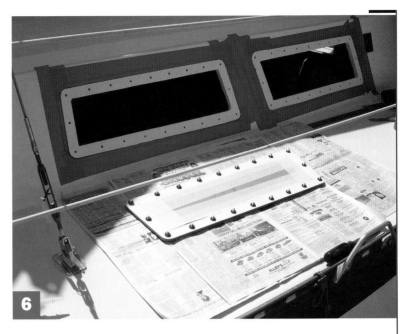

5. Blue tape is applied to the areas around the fixed-port openings.

6. The tape has been cut away where the port will be mounted.

7. The inside surface of the port. The edges are sanded and painted, and rubber washers for the fasteners are in place.

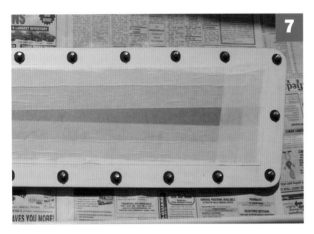

8. Apply a generous amount of sealant to the port. Don't scrimp.

9. When tightening down the port fasteners, work around the port gradually and allow the excess sealant to squeeze out.

Photos this page by Paul Esterle

Tee-Nut Installation

When I replaced my fixed ports, I wanted as few places for leaks to develop as possible. It seemed to me that through-bolting all the fasteners would leave too many places for potential leaks, so I fastened the windows in place with stainless-steel tee-nuts.

After I drilled the cabin walls for the ¼″ fasteners, I moved inside the cabin for the next step. Using a hole saw, I drilled through the inner fiberglass skin and the center core, being careful not to touch the outer fiberglass skin of the cabin wall. I popped out the center of the hole with a screwdriver, leaving a counterbore, or recess, in the inside cabin wall.

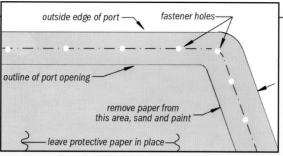

Edge layout of a fixed port.

I screwed the fixed port back in place, using truss-headed stainless-steel machine screws on the outside. The screw threaded into the tee-nuts on the inside and held everything in place. With the wide end of the tee-nut facing inward, I placed a small piece of tape over the center hole to protect the threads and the fasteners.

I placed an epoxy/filler mixture in an empty caulking-gun tube and injected a stiff epoxy mixture under the tee-nut, filling up the counterbore even with the inside cabin wall. Once the epoxy cured, I lightly sanded the filler and laminated two layers of fiberglass and epoxy over the counterbores.

The fasteners now screw into a blind hole sealed from the inside cabin by the epoxy. This eliminates a series of potential leak sites and leaves no nuts to cover on the inside of the cabin.

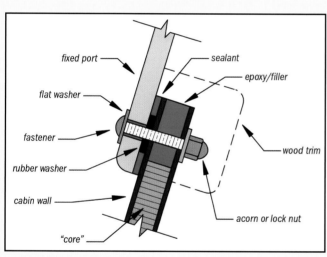

Through-bolted port fastening.

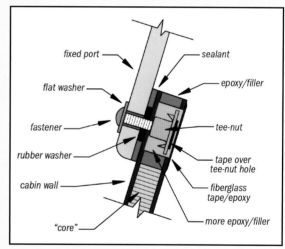

"Tee-nut" port fastening.

trim. Or you can use barrel nuts on the inside, leaving only the head of the barrel nut visible inside. I decided to bury the tee-nuts in the cabin wall so there was no direct path for water to leak through the fastener holes (see "Tee-Nut Installation").

Then I drilled out the holes in the fixed port for the fasteners. These holes need to be drilled oversize to allow for the greater expansion and contraction of the plastic relative to the cabin sides. For example, I drilled ⁵⁄₁₆″ holes for ¼″ fasteners.

Next, I drilled the holes in the cabin walls for the fasteners. Make sure the holes pass through the solid epoxy/ filler. If you hit core material, you must clean it out and fill the void with epoxy/fillers to avoid leaks.

Final steps

I trial-fitted the fixed port in place to make sure all fasteners would seat properly and everything lined up. I cut away the paper backing around the back edge of the port, down to the line of the opening. I then sanded the exposed plastic with 80-grit paper and gave the area two coats of marine paint that matched the cabin sides. This protected the sealant from UV damage and gave the edges of the

A close-up view of a tee-nut.

fixed port a uniform look. If you want to simulate a frame, you could use a dark color.

10. The ports are tightened down and ready for cleanup.

11. Cleaning up excess sealant with a tongue depressor.

12. Pulling off the protective paper.

13. The finished job—no mess, no fuss.

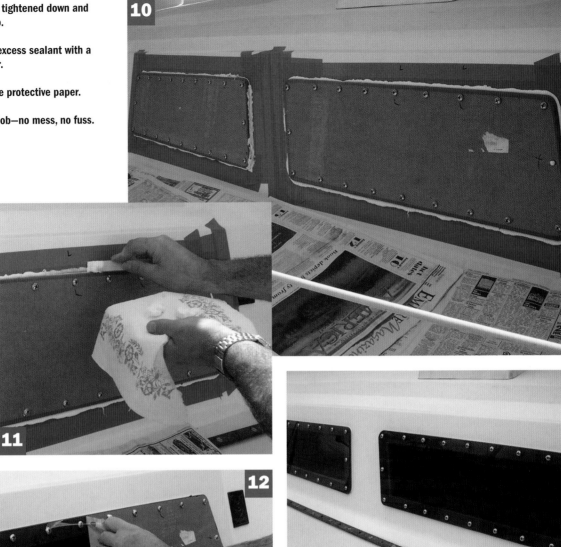

Photos this page by Paul Esterle

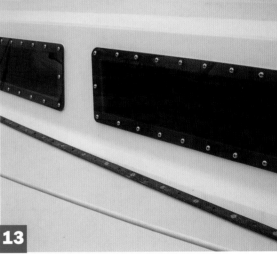

Tee-nuts installed and ready to be encapsulated with epoxy and filler.

I taped around the opening for the port with blue masking tape, put the port back in place, and traced around it. After removing the port, I cut away the tape under where the port would go. I also taped the exposed edges of the port to protect it from stray sealant.

With everything taped and plenty of newspaper protecting the deck, I applied the sealant to the port. I used Life Seal, a sealant specifically designed for use with acrylics and polycarbonates. If you use a different sealant, verify that it is compatible with the plastic material you are using.

Then I placed the port in its location and tightened down the fasteners a little at a time to allow it to settle in place without any undue stress.

My final step was to clean up the excess sealant. I used wooden tongue depressors to remove the bulk of the excess and paper towels with the recommended thinner to do the final cleanup. Taping and laying down newspaper on the deck left a clean installation with no mess. The best part is that these ports haven't leaked a drop in four years.

Peter Nielsen

Fairing a Boat's Keel

Jabberwock, the *BoatWorks* project O'Day 25, was looking very scruffy around the underparts. The boat had been standing for so long that most of the paint had just fallen off the bottom, and the keel was looking particularly seedy. There was no way we could launch the boat with the

keel in such bad condition. It was time for a makeover. A proper keel job done by a boatyard will cost upward of $1,000, but we reckoned we could do it ourselves for a fraction of that. We were lucky in that the keel was lead; a cast-iron keel would have been much more labor-intensive.

TIP

If you want to get the last ounce of performance out of your boat, you may be able to buy a set of templates for your keel (try the builder, or www.computerkeels.com). These will ensure that your keel is perfectly symmetrical and fair on both sides. Enthusiastic racers may want to do this, but for the average cruising sailor, near enough is good enough. Even an imperfectly faired keel will improve your boatspeed.

1

1. This keel is fairly typical for its age. It's taken a bit of punishment over the years, and the old fiberglass skin has lifted off in patches. Fairing it will not only improve the water flow over it and reduce drag, it will also provide a better substrate for paint.

2. Gentlemen, choose your weapons. The implement of choice is a beefy random-orbital sander—in our case a Porter-Cable—with a variety of sanding disks. It pays to buy disks in bulk, because you'll use a lot.

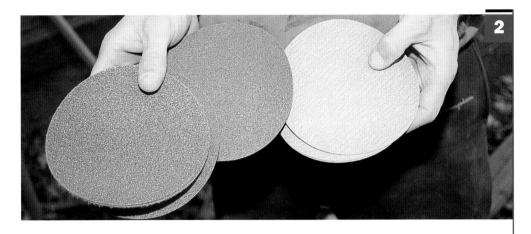

3. Make sure you have everything you need on hand before you start. Once you've started a project like this, you won't want to put down tools to go buy a brush. Stock up on resin containers, disposable brushes, gloves, scrapers, and acetone.

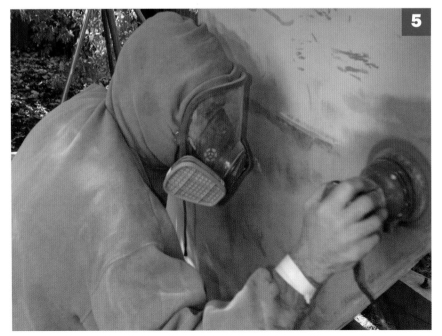

4. We'll need to seal the joint between the hull and the keel. Some work has already been done here. Over the years, impurities at the top of the lead/antimony keel casting had become brittle. They had been chipped out, and the gaps were filled with a paste of thickened epoxy resin.

5. We start off using 36-grit paper along the hull/keel joint. We'll be covering the joint with fiberglass, and the heavy grit leaves a nice rough surface for the resin and glass to bond to. The dust that results from sanding old antifouling paint, fiberglass, and lead is not pleasant, so if you do a job like this make sure you cover up as much skin as possible and use a high-quality respirator.

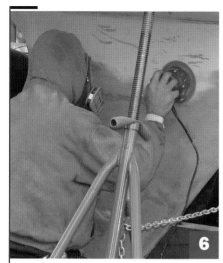

6. There's no need to go down to bare metal, but we make sure the old loose fiberglass is ground off; in many places the bond between it and the lead is still strong, so we don't need to take it all off. Next, we wipe the entire keel with acetone to make sure the epoxy has a nice clean surface to bond to.

7. Now we need to skin over the hull/keel joint. This will strengthen and seal the joint. We first cut out four pieces of 17-ounce biaxial mat, two for each side of the keel. This is equivalent to four layers of glass cloth. The second layer will be slightly wider than the first. We wet out each layer of mat very thoroughly with a 5:1 mix of West System epoxy and 105 fast hardener.

8a and 8b. One at a time, we line up the strips of mat along the hull/keel joint—it may be easier to have a helper for this—before using a rubber roller to smooth down the mat and work the resin into the weave. We repeat this on the other side of the keel.

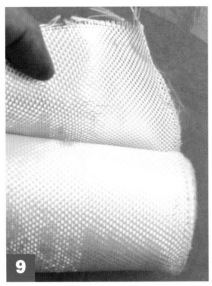

9. Next we cut two lengths of woven 8-ounce fiberglass cloth, 3" wider than the biaxial mat. This will absorb the extra resin that is oozing out of the mat.

10. We use a squeegee to smooth down the glass cloth and work the resin through the weave. Then we use a roller to smooth it out, and we tuck the edges around the front and back edges of the keel. Now we have to get the fairing compound on before the resin cures, to make sure there is a chemical bond.

12. The "goop" is troweled on thickly over the entire surface of the keel, up to and just above the fiberglass tape we've applied. You need to gauge the thickness well. Too heavy a coat will drip and sag; too thin, and you won't have enough of a substrate to sand down fair.

11. We mix up a big pot of resin, using a slow hardener because we don't want it to kick off too soon, and add fillers to thicken it up. You can use colloidal silica, microballoons, or Q-cells for this—it doesn't really matter (except that colloidal silica will be harder to sand). The mix must be the consistency of peanut butter. You should never use anything but an epoxy-based filler to fair a keel; polyester compounds like Bondo do not stick well to a keel and are much more likely to absorb water.

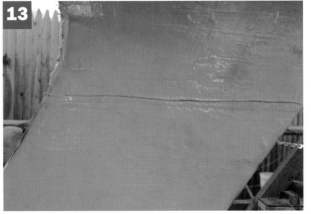

13. Next morning, inspecting our handiwork, we find only a couple of runs and sags, which will be easy enough to sand out. If we'd used colloidal silica instead of Q-cells we could probably have avoided them, but all in all it's not a bad effort.

14. Sanding down the fairing compound requires concentration and patience. It's easy to take too much off in one spot and not enough in another. Develop a method that suits you—for example, try working only in horizontal swathes and moving down the keel gradually, rather than doing it patchwork. Stand back occasionally and eyeball the keel as you go, sighting along it to check for fairness. You could also use a fiberglass batten to check for high and low spots; lay it across the keel from time to time. Don't sand through the fiberglass you've laid over the hull/keel joint.

16. After wiping the keel down with acetone, we mix up some Interlux Interprotect, a two-part epoxy primer, and roll on the first of five coats. This fills in any pinholes left in the new surface and cures hard enough to provide some abrasion resistance.

15. Phew. It's a long haul, but eventually you'll get down to the point where the keel is beautifully fair and smooth. You'll be through to the bare metal here and there, but be careful—it's easy to take too much off, not so easy to put it back. If we had been too enthusiastic with the sanding, we would have mixed up some more "peanut butter" and then sanded some more—carefully.

Thanks to **Greg Dolan** and **Joe Duplin** for their help.

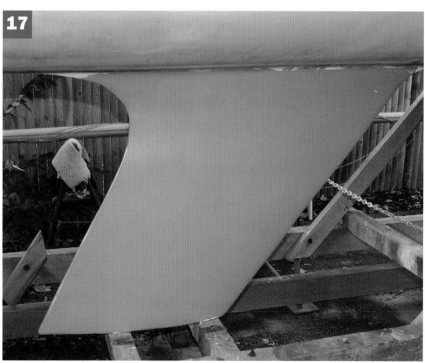

17. Finally, we stand back and admire our lovely "new" keel, which is now ready for its antifouling paint. Total time: about a day and a half. Materials cost: less than $200.

Core Repairs

Paul Esterle

No two words strike more terror in the hearts of boat buyers and owners than "core rot." The owner sees his investment going down the drain; the buyer sees that his dream boat has fatal flaws. Is core rot curable, or is it the end of the line? The answer is a firmly qualified maybe.

Most modern boats are built with cored laminates. A lightweight core material is sandwiched between two skins of fiberglass or some other composite material. The resulting structure is thicker, lighter, stiffer, and stronger than a solid fiberglass laminate. Over the years many materials have been used for coring. Among the more common are plywood, end-grain balsa, foam, and aluminum honeycomb (this is unlikely to be used in a production boat).

Two main types of problems occur. The simpler of the two to repair is delamination, in which the bond between the fiberglass skin and the core material fails because of impact or overloading the deck. The deck becomes springy and the structure weakens. As long as the core remains dry, repairs are possible. Water penetration of a balsa core is far worse. The wet core material breaks away from the fiberglass and eventually rots or turns to mush. This problem is harder to solve and, unfortunately, more common. Foam-cored

Core materials are found in the decks and hulls of many boats. Some of the most common are plywood, foam, and balsa, although plastic and even aluminum are sometimes used.

decks and hulls are rare in production boats. When foam breaks down it can turn crumbly or powdery.

If your boat's cored deck or hull is tight and dry, count your blessings—but don't expect to lead a charmed life forever. This is the perfect example of an ounce of prevention being worth a pound of cure. Inspect your boat to locate and eliminate all sources of water intrusion. This can result from poor construction practices or poor maintenance.

Preventive maintenance

Most commonly, water leaks into cores around ports, chainplates, deck hardware, and stanchions. In no case should anything—bolt, screw, whatever—penetrate the actual core. Rebedding fittings without properly sealing the opening only invites trouble.

In every case where there is a hole through the cored structure, the edges of that hole must be sealed. The usual practice is to remove the fittings and fastenings and then rout out the core between the skins. The hole is sealed from the bottom, and the space be-

tween the cores is filled with an epoxy/filler mixture. When this hardens, the hole is redrilled through the epoxy. In effect, you have made an epoxy bushing for the fitting.

Pay special attention around ports and hatches. Many times the openings are simply cut out, exposing the core to possible water penetration. You'll need to dig out the core around the opening and fill with the epoxy/filler mixture. Pay attention to the port's fasteners, which may be outside the area you have sealed around the port opening. They, too, must be dug out and the holes filled with epoxy filler.

If your hull is cored, also check and repair any of the through-hull openings, which are prime sites for water penetration and saturated cores.

I've developed a quick process for sealing chainplate slots. Most of those I've fixed have had cover plates.

Using a fiberglass-reinforced cut-off wheel in a Dremel tool, cut about ⅛″ inside the area covered by the plate. Usually this is about ½″ from the edge of the chainplate opening. After prying off the fiberglass, dig out the core material from this area. Cover the sur-

rounding deck and the top surface of the cover plate with masking tape. Carefully seal the lower edge of the opening and coat the chainplate with petroleum jelly. Then fill the void with epoxy filler and let it harden.

With careful work, the epoxy plug will need minimal sanding to bring it flush to the surrounding deck. When the epoxy has cured, apply a liberal amount of sealant around the area and press the cover plate back in place. When the sealant has cured, carefully cut around the plate and remove the excess sealant with the tape.

Taking care of these areas will prevent core rot. Remember, the sealants are there to keep the water out of the boat, not out of the core—the epoxy does that far better.

More-complex problems

It's probably best to run, not walk, away from a boat with a cored hull that is saturated. Repairing it—if it's possible—could be a thankless and expensive task. If the rot is in the deck, it may be repairable—but a professional repair of an extensively saturated deck might

1. A sure sign of trouble. The crack radiating from the chainplate indicates structural problems below and a deteriorated deck core.

2. Use a circular saw with a carbide blade for large areas and a rotary tool with a reinforced cut-off disk for smaller areas.

3. This chainplate is pitted and corroded from years of salt water leaking through the deck. Most corrosion results from salt water coming in contact with the aluminum chainplate and stainless-steel bolts.

Photos this page by Paul Esterle

Core Repairs

37

easily exceed the value of the boat. Or you can tackle the job yourself.

There are three major types of problems: delamination with a dry core, small areas of core rot or wet core, and major deck saturation and delamination. In each case, the first step is to define the extent of the problem. Here is where the services of an experienced surveyor might be well worth the expense. Sound out the deck and mark the areas to be repaired. You want to do this job only once, so be thorough. Nothing is more disheartening than fixing one area and finding later that an area right next to it also needs repair.

Dealing with deck delamination

This could be as simple as drilling a series of holes over the delaminated area and filling them with epoxy. Once you've injected the epoxy into the hole(s) using a plastic syringe, you may need to screw or bolt the layers together until the epoxy hardens. Most of the epoxy suppliers have manuals or videos demonstrating this process. Take extra time to cover the surrounding areas with drop cloths to catch the epoxy drips.

A word to the wise: Don't assume that the core is void-free. Before inject-ing large quantities of epoxy, inject a solvent like acetone or alcohol. Go below and look for telltale leaks. Better the solvent, which will evaporate, than the epoxy, which will cure to a hard lump down the back of your bookshelf.

Dealing with core rot

Strategies. You first need to decide whether you're going to do the repair from underneath or on top. There are advantages and disadvantages to both. Repairing from below will preserve the look and integrity of your deck, and the headliner will cover the repaired areas belowdecks. The disadvantage is that you will be working overhead with the attendant epoxy drips and the complication of holding things in place. You may also have to remove some of the interior joinery to get to the overhead.

Working from the topsides will be much easier in terms of accessing the affected areas, but will require replacing anti-skid areas and repainting. If your anti-skid is worn or your topsides already need painting, this could be an easy decision.

Materials. Once you've identified the areas to be repaired and have decided how to proceed, it's time to gather materials and tools. Even though the deck was probably laminated with some form of polyester resin, epoxy is best for making repairs. Epoxies will reliably bond to polyester. Visit your local chandlery or epoxy manufacturers' Web sites to gather information about the available products. Invest in the epoxy pumps, as they will soon pay for themselves.

You will need the epoxy resin and hardener, pumps, mixing tubs, fillers and additives, fiberglass cloth and/or tape for reinforcement, plus safety equipment like gloves, safety glasses, and respirators if working inside. Don't scrimp here; developing an allergic reaction to epoxy will end your boat-repairing days quickly.

Method. If the area to be fixed is relatively small, use a Dremel tool and cut-off wheel to cut back the fiberglass skin. You want to cut back either the top or the bottom, but not both. In larger areas, use a skill saw with a carbide toothed blade to cut back the skin. Set the blade depth just slightly deeper than the fiberglass skin. If you're working near the edge of the deck or the cabin side, leave a narrow strip of the surface in place. If you're careful, you may be able to save the deck surface and re-epoxy it in place over the new core.

With the core exposed, you can cut away the saturated material. Dig the core out from under the edges of the exposed area. Clean up the area where

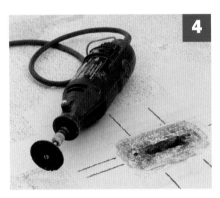

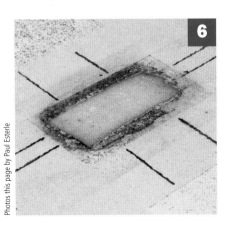

4. After the deck plate is removed, mark the slot location before cutting the deck.

5. The deck is removed around the chainplate and the core is cut back underneath the deck.

6. A cavity filled with epoxy and high-density filler.

7. The chainplate slot is recut with a saber saw (about ⅛" oversize). The chainplate, chainplate cover, and surrounding deck are covered with masking tape. Sealant is applied, and the cover plate is then pressed in place.

Repairs to the core are possible whatever the original material, but some are much easier to work with than others. Foam is the lightest and easiest to cut, aluminum the hardest.

the core material was and sand with coarse-grit paper for a good bond. Taper the edges of the deck opening and the piece of deck you cut out (if you can reuse it). If the deck is ⅛″ thick, taper back about 1″ or so.

It's now time to install a new core. Plywood, foam, and balsa are all possibilities for larger areas. Smaller areas may simply be filled with an epoxy/filler mixture. The most common replacement core is plywood. Use as good an exterior-grade plywood as you can find or afford. Void-free marine ply is best. If the area you're repairing is curved, you'll need to score the new core or cut it into squares; about 4″ to 6″ should be small enough.

Dry-fit the squares in place, fitting them under the edges and cutting them to shape where required. Plan on leaving ⅛″ or so between the squares. Number the squares or lay them out on a surface so you can easily identify which piece goes in next.

Now don your safety equipment and begin mixing the epoxy. Follow the manufacturer's suggestions for a heavy adhesive mixture. Spread a generous

layer of the epoxy in the opening and begin pressing the core squares in place.

If you're working on the underside of the deck, you'll need to get creative to keep the squares in place. Spring-loaded shower rods work wonders in situations like this.

Let the epoxy begin to harden. It needn't be fully cured, just stiff enough to keep things in place while you continue. If you are able to reuse the section of deck you cut out, clean it up and grind the bonding surface with coarse-grit paper to ensure a good bond. Dry-fit it in place to make sure it will be at the right height.

Remove the deck section and apply a layer of epoxy to the core surface, again following the manufacturer's suggestions for a thick adhesive mixture. Be sure to fill all the voids under the edges and between the core squares. Place the deck section on the epoxy and hold it in place with weights, shower rods, or even screws. If you use screws, don't overtighten them and squeeze out all the epoxy. Clean up any ooze around the edges.

Once the epoxy has cured, sand the tapered area between the existing deck edge and the replaced section. Then laminate several layers of glass tape in place, using 1½″ or 2″ tape. Sand level and fill with epoxy filler if needed. You can then repaint the deck and/or apply new anti-skid.

If you were unable to save the section of deck you cut away, you have a little more work to do. Once the core squares are all bonded in place, you need to apply a layer of epoxy and filler over the squares, being sure to fill all voids. You then build up a new deck surface using layers of 9- or 10-ounce fiberglass cloth. Be sure to lap the cloth over the tapered edges of the opening. Once you've built the surface up to almost the original height, you can use epoxy and filler to fair the surface into the existing deck level. Then it's time to paint and apply anti-skid.

Is this all really practical and feasible? Yes, in many cases it is. It all depends on your abilities. Is it economical? If you do the work yourself, it can be.

Working with Epoxy

Epoxy resins have been around quite a while, and you're probably familiar with the basic concept: two components, a resin and a hardener, are mixed together and chemically combine to make a very strong adhesive. Just how this works is pretty arcane; all you need to know is that once the two components are mixed and the chemical reaction starts, there is no going back—the cure is inevitable.

What makes epoxy so versatile is that it can be modified by mixing in various filling and fairing powders with no loss of strength. Which specific filler you use depends mostly on what you're using it for. For example, high-density filler forms very strong joints but is very hard to sand when cured. On the other hand, epoxy mixed with a fairing powder is very easy to sand and can be used to fill imperfections on the surface of the hull. With the correct techniques, epoxy can be used to bond hardware—even winches and cleats—to the deck in place of traditional mechanical fasteners provided the deck is strong enough to cope with the loads imposed.

Safety is an important consideration when using epoxy, though the risk it poses is slight if you take reasonable precautions and follow safe working practices. You should always wear latex or nitrile gloves when handling epoxy, as it is possible to become sensitized from prolonged exposure. It's also much easier to throw away a pair of gloves than it is to get epoxy off your

hands. Acetone will remove uncured epoxy from tools but should never be used to clean epoxy off your skin; it is absorbed immediately into the body and can do irreparable damage to internal organs and the central nervous system (white vinegar will safely clean uncured resin from skin). Safety glasses will keep epoxy out of your eyes. You'll also need to wear a respirator with an organic filter when sanding hardened epoxy and fillers.

Epoxy takes several days to fully cure, and you need to be especially careful when it is only partially cured. It is possible to sand during this time, but this is when the dust is most irritating to nasal passages. Be sure to read and follow the manufacturer's instructions, and you'll have no problems.

If this is the first time you're working with epoxy, a basic kit (foreground) is probably the best option. Gallon containers are more economical for larger jobs.

I've found through bitter experience that I'd have been better off if I'd practiced epoxy techniques before starting on a major project. Making an epoxy joint using a couple of pieces of wood is a good way to start the learning process.

Photos by Mark Corke

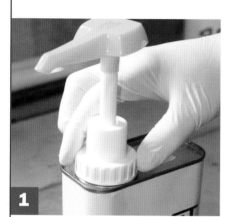

1 and 2. Dispensing pumps
Dispensing pumps make measuring out the exact ratio of resin and hardener a simple and clean process. The pumps can be left attached until the can is empty.

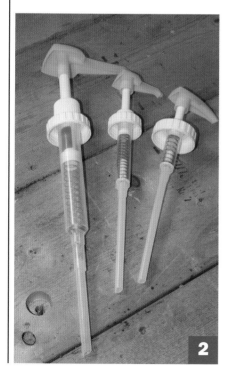

3. Dispensing resin
Press the pump for resin and the pump for hardener just once each to ensure that the correct mixing ratio is maintained. Slowly depress the pumps, decanting first the resin and then the hardener into a plastic cup.

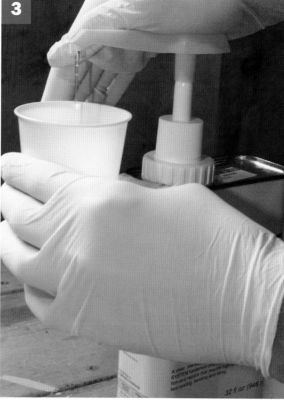

4. Mixing
Thoroughly mix the components together, making sure to scrape the sides of the cup. Wooden or plastic tongue depressors make ideal mixing sticks. As epoxy will not stick to polythene plastic, these can be reused.

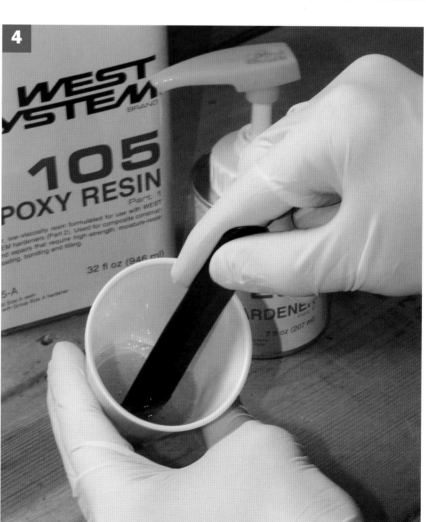

Working with Epoxy

5. Wetting out

Spread a generous layer of glue on both sides of the joint. Use a disposable glue brush or a foam roller if the gluing area is particularly large. This stage, called wetting out, prepares the surfaces for the actual gluing. It prevents the wood from sucking the epoxy out of the thickened mix, as would happen with a dry surface. It also allows the epoxy to flow better over the surface.

5

6b

6. Fillers

After the two parts of the joint have been wetted-out, mix some filler powder into what is left in the plastic cup (6a). If you used up all the resin on wetting out, put another couple of squirts of resin and hardener into the cup and use a clean stick to mix in some colloidal silica. Keep adding and mixing filler powder until the mixture reaches the consistency of ketchup (6b).

6a

7. Spreading the mixture
Spread a generous layer of the thickened mix onto the previously wetted-out surface, as shown.

8. Gluing the parts together
When both edges have been coated with the thickened mixture, bring the two parts together. You don't need a lot of clamping pressure (epoxy will bridge quite large gaps with no loss of strength)—just enough to prevent the parts from sliding around.

9. Scraping off the excess
Before the epoxy sets, use a sharpened mixing stick or an old chisel to scrape off the excess that has squeezed out of the joint. If you don't do it now, the epoxy will set up rock hard and will have to be sanded back. Take the time to do this; it will save hours and tempers later.

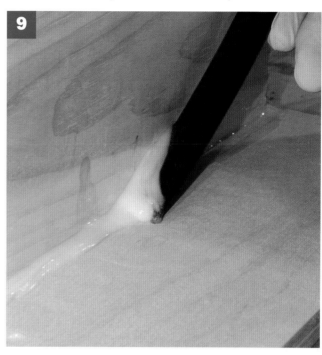

10. Forming a fillet
The next stage in the process is to form a fillet. Much like a welded metal joint, a fillet increases the size of the glued area, makes a neat internal corner, and makes the joint even stronger. Mix up a fresh batch of resin and hardener, but instead of adding silica, mix in some filleting blend (a brown substance). This should be stiffer than the previous mix—about the consistency of stiff mayonnaise. Spread it into the corner of the joint with the end of the mixing stick.

11. Finishing the fillet
Hold a mixing stick with a rounded end at 45 degrees to each of the components and drag it over the filler to form a neat fillet. Scrape off the excess into the cup for reuse farther down the joint.

11

12. Clean up the excess
Without disturbing the neat cove you've formed, again clean up the excess on either side of the fillet with a sharpened mixing stick or an old wood chisel.

12

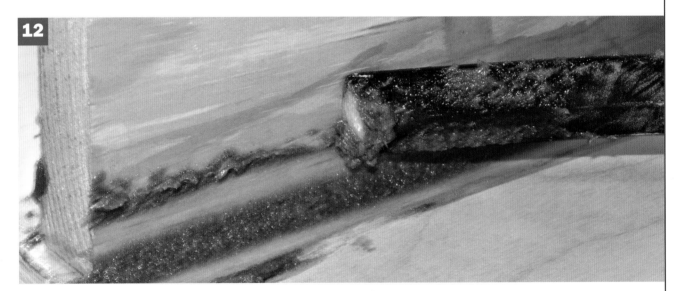

13

13: Finished joint
With both sides done, the joint is now complete. When fully cured it will require minimal sanding to ready it for finishing with paint or varnish.

RESOURCES

West System
www.westsystem.com
866-937-8797

System Three
www.systemthree.com
800-333-5514

MAS
www.masepoxies.com
888-627-3769

Epiglass (Interlux)
www.yachtpaint.com
800-468-7589

Repairing Gelcoat

Peter Caplen

The materials and tools used in this project.

Photos by Peter Caplen

Although fiberglass is a strong and durable boatbuilding material, its exterior gelcoat finish is prone to cosmetic damage. Repairing gelcoat isn't difficult, but matching the color can be. Some boatbuilders provide small quantities of pigment gelcoat for repair purposes, but even these are unlikely to yield an exact match, both because of the vagaries of the mixing process and because the existing gelcoat is likely to have faded after prolonged exposure to sunlight.

With minor repairs, a near-match will be almost invisible after the entire area is properly polished. Large repairs involving major structural work will be hard to hide. In these cases you should consider painting all your gelcoat with a two-part polyurethane; it's not difficult to achieve a good-as-new finish.

The most important factor in a gelcoat repair is speed—not the time taken to do the job, but how quickly the repair is made after the damage has occurred. Deep gouges that penetrate the gelcoat, especially those below the waterline, will eventually cause structural

damage as moisture leaches into the laminate if the gouges are left untreated. Even shallow scratches will allow dirt and grease to permeate the surface over time, making a successful repair more difficult.

The second important consideration is cleanliness. Unless the damaged area is perfectly clean, the new gelcoat will not adhere properly and the repaired area may be discolored by dirt.

Gelcoat filler is a thickened resin rather than a powdery filler. The thickening helps to inhibit "slumping" of the filler on vertical surfaces—in other words, it stays where you put it. Clear filler can be used with an appropriate pigment.

Follow the manufacturer's mixing instructions closely. This is less critical with purely cosmetic repairs than it is with structural work. Many DIYers add extra catalyst when working in lower temperatures to make the new gelcoat cure faster, and in practice this does no harm.

For small jobs it is difficult to measure amounts accurately. The correct mix

for most gelcoat fillers is 1 part pigment to 10 parts resin, followed by 10 milliliters of catalyst to 1 pound of resin. The pigment is always added before the catalyst. As a general guide,

---

🕐 **Approx. job time: 4 hours**

📖 **Skill level: Easy**

✂ **Tools you will need**

- **Gelcoat filler and catalyst**
- **Resin-proof tape**
- **Pigment**
- **Acetone (for cleaning)**
- **Wood chisel (optional)**
- **Stripper knife**
- **Wet-and-dry sandpaper: 180-, 240-, 400-, and 600-grit**
- **Sanding block**
- **Rubbing compound (ammonia-free for use on fiberglass)**

Repairing Gelcoat

1. Gelcoat damage can occur anywhere. If the boat has a wide bow section, this area is particularly prone to damage.

2. Gelcoat is often weak at the knuckles and can chip easily, often exposing the underlying laminate.

3. Transom corners are prone to both scuffing and chipping when coming alongside or moving away from a mooring. Careful close-quarters maneuvering always pays dividends.

4. The topsides can suffer all sorts of damage, from deep scratches to chipping.

5. It is clear these damaged transom corners have been neglected for a long time. Dirt is ground into the damaged areas and must be completely removed before filler is applied. It is best to use hand tools when making cosmetic repairs. This wood chisel works well for cleaning up edges and scraping out dirt. Rinse the area with acetone applied with a clean brush; be careful not to let the acetone run down the hull.

6. Use a stripper knife to trowel the gelcoat filler/pigment mix into the cleaned area. Start at the bottom and work up, being careful to avoid trapping air in the mix. Trowel in enough filler so the repair is higher than the surrounding area; it will be sanded down later.

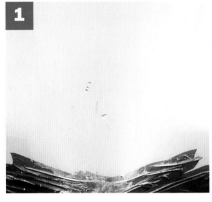

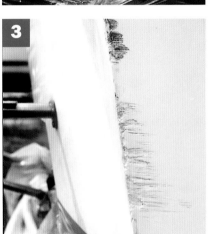
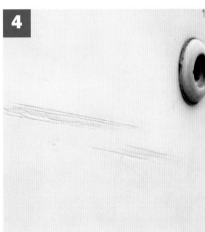

7

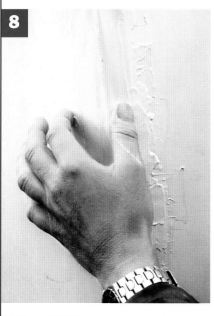

8

9

10

11

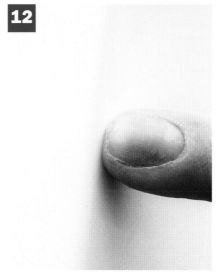

12

7. To prevent the filler from running out, carefully apply resin-proof tape over the top of the repair. Stick the edge of the tape onto firm gelcoat down the side of the repaired area and parallel with it. Then smooth the tape lightly over the repair and, in this case, around the transom corner.

8. If the tape isn't wide enough to cover the entire repaired area, simply apply another piece edge-to-edge alongside the first. Continue smoothing until you reach the other side of the repair and can stick down the edge of the tape onto the surrounding dry gelcoat. It is important to use only light pressure, since it is very easy to squeeze the filler out of position.

9. Allow the filler to cure overnight. The resin-proof tape can be removed before sanding. You'll find that it can be difficult to remove. Scrape one end free using the chisel or filler knife to give you something to hold onto; it will usually pull off in one piece.

10. Wash down the surface with acetone to remove any remaining adhesive from the tape. Use wet 180-grit wet-and-dry paper on a sanding block to remove excess filler. Follow with 240-grit, followed by 400-grit, and finish with 600-grit; all should be used with plenty of water.

11. Unfortunately, a near-perfect finish can be marred by small indentations or voids in the first coat. You'll need to repeat the process on them after roughening and thoroughly drying the areas to be refilled. It's much easier to deal with small voids than with the large initial area of repair.

12. When you've finished sanding and the surface is perfectly smooth, polish it with rubbing compound on a damp rag. Use an ammonia-free rubbing compound to avoid staining the finished surface.

13. Using the same technique, trowel gelcoat filler into the void in the knuckle area.

14. Next, apply the tape. Again, take care to avoid squeezing the filler out of place while ensuring the whole area is covered.

15. A small repair like this can be almost perfectly formed by gently smoothing the tape until the rough shape of the knuckle is achieved.

16. Light sanding with progressively finer wet-and-dry paper produces the final shape.

17. Some tiny pinholes are (barely) visible in the final polished finish. Pinholes like these are often found in undamaged gelcoat; you can ignore them or fill them after the rest of the knuckle is repaired.

when working at temperatures around 55°F you want to mix a golfball of resin with a pea of catalyst; use less hardener when it's warmer (or if you need to work faster).

When working with fiberglass products, wear protective gloves. Some people find it difficult to work with gloves and instead rely on barrier creams.

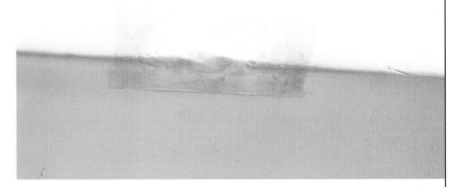

RESOURCES

Laminex
www.bondo.com
800-421-2663

TAP Plastics
www.tapplastics.com
800-246-5055

Sea Hawk Paints
www.seahawkpaints.com
800-528-0997

48

James D. Phyfe

Rebedding Deck Hardware

ittle wears on a sailor as quickly as water in the cabin. Be it at night in a rainy anchorage after a long day's sail or in a gale offshore, a constant dripping of moisture into what should be the one warm, dry haven on board can ruin any crew's spirits. Many a sailor has spent years chasing deck leaks in order to make his boat completely dry.

Aside from the effect on crew morale, deck leaks can do long-term damage to the deck itself and, in severe cases, can be dangerous. As most fiberglass boats built in the last 40 years have decks with wood cores to save weight and provide rigidity, consistent water penetration can cause rot and, ultimately, failure. It can also harm joinery, cosmetic finishes, personal gear, and other equipment on board (I've lost at least one laptop this way).

Most leaks are caused by through-deck fasteners that secure winches, cleats, and other deck hardware (toe-rails and sheet tracks included). The bedding compounds used years ago were not as effective as those used today, and years of wear can cause even the best compounds to eventually break down. As a result, water can find its way through what might be a tiny channel in the bedding and down to the world below.

It pays to have a helper belowdecks when removing and tightening deck hardware.

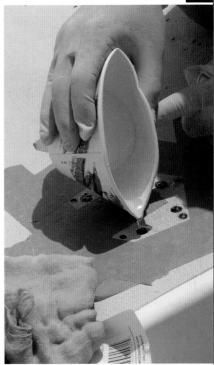

Wear latex gloves when working with epoxy. A tongue depressor makes a handy spreader.

With the underside of the deck taped off, pour in thickened epoxy to make a solid plug.

Rebedding hardware properly isn't a particularly difficult job. Short of there being a crack or hole in the deck, there are few leaks that cannot be fixed by a diligent boatowner with a tube of caulk.

Any rebedding job starts with removal of the hardware and associated fasteners. Although usually not difficult, this does require a set of hands on deck and another below. Good access from both sides is important, and, depending on the boat, a significant amount of interior disassembly may be required. Occasionally a stubborn fastener will have to be addressed with a hacksaw or drill bit, but since you will not be reusing any fasteners, these can be destroyed if necessary. Inevitably, some old bedding compound will be left behind when a piece of hardware is removed. There are many products for lifting old bedding, most of which probably work to some degree or another. I use paint thinner and a soft wire brush in places where the compound really sticks to the anti-skid. As with so many things in life, patience and persistence are what you need most to succeed.

Once the hardware and all traces of old compound are removed, the hard part is over. Now the job becomes fun. The next step is to drill out the fastener holes to roughly three times their original size—for example, a ³⁄₄″ hole for a ¹⁄₄″ fastener. Good results can also be obtained by using a bent nail with the head sawn off in an electric drill to re-

move some of the core between the inner and outer laminate skins. Obviously, this works only for soft cores, such as balsa and foam. The idea is to remove the core and replace it with an epoxy plug through which to drill new fastener holes. This has the added advantage of thoroughly sealing the core against water ingress.

Run a round file through the new hole a few times to roughen up the edges, then clean it thoroughly with solvent. After all is clean and dry, tape over the underside of the hole (duct tape works well for this) and mask off the area surrounding the hole on deck. Next, mix up some epoxy and thicken it with filler to the consistency of a heavy

Drill holes slightly undersized, then screw the bolt home.

These holes in the overhead have not yet been filled with thickened epoxy.

A helper with a square ensures holes are vertical. Use a sharp drill at a slow speed.

syrup. Pour the mixture into the hole(s) and let it cure.

You have now created a plug of epoxy through which to pass the new fasteners. These plugs will provide non-compressible surfaces onto which fasteners can be tightened. Many deck leaks occur when new hardware is mounted in an area cored with a soft material such as balsa or foam. Tightening the fasteners squeezes the deck and compresses the core, creating small cracks in the fiberglass that allow water to penetrate the laminate. The solid epoxy plug will also isolate the surrounding core if a leak down the fastener hole does develop later. This is particularly important when working with decks cored with plywood, because once water comes in contact with the wood, it will migrate quickly through the deck.

After the epoxy plugs have set up and the tape has been removed (be sure to remove the masking tape on deck before the epoxy is fully cured, as hardened spillage will make it difficult to remove), you can drill the new holes. Using a template or the hardware itself, line the holes up exactly where you want them and then dimple their centers with a punch. This is the best way to guide the bit when drilling. Keep the holes as close to the center of the epoxy plugs as possible so no core will come in contact with the fasteners when the hardware is installed.

I like to drill the holes slightly smaller than the fasteners so that the fasteners can be threaded into the deck. This way there is even less room for water to find its way below. Doing this, however, can make it difficult to align the heads of the fasteners in the proper direction in the end. With liberal use of a bedding compound, a slightly larger hole can also be properly sealed.

Removing Ornery Hardware

Once when attempting to remove an anchor windlass from the foredeck of a large cruising boat, I was confronted with a very "sticky" problem. After removing the through-deck fastening bolts, I found the windlass base had been bedded with a tenacious adhesive sealant similar to 3M's 5200 and was still firmly glued in place. To lift the windlass off the deck, I carefully drove a wood chisel and a large screwdriver under its base and pried it up enough to get some wedges under the perimeter. As I gained clearance, I cut exposed strands of adhesive with my pocketknife and maintained constant upward pressure with the wedges until at last the windlass came free. Unfortunately, the adhesive had peeled back several sections of gelcoat and some chips and chunks of fiberglass. Though it was only minor damage, I hated to see any at all.

Later, a fellow boatowner who is a machinist by trade suggested a way to avoid such collateral damage. He recommended looping a long piece of piano wire or guitar string around the base of the hardware to be removed. Then, with a stick or length of broom handle, the ends of the wire can be twisted tourniquet fashion to slowly tighten the loop and cut through the adhesive without damaging the deck. It may be necessary to pause to allow time for the cutting action to take place. In some cases, you'll need to tighten, wait a little bit, then tighten some more before all the adhesive is cut through.

Arthur R. Lee

Use plenty of compound when rebedding deck fittings. Wipe off excess with clean rag.

Get a helper to hold the screw heads while you tighten from below with a wrench.

Many different compounds can be used to bed hardware, and deciding which to use depends on several factors. On wooden boats that will swell and shrink, for example, you would do well to use a soft compound such as Dolphinite. If you are dead set against ever doing this job again and are confident you will never want to move a piece of hardware after rebedding it, an indestructible compound such as 3M's 5200 could be used, but be warned—I have seen 5200 take out chunks of deck with it when hardware is removed. For general purposes, a less-aggressive polysulfide caulking compound, such as LifeCalk, will work just fine.

The final step is to reinstall the hardware. Remember to always use new fasteners. Fasteners that have been well tightened and then subjected to loads will have stretched and will have lost strength and form. For any hardware that will be subjected to serious loads, always use large backing plates that span the entire area between fastener holes with a generous margin be-

Fender washers spread the loads imposed by the bolts. Always use new fasteners.

yond them. Assemble the pieces first in a dry run, with no bedding compound, so that you are sure the holes are properly sized, the fasteners fit, and the hardware is exactly where you want it. It is best to use over-long bolts with washers on both sides and lock-washers or lock nuts. You can always cut off the excess bolt with a hacksaw afterward.

Once everything is laid out and you have a helper at the ready, apply a liberal amount of bedding compound (it's a lot easier to clean up excess goo than it is to add more later) and press the hardware in place. Tighten the nuts on the bolts while your helper holds the head in place with a screwdriver. Don't kill yourself trying to get the fastener as tight as you can, but be sure to get it good and snug.

Cleaning up is no big deal. Usually solvent and lots of small (about 3″ × 3″) rags are all you need to do the job. If working around Plexiglas or Lexan, use mineral spirits instead of paint thinner, as it is less likely to scratch these sorts of surfaces. Be very careful with acetone. When you are sure the bedding compound is fully cured, give the fasteners another quarter turn as some caulking compounds shrink slightly when curing. If you have done the job correctly, the hardware will now be able to stand up to heavy strain and a good dunking with no signs of any leaks.

Paint and Varnish

s there anything quite as beautiful as a traditional bright-finished yacht—whether a sailboat or a powerboat—her varnish gleaming under the sun, turning heads wherever she goes? I don't think so. The beauty of perfectly finished woodwork is, for many people, a large source of the satisfaction of owning a boat.

Who better to give you the lowdown on how to achieve that perfect finish than Don Casey? I don't think anyone knows more about paint and varnish application and techniques than he does. In this section Don tells you what to use in which situations, and he offers his top tips for saving yourself time and money.

Our other contributors have served their time up to their elbows in various kinds of paint, too. Whether it's choosing and applying antifouling paint, deciding whether or not to spray a polyurethane finish, or marking out a perfect waterline with a laser level, they've done it all, and reading their advice could save you a lot of time and heartache.

We'll also show you some tricks to help you get old finishes off; it's nasty work, but someone's got to do it. And hopefully you'll find our piece on painting a plywood dinghy with modern finishes inspirational, too.

Painting and Varnishing Tips

Always dewax a hull before sanding. Otherwise the wax will be dragged into the sanded surface, making it harder for paint to adhere to it.

Peter Nielsen

Spring is the season when a sailor's thoughts turn to gloss. If this is the year you think you're finally going to restore the shine to your hull and put the bright back into your brightwork, here are a few hard-won truths that should yield great results. A spectacular finish takes only a little more time and effort than a mediocre finish. The difference is mostly in technique. Follow these tips, and you should see your own undistorted smile of satisfaction reflected back at you.

Painting

Use *only* two-part linear polyurethane (LPU) to paint your topsides. LPU is no more difficult to apply to an uninterrupted expanse of topsides than other paints, but yields a finish that retains its gloss at least twice as long as any other paint you can apply. And what gloss! Applied with a foam roller and tipped with a dry badger-hair brush, a two-part polyurethane finish will look shinier than brand-new gelcoat. LPU is also quick-skinning, which makes it less vulnerable to boatyard dust and grit.

• **Dewax first.** Regardless of the paint you use, wax on the hull will prevent it from adhering and will ruin the finish. Sanding does not remove all the wax,

Varnishing Do's and Don'ts

- Do start with smooth wood. If the wood is discolored, bleaching will be necessary, followed by sanding to smooth the surface.

- Don't use urethane varnish for exterior wood. Oil-based varnishes maintain their grip better on exposed surfaces.

- Do varnish at anchor or on a mooring. Moving your boat away from land avoids most airborne contamination.

- Don't varnish when you know you shouldn't. Rain, fog, dew, or a sudden temperature change will spoil the finish.

- Do wipe raw teak with acetone prior to varnishing. It is essential to remove as much surface oil as possible for good adhesion.

- Don't varnish without masking. Masking allows you to varnish more quickly, which improves the quality of the finish.

- Do thin the first three coats. Thinning allows the initial coats of varnish to double as a sealant, extending the life of the finish.

- Don't varnish from the can. Decant the amount of varnish you need, always pouring it through a mesh paint filter.

- Do try a foam brush. Foam brushes do not shed, and they tend to prevent you from applying varnish too thickly.

- Don't make one more stroke with your brush than necessary. Worrying the varnish degrades the finish.

- Do sand between finish coats. Sand, and the only flaws are those in the final coat; don't sand, and the flaws of every coat show through.

- Don't sand within 24 hours of laying a coat on. Let each finish coat dry 48 hours or longer before sanding but drags it into the scratches the grit makes. You must dewax *before* you sand. Even if you know your hull has never been waxed, the first coating in the mold when your boat was being laid up was a wax mold release. Use a de-waxing solvent and "sweep" a saturated rag in one direction to dissolve and lift the wax residue. Turn the rag often, and change it when you run out of fresh areas.

• **Glossy paints accentuate flaws.** Genius may be 99 percent perspiration (I wouldn't know), but brilliance is 99 percent preparation. LPU paint is not like the thick one-coat stuff you roll on the living room wall. It goes on milk-thin and won't hide anything. Instead, it will accentuate every underlying flaw. If you want a perfect finish, the surface you are painting must be perfect. Fill dings and scratches with epoxy putty. Cover crazing and/or weathering (porosity) with a coat or two of epoxy primer. Sand the entire hull billiard-ball smooth with 120-grit paper.

• **If you are sweating, it is too humid to paint.** The curing of two-part polyurethanes is accelerated by moisture. If the air is humid, the paint gels before it has a chance to flow out to a mirrorlike finish. Do not paint when the humidity is above 70 percent. Ignore this edict and you will see brush strokes in your finish. Dew has the same effect. Don't paint in the early morning or late afternoon. Don't paint when rain is forecast. It is best to paint when there is little wind and the temperature is between 50°F and 80°F.

• **Thinning is the key to a stroke-free finish.** The amount of thinner you need to add to mixed paint varies with

changes in humidity and temperature. To get it right, you have to sneak up on it. Use a piece of clean window glass or some other perfect surface to serve as a test panel. Starting with slightly less thinner than recommended, brush a small amount of thinned paint onto the vertical glass. If the brush strokes do not disappear entirely in a couple of minutes, add around 1 percent more thinner by volume and test again. Continue this process, thinning in 1 percent increments, until the stroke marks just disappear. Try not to go too far; too much thinner diminishes the gloss and creates sags and runs. When the mixture passes the brush test, pour some into a paint tray and try your foam roller on the glass. Lightly drag a dry badger-hair brush through the paint to smooth it and eliminate bubbles. If the paint is mirror-smooth in a minute or two, you are ready to go.

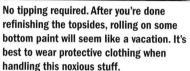

No tipping required. After you're done refinishing the topsides, rolling on some bottom paint will seem like a vacation. It's best to wear protective clothing when handling this noxious stuff.

• **Paint fast.** Two-part polyurethane paint begins to set almost immediately, so the faster you roll it on and tip it out, the better the finish will be. Try to apply LPU in no more than 45 seconds per linear foot on a boat with less than 4 feet of freeboard. That translates into less than 30 minutes to paint one side of a 38-foot boat. Keep telling yourself "faster, faster, faster." It is best to have one person rolling and a second tipping. Once you've tipped the paint, don't even think about going back. Correct mistakes with a second coat.

• **Brush out, not in.** When tipping LPU, you should always brush in only one direction, toward the unpainted surface. The first stroke should be at the rail, the last at the bootstripe, with each stroke only slightly overlapping the one above. Start your forward brush stroke in the air and let the brush touch the paint just inside the previously tipped area. Drag it smoothly across the rolled-on paint and lift it off again as it pulls out of the paint onto the unpainted surface. The idea is to move the extra paint forward rather than back onto the already painted surface, where it can cause a ridge.

• **Lacquer-mist between coats.** You should wet-sand with 340-grit paper between coats. But it can be very hard to

A glossy finish accentuates minor surface flaws. If you want a shiny hull, be prepared to do the necessary prep work.

Spraying on paint is best left the to the professionals. The equipment is expensive, and respirators are an absolute must.

see where you have sanded, especially on white paint on a bright day. The solution is to lightly mist the surface with a contrasting color of spray lacquer. The lacquer dries instantly, comes off as you sand, and thus makes sanded areas very distinct from those not sanded.

• **One edge at a time.** The "wet edge" is where painted and unpainted surfaces abut. If you roll the topsides from waterline to rail, you have only one wet edge, which will move across the hull from bow to stern or vice versa. Maintaining a single wet edge when painting the deck requires some forethought; the payoff is that you can use LPU on the deck. Anywhere the surface you're painting takes off in two directions, mask off one of them. Mask off the other side the next day and paint the sections individually. The result is perfect finish everywhere,

The key to a good varnish job is to go heavy on the sandpaper when prepping the surface to be varnished. Suffer now, or suffer later.

with (perhaps) a very faint line between sections.

• **Sift, don't mix.** When adding grit to your deck paint to create an antiskid finish, you'll get better looking results if you sift the grit onto a coat of wet primer rather than mixing it in with the paint.

Varnishing

Varnish on a mooring or at anchor. Dust is the enemy. The amount of dust that gets into your varnish is inversely related to your distance from shore when the varnish is applied. A boatyard is the worst place to work. Prep the wood in the yard, but keep the varnish can tightly sealed until your boat is in the water.

• **Always bleach raw wood.** Even the most colorless varnish darkens wood after six or eight coats, and all oil-based varnishes darken with age. If you really want bright brightwork, the raw wood, especially if it's teak, should be as light as possible before the first coat of varnish goes on. Dissolve half a cup of oxalic-acid crystals in a quart of warm water to make a strong bleach solution. Wet the raw wood with this solution, applying it with a sponge or paint brush. (Mask adjoining surfaces as necessary; this solution will etch both paint and gelcoat.) Let the wood dry completely, then vacuum or carefully brush away the powder that remains.

Wet the wood with a borax or soda-ash solution (1 cup borax to 2 gallons water) to neutralize the remaining acid. Rinse the wood and neutralize it a second time. The wood should dry to a uniform light color.

• **Don't skimp on sanding.** If you want your varnishing to be worth the effort, the bare wood must be smooth. "Plane" rough wood with 60-grit or 80-grit paper until it is smooth to the touch; then sand the wood ivory-smooth with 120-grit paper. The sanding you don't perform on the wood will be paid for with additional sanding on the varnish.

• **Build-up coats should always be gloss.** When applying a satin-finish or rubbed-effect varnish, you will get better results using a high-gloss varnish for the build-up coats. This is because rubbed-effect varnish contains pigments that "muddy" the finish. The more coats, the muddier the look. Gloss varnish is clear, so build-up coats of gloss highlight rather than obscure the finish. Covering clear varnish with one or two top coats of rubbed-effect varnish eliminates the gloss without reducing the depth.

• **Mask, mask, mask.** I am astonished by how many sailors I see applying varnish without masking adjacent surfaces. This is false economy. No matter how steady your hand, you will get better results with less effort if you mask. Not only does the tape protect your gel-

Malcolm White

Avoid varnishing in a boatyard whenever possible. Working on a mooring or at a dock is always preferable.

coat or paint, it also allows you to apply the varnish more quickly, which pays dividends in the quality of the finish. Cheap masking tape is another false economy. If you use long-life tape (3M 2080 or its equivalent), you only have to mask once.

• **Thin the first coat 50 percent.** On raw wood you want the varnish to penetrate as deeply as possible. Thin the first coat with ½ ounce of thinner to every ounce of varnish. As soon as this penetrating coat is dry to the touch, apply a second coat thinned about 25 percent by volume (¼ ounce thinner per ounce of varnish). Let this coat dry overnight, then apply a third coat thinned about 10 percent. If you get the third coat on within 24 hours of the second one, you won't need to sand between the two. After the third coat, sand with 220-grit paper between build-up coats and with 320-grit between the final two coats. All coats after the third one should be applied at full strength, except in hot weather when small amounts of thinner may be needed to keep the brush from "dragging." It will take at least six coats of varnish to provide lasting protection for the wood; as many as eight or nine coats are needed to achieve that much-admired "foot-deep" look.

• **Use foam or badger-hair brushes.** Next to dust, your worst enemy when varnishing is loose bristles. Don't use cheap bristle brushes. You can buy a $15 badger-hair brush for your varnish work and take meticulous care of it, or you can buy a bag of 50-cent foam brushes and throw them away when you're done. Either way you keep bristles out of your varnish. If you get better results with badger hair, that's what you should use. In my hands, foam delivers the better finish.

• **Don't worry the varnish.** Laying on varnish is more like penmanship than painting. Ideally you want to transfer a brush-width of varnish to the wood with a single stroke, like drawing a smooth, even line with an ink pen. If the area you are coating is wider than your brush, make parallel strokes in the same direction, overlapping them slightly. Try to allow yourself no more than two additional strokes per brush width to even out the varnish. With each additional stroke of your brush, you introduce air bubbles into the varnish, some of which will become trapped. Finish each brush width of varnish with a single long stroke, "landing" your forward-moving brush just inside the old wet edge and dragging it just beyond the new wet edge.

• **Wait 48 hours between finish coats.** Most varnishes can be safely recoated without sanding within about 24 hours. But when you recoat without sanding, each successive coat accentuates the flaws of the previous coat, plus adds its own. Sanding removes surface flaws from the previous coat, limiting flaws in the finish to those in the top coat. Sand between coats and the top surface gets progressively smoother; fail to sand and it gets progressively rougher. But varnish is rarely dry enough to sand in 24 hours. If sanding between coats, wait at least 48 hours. Three days is even better. You will be rewarded for your patience with a dry surface that sands easily without loading the sandpaper or "rolling" the fresh varnish. For the best possible finish, open a new can of varnish for your final coat.

• **Bonus tip: Never polish brightwork!** Maintaining varnished interior wood with furniture polish will cause you grief when the time eventually comes to put down a fresh coat of varnish. Instead, it is better to wipe brightwork with a 3-to-1 mixture of water and distilled vinegar to clean it and keep it bright.

TIP

Sometimes you need to keep wet paint or varnish brushes for a few days or even weeks. One method is to wrap them in plastic wrap—they'll keep for a week like this. Another is to drill a small hole through the handles and use a piece of wire to suspend them in enough thinner to cover the bristles. Keep paint and varnish brushes separate.

Choosing Brightwork Finishes

The greatest investment in varnishing is the time put in to applying it, so a cheap $20 varnish may not be such a bargain. It's worthwhile spending extra for a top-quality varnish and having the finish last as long as possible. Be sure to use a varnish that is designed for marine use.

Finish types

One-part varnish. There are three basic finishes for wood: one-part varnish, two-part varnish, and oil finishes. Within these categories are a number of variations—clear, satin, gloss, and matte finishes; polyurethane and tung oil bases; products that do and don't require sanding between coats.

One-part varnishes can be used straight from the can. Their three main components are an oil, a solvent, and a resin. These varnishes are somewhat flexible and can expand and contract as weather affects the wood they protect. This makes them an ideal choice for covering large areas on boats.

Two-part varnish. These finishes come in two parts—a clear coating and a hardener or catalyst. When they're mixed together in the correct ratio, a chemical reaction occurs that results in a very hard, tough finish. Once mixed, the application process for a two-part varnish is the same as for a one-part varnish.

Oil finishes. An oil finish has a higher oil content than a varnish and less solvent and resin. One of the great virtues of an oil finish is speed of application, even if numerous coats are used. But oil finishes must be applied more frequently than varnish. I've had good results using an oil finish belowdecks, where it holds up well.

Compatibility

Suppose you've just bought a used boat. How can you tell what surface coating has been used and whether a new coating will be compatible?

One way to check whether the surface treatment will be compatible is to tape off a small, inconspicuous area and try applying a thin coat of the desired finish. Leave it for 24 hours and if

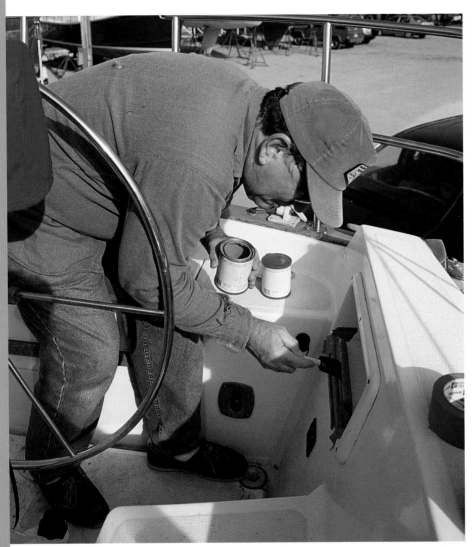

Some finishes contain pigments, which color the wood as well as provide a protective coating.

Alison Langley

There are few boatowners who have never walked the docks and marveled at a beautifully varnished rail or hatch cover. Even boats with no exterior varnish often have some brightwork down below; fiddles, door frames, bookshelves, and mast supports are often finished bright to break up a stark white interior. Any brightwork on your boat, inside or out, needs regular maintenance to stay in top condition.

Varnishes are expected to fulfill two important functions—they enhance the natural beauty of the wood and protect

it from the elements. One of the greatest threats to varnish is sunlight. Though all exterior varnishes should contain UV inhibitors, all finishes will eventually break down when continuously exposed to bright sun. As the sun penetrates the finish, it lifts the varnish from the wood. You've probably seen a teak toerail whose wood is turning black under a smooth exterior. Because the varnish is no longer adhering to the wood, it must be removed and replaced to restore the finish and provide the necessary protection.

Oil finishes are becoming increasingly popular. If you are new to these products try them out on scrap wood to ensure that you understand how to use them.

it dries with no signs of crazing or alligatoring then the two should be okay together. It is worth noting that two-part varnishes are hard and can be over coated with a one-part finish but the reverse is not true. A two-part product used over a one-part finish will crack and flake due to the movement of the flexible undercoats.

The one sure way to solve compatibility problems is to remove all the old finish and start fresh. This sounds like a lot of work, and it can be—especially if you have acres of varnished wood

aboard. But it's the best way to revive an existing surface in poor shape, and it could save you time (and money) in the long run.

Overcoating an oil finish with varnish is often less of a problem, as oils are often present in the composition of the varnish. Even so, you should try the two together on a small test area.

Preparation

One thing I've learned over and over is that the best finish starts with meticulous preparation. Starting off with bare wood is in many ways easiest, because you don't have to worry about compatibility with any previous coatings. Especially if the old coating is in a state of disrepair, it's best to remove it completely. I like to use a hot-air gun and a sharp scraper. Use sandpaper only as a

Pros and Cons

One-Part Varnish
PROS: Less expensive than two-part varnish; flexible; easy to apply
CONS: Not as durable as two-part varnish; must be applied in warm conditions

Two-Part Varnish
PROS: Very hard surface; ideal over an epoxy finish
CONS: Expensive; can be tricky to apply properly

Oil Finishes
PROS: Easy to apply; economical
CONS: Can look artificial, especially if a stain is added; needs to be redone more often than varnish

I have had excellent results with wipe-on oil finishes for interior woodwork. They are easy to apply, and many provide a low luster sheen.

Photos this page by Mark Corke

Available as either two-part or one-part products, all varnish should be applied as recommended by the manufacturer. You can overcoat a two-part with a one-part varnish, but not the other way around.

last resort; it's slow and expensive, it gums up, and it creates a lot of dust.

If the previously varnished surface is in good condition, you can give it a thorough wash-down with plenty of clean water and then sand the surface with either 320- or 400-grit wet-and-dry paper. Use it wet to smooth and prep it for additional coats of varnish.

Application

Using the correct application technique is the key to a perfect finish, which is why it's imperative to follow the instructions on the varnish can to the letter. Don't varnish on a damp day or when the air is full of dust. It pays to use the best brushes you can lay your hands on;

natural bristles are best. Keep the brushes you use for varnishing separate from paint brushes and use them only for varnishing.

Conclusions

After many years of varnishing, my personal preference is to have a rubbed oil finish belowdecks and a gloss-finish one-part varnish on all above decks brightwork. I know many varnishers who swear by their own favorite brand, and they get nice results. I strongly recommend that you choose one finish and then stick with it. Get to know one product well, learn how to apply it properly, and you'll be rewarded with a finish your boating neighbors will admire.

There's a lot of advice on varnishing available. My favorite is *Brightwork: The Art of Finishing Wood,* by Rebecca Wittman (International Marine). Lavishly illustrated with stunning photography, it contains a wealth of knowledge on all things that deal with varnishing.

Photos this page by Mark Corke

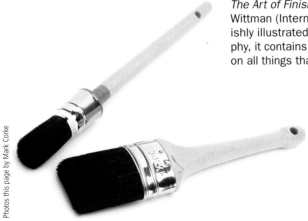

Good varnish brushes go a long way to achieving varnish perfection.

PAINT AND VARNISH

Peter Caplen

Bottom Painting

Applying bottom paint is one of the more onerous chores of boat maintenance, but it is essential if the boat is to perform properly. These paints aren't cheap, so it's worth spending the time to do a good job.

When you're working with antifouling paint, remember that it is a poison and that prolonged exposure without adequate protection can cause irreparable damage to your health. Dry-sanding is

When applying antifouling, follow the manufacturer's guidelines, especially with regard to safety. Gloves, a Tyvek suit, and a respirator are essential for safe application.

the most lethal way to remove antifouling; don't do it unless you use a dedicated antifouling sander with a dust extracter. Without the proper equipment, dust entering the lungs and eyes will have disastrous long-term consequences for the operator and bystanders. Always wear protective clothing—goggles, a particulate dust mask with an organic filter, gloves, and a Tyvek suit—when preparing the hull for bottom paint.

Antifoulings removed by any method are harmful to the environment if not properly disposed of. Many marinas now have settling tanks installed in their DIY areas for proper disposal of the residue.

As soon as the boat is hauled, clean the hull to remove all the weed, slime,

and shellfish that have attached themselves. A high-pressure washer is easiest for this job, but an equally effective (though more labor-intensive) finish can be achieved with a garden hose and a scraper.

Products used

- antifouling-paint remover (must be a type harmless to fiberglass)
- antifouling barrier primer
- hard racing antifouling paint
- brush cleaner

Bottom Painting

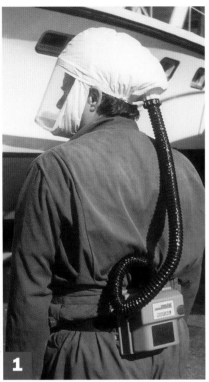

Photos by Peter Caplen

1. The ultimate protective headgear is 3M's Dustmaster. It costs a couple of hundred dollars, but wearing it may extend your life by a number of years.

2. The equipment you need varies depending on the standard of finish required, but may include the following:
- Brushes: Standard bristle for antifouling application (as large as practically possible), plus nylon bristle for antifouling remover.
- Rollers: large and small (or paint pads) and tray.
- Stripper knife, masking tape, brush cleaner, cleaning rags.

3. Once the hull is clean and dry, inspect it for damage. Fiberglass boats should be checked for osmotic blistering and impact damage. Steel boats may have damaged paint coatings, corrosion, and rust. Check a wooden hull for damaged paint, soft spots, and loose caulking.

When all the necessary repairs have been made, the next step is to examine the existing bottom paint to determine the extent of prep work required. If the paint is perfectly sound, you can simply use a compatible paint type and apply an overcoat. All the major manufacturers of antifouling bottom paints provide compatibility charts to indicate which of their products can be used with those of other manufacturers.

4. If you want a very smooth bottom for racing, take extra care at the inspection stage to ensure there are no areas where the previous coating is flaking off. If the previous coatings are sound, you can be a bit less fastidious with the surface finish. If there is evidence that they are flaking off, cracking, or bubbling, it's best to strip off all previous coatings down to the bare hull.

5. It is equally important to remove all rough patches in the old antifouling layer.

6. There are several methods of removing old antifouling; none is very pleasant. Sand-blasting is safe and effective, though care is needed to avoid cutting into the hull surface. The alternative is to use a proprietary antifouling stripping solution. This is usually applied in one thick layer with either a stripping knife or a nylon bristle brush. It must be left on the surface long enough to react. This can take several days if the antifouling is particularly thick or temperatures are very cold.

7. It is important to apply the stripper very thickly to penetrate many layers of antifouling. Once all the layers are softened, they can be washed off with a pressure washer and scraper. Stubborn areas can be treated with further applications of stripper.

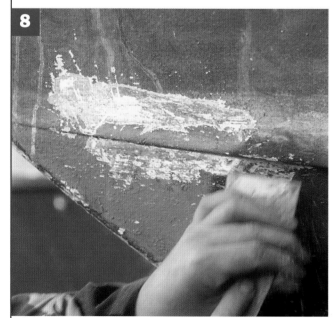

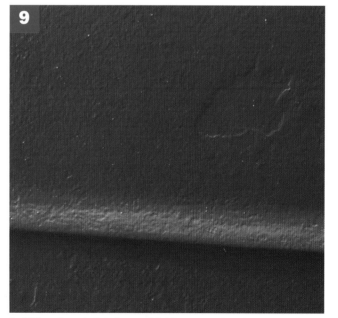

8. If the hull was not properly prepared originally, try dry-scraping. You can often lift off large areas of antifouling in one go where it has not adhered properly to the hull or to previous coats.

Sanding is another removal method, but it is tiring and time-consuming and is better suited to surface preparation than removal. Health and safety issues must be considered when using this method.

9. If there is an isolated area of flaking on an otherwise good surface, removal can be restricted to that one area. However, this leaves an uneven surface and "craters" when the new antifouling is applied. After the surface in the damaged area has been prepared, build up the antifouling by patch-brushing until it is level with the rest. This may require several applications. The entire hull is then ready for antifouling as normal.

Preparation

Hulls with bottom paint. Unless the underlying antifouling surface is good, removal of the old antifouling is the first step in preparing a rough or flaky surface. If the surface is smooth and sound and the new antifouling is compatible with the old coating, the only preparation required is to wash down the hull with fresh clean water and allow the surface to dry before masking off the anodes and waterline prior to applying the first coat.

New hulls. A new fiberglass hull must be completely dewaxed and then sanded with 280-grit wet-and-dry paper to roughen the surface. Once this has been done, the hull is ready for antifouling application. However, applying an anti-osmosis epoxy undercoat before painting is well worth the effort.

Steel or wooden hulls will, as a matter of course, have been properly protected prior to antifouling and should require only a freshwater washdown prior to painting.

10. The waterline and anodes are first masked off with 2" tape.

11. If a different brand of antifouling is to be used over the old coating, or if the old make and type are unknown, apply a barrier coat to form a seal that prevents an adverse reaction between the two antifoulings.

12. Although most paint manufacturers recommend two coats, I have often found one generous coat to be sufficient. When using a barrier primer, following the manufacturer's instructions is essential. Using a brush ensures the best thickness and the smoothest finish, but rollers—large short-pile types for the main areas and small short-pile (radiator) types for confined areas—are much quicker. Brushes can be used for final touching up of awkward areas.

Finishing Touches

Special applications. Special care must be taken when selecting an antifouling paint for an aluminum boat or any boat with a saildrive or outboard engine. These require copper-free paint to avoid setting up galvanic corrosion.

Cleaning up. When the job is complete, immediately clean the brushes and tray with a good-quality brush cleaner. I generally discard roller heads but like to keep good brushes.

Relaunching. It is important to follow the manufacturer's recommendations. Some paints require relaunching within days of application, while others (generally the more modern types) can be left ashore for several months.

13. When the required number of coats have been applied, remove the masking tape immediately; otherwise it becomes difficult to remove and may tear away some of the paint after it has dried. If the job is being performed over several days, use a Long Mask masking tape (available in all standard widths) from 3M. It is several times more expensive than standard masking tapes but can be left in place until the job is completed.

Mark Corke

Choosing a Bottom Paint

Illustration by Tadami Takahashi

The chances are that unless you have a small daysailer or dinghy that spends most of its time out of the water, your boat will have some form of antifouling paint below the waterline. Antifouling paint is poisonous to marine life and prevents it, as much as possible, from adhering to the bottom while the boat is in the water. Sailors early on recognized the importance of keeping the bottom of their craft free of fouling as a hull covered with barnacles and weeds loses significantly in terms of speed and performance. To deter marine growth, they nailed sheets of copper (poisonous to marine life) to the undersections of their boats.

It's certainly more convenient to apply a paint offering similar properties to those of the copper sheets. In fact, most antifouling paints contain large amounts of copper in the form of cuprous oxide,

which repels marine growth and is held in a binder to make it into a paint that can be applied to the boat. The rising cost of copper is one reason why antifouling paint is so expensive.

Unlike the copper sheets of old, antifouling paint often needs to be reapplied every year—sometimes less often, depending on where the boat is sailed and whether it is left in the water all season.

Which type?

It's a good idea to think in terms of the type of paint you need before getting mired down in cost and manufacturers. There is a confusing variety to choose from—ablative/self-polishing, traditional, hard modified epoxies, vinyl, thin film, and a number of specialized varieties, each targeted at a specific application.

Ablatives/self-polishing

Ablative paints are formulated to wear away exposing fresh biocide, usually copper, as the boat moves through the water. They depend on water washing away the paint surface, so they are not a good choice for a boat that stays at the dock or on a mooring for extended periods of time. Because the rate of wear varies with the water flow, extra coats are needed on leading edges that see higher velocities.

Copolymer ablatives can provide multi-season protection. Their antifouling properties are not degraded by drying out, and these paints are recommended for trailersailers. It is desirable to have the first coat of antifouling of a different color than subsequent ones to serve as a flag coat. When the flag coat begins to show, it's definitely time to repaint. Because the paint film wears away over time, minimal prep work is required before re-painting.

Ablatives are produced by all major bottom-paint manufacturers. At least one manufacturer has a copolymer paint that does not rely on the boat's movement to release fresh biocide, but it is sold for professional use only.

Traditional soft/sloughing

Older formulations are based on rosin or rosin/resin blends; they vary from soft to semi-hard and are in general the lowest-cost antifouling paints. The softer of these don't stand up to abrasion and are sometimes referred to as "sloughing," although their primary action is the result of the biocide, almost always cuprous oxide, leaching out of the paint. These single-season paints are an economical choice for cruising boats that are hauled for the winter.

Hard modified epoxies

Based on epoxy resins, these are hard one-part paints that in some cases can be burnished. Their effectiveness and cost vary with the percentage of biocide (usually cuprous oxide without additives). They are the most likely to be compatible for overcoating other types of antifouling, other than those that are soft or contain low-friction components like Teflon. They require launching within 24 hours or less (varies from paint to paint) after the final coat. While they lose effectiveness when out of the water for extended periods, this does not happen immediately, so haulouts are practical. They work by releasing the biocide from the paint over the course of the season, so the effectiveness drops as the biocide needs to come from deeper within the paint. This can be offset to some extent with periodic scrubbing. Because the paint film does not wear away, it must be removed from time to time to avoid excessive buildup.

Vinyls

The hardest of antifouling paints, they are often used on racing boats as they can be wet-sanded and burnished to a polished surface. Because their strong solvents are capable of attacking other paints, all other types of antifouling must be removed before vinyls are applied, since tie coats are not a viable solution. Vinyls also must be launched soon after application.

Use cheap brushes and roller covers when applying antifouling paints.

Thin film

These paints are described as low-drag/high-performance paints, suitable for freshwater use, that incorporate low-friction components like Teflon in addition to copper-based and chemical biocides. One such paint is stated to dry within 2 to 6 minutes and require launching within 10 to 30 minutes.

Specialized antifouling paints

Aluminum safe: These employ copper thiocyanate in lieu of cuprous oxide to avoid galvanic attack on aluminum hulls and other underwater components. Often available in spray cans for use on the lower ends of saildrives.

Boottop: Hard scrubbable antifouling also using copper thiocyanate, but compatible with bright colored pigments instead of the dull muted colors of paints using cuprous oxide.

Transducer: Usually sold in spray cans, these antifoulings are formulated to not degrade electronic performance. They may have zinc as a biocide.

Inflatable: Flexible antifouling formulated to bond to nonrigid coated fabrics.

How do you choose?

Choosing your antifoulings requires making several decisions: What type is your existing antifouling, and how much maintenance do you want to do? Is your boat a trailersailer, or will it remain in the water for an extended period of time? Is the water salt or fresh? How important is speed, long life, or both? Since the severity of fouling can vary significantly from area to area, it's useful to consult with other sailors in the area, with local boatyards, and/or with the guys behind the counter at the local boat store.

Don't buy on price alone; a cheap antifouling may not give you the protection that you need and might cause headaches later in terms of additional stripping and preparation time before applying the next coats. Most of the ma-

Use 80-grit wet-and-dry paper (drywall sanding mesh works well, too), and use plenty of water from a hose. In most cases it is not essential to remove every last scrap of the old stuff, but you do need a smooth surface to apply the new paint to. Now is also a good time to repair any dings in the hull surface.

You should dry-sand antifouling only if you have a sander that is intended for the purpose and connected to a vacuum cleaner. The dust is poisonous and very invasive, and you will coat everything within a 50-yard radius—more if it's windy. Also, the health risks of breathing the dust cannot be over emphasized; do everything you can to keep dust under control.

Application

It should go without saying that when applying any paint, you should follow the manufacturer's recommendation to the letter. Read the label carefully; the paint is expensive, and application on a poor undersurface will cause the paint to underperform or, worse, fall off. I'm the first to admit that on several occasions I thought I knew better than the makers and ended up getting a sloppy finish.

Applying antifouling paint is more straightforward than applying topside paint, but you must be careful to adhere to the application and safety recommendations. Mask off the hull by taping along the boottop and as necessary around depth or speed transducers. Protect yourself—a Tyvek suit is ideal—and roll on the paint with a short-nap solvent-proof roller. You'll probably need a couple of coats; follow and adhere to the overcoating times stated on the can. With ablative antifoulings, add an extra coat at the stem, the front of the keel(s), and the trailing edges of the rudder(s), which tend to wear more rapidly than other parts of the boat. Pull the tape while the paint is still soft to get a sharp edge, and use a cheap brush to coat areas you are unable to reach with the roller.

How often to reapply

Many antifoulings have a limited lifespan. Even though some copolymer ablatives will last for a couple of years, most owners will reapply at least one coat in the spring before relaunching if the boat has been out of the water throughout the winter. If you live in a warm climate and the boat stays in all year, you should keep a close eye on its underbody; if the fouling gets harder and harder to scrub off, this is often an indi-

Apply additional coats to rudders, centerboards, and leading edges, all of which are subject to water turbulence.

jor marine-paint manufacturers have Web sites and telephone help lines; they can be an invaluable source of help, particularly with respect to what types of antifouling can be used to overcoat other types. In some cases either a

special primer coat or complete removal is required.

Getting the old stuff off

Removing years of old antifouling can be a real chore. Bear in mind that the antifouling is toxic to humans too, so make sure to wear a proper respirator and a full bodysuit. Use a chemical stripper; they're expensive but will save you lots of time. Wet-sanding is another possibility, but it's messy and may be illegal in your area because of the toxic waste.

RESOURCES

For a list of suppliers see the Sailboat Buyers Guide Web site: www.sailbuyersguide.com

cation that the antifouling is losing effectiveness and the time has come to recoat.

Special considerations

Under no circumstances should antifouling containing cuprous-oxide biocide be applied to outdrive or saildrive legs. These are made of aluminum and will be subject to galvanic corrosion caused by the copper reacting with the aluminum. Special antifoulings using copper thiocyanite are available in spray cans for aluminum and seem to produce good results when correctly applied. There is no need to coat regular outboard legs, which spend little time in the water. Do not paint your bronze propeller as it too will be affected by galvanic corrosion. Zinc anodes should never be painted; these are meant to be exposed and waste away throughout the season.

Other coatings

In an effort to reduce the time and effort required in applying antifoulings, one or two alternatives appear on the market each year. One such product is an epoxy coating with copper nickel held in suspension. The theory is that the hard epoxy will last longer than a painted surface, but reports on the effectiveness of these coatings are mixed. Although they appear to have a lifespan of 5 to 7 years, they need to be burnished with a Scotch Brite pad each season to expose a fresh copper surface. If burnishing takes longer than wielding a paintbrush and roller, then the savings may not be as significant as it first appears.

Antifoulings come in many formulations from many manufacturers. Cuprous oxide is usually the main active ingredient.

Virginia Schultz

Spray Painting Your Boat

⏱ **Approx. job time: 40 hours**

📖 **Skill level: Intermediate**

✂ **Tools you will need**

- Sandpaper: #50 and #60 dry; #320, #300, #600 wet/dry
- Newspapers and/or masking paper for covering the top part of the lower hull
- Masking tape: 3M blue (1" and 2"), plus regular masking tape (for newspapers)
- White epoxy filler
- Flat sanding block
- Electric sander
- Pettit Brushing Thinner (No. 12120) for use on painted surfaces; it will not cut the paint or remove the gloss. (Do not use acetone, which will remove the paint)
- Several cotton rags and old towels for cleanup and waxing
- Electric polisher (not essential but will save time with the final buffing)
- Cans of white primer and enamel. The amount of primer you use will give you an idea how many cans of enamel you'll need

A "three-foot paint job" is how a friend described the finish on the hull of *Beau Geste,* my Bristol 24 (built in 1966 and purchased in 1990), after I painted it. The original white gelcoat had chalked terribly, leaving streaks down to the keel and me with limited options. I considered waxing the hull, but figured it would probably soak up the wax like a sponge. Plus, there would be considerable buildup that would make future painting difficult.

Over a period of 15 years, I had twice painted the topsides of *Virginian*, my previous boat, a South Coast 22, using two-part polyurethanes. While the paint worked well, this time I wanted to avoid the extra effort and expense of using the special thinners and equipment required. I had already used Krylon white spray primer and enamel on the stern of the Bristol, over which I painted "Beau Geste" in red letters. It worked so nicely that I decided to try it on the hull—just to see if it was possible to paint the entire boat with spray paint from my local hardware store.

Preparation

Wash the hull with a mild detergent or boat soap and rinse well with plenty of clean water to remove dirt and wax. Repair any damage and/or dings using Marine-Tex or a similar product, troweling it in with a plastic putty knife so that it is slightly proud.

Allow the putty to cure for the recommended amount of time before using a sanding block and #50 or #60 paper to take down the high points from the repair. When all repairs have been faired, sand the entire hull with #320 paper. This is crucial and the secret to a good finish—the more time you spend on preparation, the better your paint job will be. Run your fingertips over the hull to examine the hull for bumps, rough spots, and hollows.

Spray paint from a can gave *Beau Geste* smooth, glossy topsides.

Painting

If you're painting the boat outdoors, it's important to pick the right day. Ideal weather conditions include no wind, a moderate temperature, and low humidity.

Hose off the sanding residue and dry the hull with a towel. Then allow it to air-dry for at least 30 minutes. Mask off everything that will not be painted. While newspaper is commonly used for masking and works fine, it's better to use proper masking paper, which is slightly thicker and has no black newsprint that can transfer to finished surfaces. Either way, spray paint is notorious for spreading onto areas that aren't supposed to be painted, so be careful.

Applying the primer

Carefully read and follow the directions on the paint can. I found that the nozzles on most cans of primer create a fan-shaped spray pattern, which covers quite easily. Most nozzles on cans of enamel topcoat, on the other hand, seem to have a narrower spray pattern, which requires more attention in order to achieve a smooth finish without telltale horizontal lines showing between strokes. If there is any breeze, make sure to spray with the wind behind you; the overspray will continue to cover the hull area and will not blow back onto fresh paint or you.

If the air is too cool, humid, or warm, the paint will drip from the nozzle aperture as it sprays. If any blobs are accidentally sprayed onto the hull, leave them for later; they can be cut back with 600-grit wet paper before you apply subsequent coats. You may also discover that one or two cans don't spray properly and are unusable. It's annoying, but unfortunately, that's just the way it is.

I practiced on a large piece of cardboard before starting on the boat. This might seem like a waste of time and paint, but it paid dividends in learning how to spray the paint evenly. Paint the transom first for additional practice. (Keep a cloth moistened with Pettit Brushing Thinner at hand to whisk away bugs or specks while the paint is still wet. You may need to return to the spot when it's dry; sand lightly with dry #320 and, moving horizontally, flick on a little primer.)

Now that you're getting the hang of it, paint one side of the hull, beginning at the stern. (You're still practicing; the bow is where you want your best work to shine.)

TIP

To get the sharpest edge possible along the gunwale and boot top, ensure that the masking tape is pressed down tightly so paint can't creep underneath. Use blue painter's tape, which can be left on for several days without leaving behind a sticky residue. Avoid using cheaper white crepe masking tape, which delaminates. When masking and covering over large areas, especially on topsides of two different colors, I recommend taping around all hardware edges and painted areas with 1" tape. Then use 2" tape to affix the covering paper to the tape already in place.

Mask off everything you don't want painted.

You can use newspaper, but masking paper is a better bet.

RESOURCES

Krylon
www.krylon.com
800-457-9566

3M
www.3M.com
888-364-3577

Interlux
www.yachtpaint.com
800-468-7589

Pettit Paint
www.pettitpaint.com
800-221-4466

If a second coat of primer is needed, wet-sand the hull thoroughly and lightly with #400 paper. Be very particular here. Feel the hull for rough patches. Your fingers will tell you what your eyes can't see. When you have finished sanding, hose down the hull to remove residue and dust. Dry with an old towel, turning it often to avoid spreading dirt from one area to another.

Applying the enamel

As with the primer, practice on cardboard and then the transom. When you are confident of your technique, start to paint the hull. Occasional light breezes may cause the paint to "mist" as it meets the hull surface. After the paint has dried thoroughly, wet-sand *very* lightly with #600 paper if this is the finish coat. If a bug spot needs to be smoothed over, sand, then give the area a brief shot of primer, beginning and ending a few inches beyond the spot. Now, wet-sand with #400 paper and repeat the process with enamel. (It won't hurt to practice on newspaper first.)

From here, simply follow these steps:

- Paint the rest of the hull.
- Wet-sand with #400 paper.
- Hose off and dry the hull.
- Apply a second coat.
- Wait several days for the paint to cure.
- Hose and dry the hull.
- Wax the hull. (I rubbed the hull of *Beau Geste* with white rubbing compound first, but that may not be necessary on your boat.)

A final thought: You'll probably examine your work from every angle, squinting down the sides with your cheek pressed against the hull. And you'll probably see a few imperfections. Don't get upset over it. If a buddy stops by, looks the boat over, steps back a few paces, and says, "That's a three-foot job!"—well, you'll know you've done work you can be proud of.

Postscript

The paint job is now 10 years old and has held up well. I have since discovered ACE appliance epoxy paint, available in white and almond. In 2003, I painted the white areas of *Beau Geste*'s two-color topsides, sanding and priming as before, before applying two coats of white epoxy enamel. In this case, the second coat *must* be applied within two hours. If not, you should wait at least five days. There is no need to sand between coats if you achieve a good finish on your first coat.

In 2004, I painted the antiskid areas with the almond epoxy and used a covered paper cup with pinholes in the top to sprinkle very fine sand onto the first coat while it was still sticky. The paint is excellent—glossy, very durable, and easy to clean. The worst part of the job is masking everything. But what a joy when you pull that tape and paper off.

With the masking tape removed, the deck looks like new.

Removing Old Paint and Varnish

Illustrations by Steve Sanford

Sooner or later, if you keep your boat long enough or purchase an "experienced" boat, you'll have to deal with removing old paint or varnish. Removing old finish correctly is the key to achieving a lasting and good-looking new finish. Choosing the right way to remove that old finish can minimize the time and effort involved and will help make the task as bearable as possible.

There are three basic methods of removing old finish: mechanical, chemical, and heat. Most jobs involve several of these processes; selecting the right combination is essential.

Start by determining the scope of your project. If it is part of an overall re-fit, you should time the finish removal so you don't impact other aspects of the project. Removing finish is usually a messy, dirty job; good planning will keep you from having to go back over completed work.

Do your homework. List the finishes you'll be removing, and to find out the best way to remove them, talk to the manufacturers to learn what they recommend. Remember that the name of the finish may not relate to the actual chemical nature of the product. For example, Interlux Perfection Varnish is actually a two-part polyurethane, and Pettit Easy-Poxy paint isn't epoxy based.

Test the effectiveness of the removal method(s) you're considering on small areas before you start the job in earnest. Shop around for the best prices on materials you need. Buying sandpaper a sheet or two at a time from a local boatyard may not be the most cost-effective way to run things.

Be sure to learn about any environmental and health issues before you start the job. Most yards require that you use a vacuum sander and tarps at a minimum. You may need a respirator, a "bunny" suit, protective goggles, and appropriate gloves for your own protection.

Mechanical: sanding/grinding

Most DIYers simply reach for a sander when they're ready to remove a finish. This is probably one of the most common methods; it can also be the least effective, and it's the one I would consider last.

Angle grinders are sometimes used for tough jobs requiring removal of a thick coating. They range in size from small grinders with 4-inch disks to large ones with 9-inch disks. The latter are truly heavy-duty and will remove a lot of finish very fast. If not carefully controlled, they will leave deep circular swirls and gouges that will have to be filled, faired, and resanded. They are also heavy, which makes them tiring to use on a large job, especially if it involves overhead work.

Sanders, too, come in a wide variety of sizes and types. Belt sanders will remove a great deal of material very quickly. Unless the sander is held perfectly level with the surface you are sanding, it's very easy to leave ridges. Belt sanders will also rapidly change the contours of a surface when used on corners or curved surfaces.

If you plan to buy a belt sander, look for one with good tracking controls for the belt. Constantly having to adjust the sander to keep the belt tracking properly will drive you to distraction.

A good all-around choice for medium-sized jobs is a 6-inch right-angle random-orbital sander with a foam pad. The random-orbital feature decreases the depth and number of swirl marks left by the sanding pad. The foam pad will also accommodate curved surfaces better than a rigid pad. These units are heavy enough to get the job done, but are light enough to handle easily without tiring your arms.

Most tool manufacturers also offer smaller, lighter random-orbital sanders, which are great for intermediate-size jobs. Most of these have either pressure-sensitive adhesive (PSA) or hook-and-loop sanding disks. PSA disks have a coating on the back; you simply slap the disk onto the pad. Hook-and-loop disks have Velcro on the back.

PSA disks can be hard to remove; you may even have to resort to a heat gun to get them off. The disk may slip if it gets hot while you're sanding. The hook-and-loop surface can get dirty and may need to be cleaned to keep the disk firmly on the pad.

Random-orbital pad sanders are useful for smaller areas and reduce the number of swirl marks. Look for a sander that makes economical use of a sheet of sandpaper. Some pad sanders can use precut sheets, which is convenient but more expensive.

Detail sanders have a triangular or contour-shaped pad that vibrates back and forth. They are the ticket for sanding in tight corners and narrow spaces.

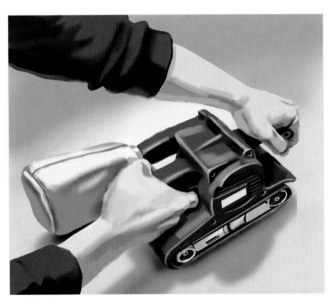

Sanders and sanding blocks are often used to smooth a surface finish prior to reapplication. They are generally the least effective at removing an old finish.

PAINT AND VARNISH

72

A sharp two-handed scraper can remove a lot of finish very quickly.

face you're scraping. For some areas rounding a blade's corners on a grinding wheel may be worthwhile.

When using a scraper, pull it toward you. Putty knives, chisels, and the like are not scrapers and have the potential to gouge and damage the surface being scraped.

You can buy cabinet scrapers at woodworking supply stores. You'll need to form a burr on the scraping edge; this takes a little practice, but it will leave a very clean finish. Most good woodworking books will describe the proper sharpening technique.

Blasting

Blasting is a *very* aggressive way to remove a finish. Air pressure is used to blast an abrasive compound against the surface being cleaned. In the old days the abrasive was always sand, but these days there are more options. Walnut shells, corncob bits, and bicarbonate of soda are all used now as less-aggressive blasting mediums.

Another new development is the use of chipped dry ice as a blasting medium. The dry ice evaporates into a gas and leaves only the paint residue behind on the tarp.

All blasting requires lots of preparation. Both the blasting medium (except dry ice) and the residue from the blast must be contained, gathered up, and disposed of properly.

Blasting is most commonly used for removing old bottom paint, and it takes an experienced operator to do an effective and safe job. Many experts do not

Many come with various pads of different shapes. I used one of these, for example, to sand the louvers on louvered doors.

Make sure any power sander you buy has an attachment for a vacuum-cleaner hose. Your lungs will thank you, and your boatyard may require it.

Sanding blocks or pads are more labor-intensive than power sanders, but are sometimes the only tools for the job. For example, you can wrap sandpaper around a shape to work on details like moldings and trim. Long boards (also known as misery boards) are long, narrow sanding pads used to fair hulls. If you are too aggressive with your grinder, you may need to learn to use one of these.

Hand sanding with sheets of sandpaper is also an option. The tactile feel of the sandpaper as you work it over the surface you are sanding allows you to locate bumps and lumps.

The automotive-repair industry has spawned a wide assortment of air-powered refinishing tools. If you have access to a decent-sized air compressor, some of these are quite economical. Make sure the compressor has proper filters to keep water and oil out of the air supply.

A final thought on sanding: Life is too short to use poor or worn sandpaper. Change paper frequently, as soon as it becomes clogged or loses its edge. You'll spend a little more on sandpaper,

but the job will move more quickly and won't seem as hard.

A final tip about sanding: If you are sanding next to an area that you don't want sanded, mask it off. Apply several layers of good-quality masking tape (not the cheap tan stuff) to protect the adjacent surface.

Scraping

One of the oldest ways to remove a finish is to scrape it off. Long before there was sandpaper, cabinetmakers and woodworkers were using scrapers to smooth and refinish surfaces. A properly sharpened scraper will remove a finish quicker and more neatly than other methods, but it takes a lot of arm strength and some practice.

Most hardware and marine stores carry a variety of scrapers. Look for scrapers with carbide blades. A sturdy handle with a knob allows more pressure to be applied for heavy-duty jobs like scraping bottom paint. Scrapers come in different shapes for getting into hard-to-reach places. Be careful of the sharp corners of the cutting edge on most scrapers; they can dig in and gouge the sur-

Strippers can be an effective though messy proposition.

recommend sandblasting a boat bottom because the process may expose the glass fibers, leaving them subject to water intrusion and blistering.

Chemicals

Paint and varnish strippers are a common chemical means of finish removal. They work by softening the finish so it can be more easily scraped or washed off. The base chemical in some strippers is methylene chloride that's been combined with other chemicals to thicken the mix so it will adhere to the surface being stripped.

There are other, more user-friendly strippers on the market. Some are citrus based; others are water soluble. They are not as effective as the harsher strippers and so take longer to do the job.

Caustic-based strippers are primarily used on bottom paint. In consistency, they range from a thick liquid to a gel paste. With some you apply a layer of paper over the coating to retain the caustic agent and improve its effectiveness. Boat bottoms with many coats of paint may require multiple applications.

Most strippers contain nasty chemicals and should be treated with respect. You need to protect your eyes and hands and work only in a well-ventilated area. Read the instructions on the container carefully, and follow them with care.

An oil-based finish, such as teak oil, presents a special problem. These finishes penetrate the grain of the wood and are hard to remove. The only effective way is to use an acid-based two-part teak cleaner—TE-KA, for example. Follow the directions carefully. The acid part must be neutralized with the second part, and the surface must be thoroughly flushed with water.

Keep these products away from fiberglass, metal, and any other surfaces you don't want damaged. Some of the strippers will permanently damage aluminum anodizing, for example.

If a wooden part can be removed from the boat, consider taking it to a professional wood stripper. He can submerge the item in a stripper bath, pressure-clean it, and give it back to you ready to have a new finish applied.

Heat

Applying heat has long been a popular method of finish removal. Back in the days of wood boats and oil-based paint, pressurized gasoline blowtorches were used. Later, propane torches became common. These days electric heat guns are the weapon of choice.

The heat softens the finish and allows it to be scraped off much more easily. Torches can damage underlying surfaces, but heat guns are much less likely to do this. They just don't get hot enough to damage most wood surfaces. Thicker fiberglass components are less susceptible to damage, but be careful not to apply excessive heat to thin sections. Keep the heat gun moving so you don't overheat any one section. Apply the heat just long enough to soften the finish, and then scrape it off. Wear gloves—the scrapings will be HOT.

A heat gun can quickly remove a finish, but may well leave a residue of the finish in the grain of the wood. A final treatment with a chemical stripper will remove the last vestiges of the old finish and leave the wood ready to be refinished.

Used with care, heat is a cheap and fast way to remove many finishes.

So what's the best way?

Each of the removal methods has pros and cons. Issues to consider include protection of adjacent surfaces while you work, guarding against health risks, and ease of use. I prefer, in this order, heat first, chemical strippers a close second, followed by sanding.

Final considerations

Take your time, plan out your project, and, above all, be safe. Proper protective gear is cheap compared to the cost of a trip to the emergency ward. Be careful of your boat and the environment as well; some of the paint residues and chemicals used are toxic and should be treated as such. Take care in removing the old finish. If you damage the underlying surface, repairs will complicate and lengthen the project. Good luck!

WHAT'S THE BEST WAY?	Heat	Scraping	Sanding	Blasting	Chemical strippers	Acid-based teak cleaners
Traditional oil-based enamel paints	● heat + scraping	●	●			
One-part polyurethane marine paints	●		●		● test effectiveness first	
Two-part finishes	●		●		●	
Varnish	● followed by stripping	●	● last resort			
Oil and other penetrating finishes						●
Epoxy			●			
Bottom paint		●	●	●	●	

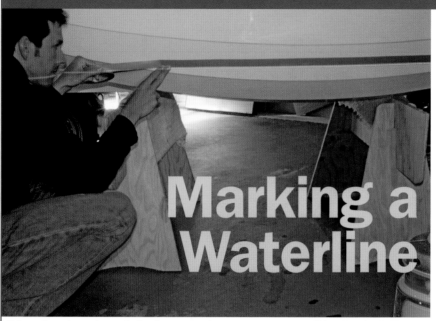

Marking a Waterline

Using a laser to mark a waterline has many advantages over more-traditional methods. The beam stays true and straight no matter how much curvature there is in the bottom panels. The bright-red beam is easy to follow when taping the hull in preparation for painting.

There are any number of reasons for marking or re-marking the waterline on your boat—perhaps the boat is new, or it's just been repainted. Or maybe you've loaded it up with so much stuff that the original marks are now 3 inches under water. Whatever the reason, re-marking the waterline fills many sailors with dread. Get it right, and the resulting perfect boottop between contrasting bottom paint and the hull will be stunning. Get it wrong, and your shaky paint job will stick out like the proverbial sore thumb.

The boat needs to be out of the water for waterline work. The boat in this example is the *BoatWorks* dinghy, but the principles apply to any boat. Set the boat on the ground or on its trailer, and chock it well with wood blocks or jackstands. Next, use a spirit level to make sure that the boat is level athwartships—from side to side. Place the level across the cockpit seats or on the cockpit sole. Level the boat by raising the jackstands on one side of the boat and lowering them on the other side. If you're using wood blocks, you'll have a bit more work to do. Use thin wedges to level the boat, and tap them in gently to avoid damaging the laminate. Do this a little at a time, and constantly check the bubble on the level. Stop when it sits between the marks on the vial.

Getting the boat to sit level end to end is a bit more complicated. If your boat is new, the waterline should be marked on the designer's drawings. If your boat is older and these drawings are not available, contact the owners' association or the designer. If this doesn't work, take the measurements from a similar boat or make a best guess. If the boat has been in the water for even a few days, there should be some marks on the hull you can refer to. With a wax crayon, make a mark on the stern at the waterline and make another at the bow.

When the boat is aligned athwartships, set up the laser tripod about 15′ abeam of midships. The exact spot is not critical providing the laser beam can see the whole side of the boat (if you can see it, so can the laser beam). Turn on the laser and adjust the height of the beam until it touches the marks you made at the bow and the stern. If it touches the mark on the bow but the stern is too high, lower the jack-

stands at the stern or raise those at the bow—vice versa if the stern is low. Double-check the spirit level in the cockpit to make sure you're not tilting the boat.

When everything lines up, you're ready to start taping in the waterline. Start at one end of the boat and work to the other, keeping the tape continuous. Fine-Line masking tape is ideal for this because it has some stretch and conforms very well to hull shape, especially if the hull has a lot of reverse turns. Since the boat is already level, all you have to do for the second side is to set the level at the correct height and mark the stern with a piece of tape or transpose the wax crayon mark. Adjust the height of the tripod until the red laser line just kisses this transposed mark, and you're ready to tape in the waterline.

The Black & Decker laser (BDL 300S) I used came with an adjustable-height tripod that made it easy to raise and lower the beam and get it perfectly aligned, but almost any make of rotating level will work. Many laser units that do not include a tripod do have a ¼″ bushing in the base. This is the standard thread size for a camera tripod, which means you can use that instead.

TOP TIP

When you look at a boottop from waterline level, the width should appear constant. Simply measuring up or down from the taped line will give an incorrect reading and a disappointing result. Because of the curvature of the hull, the width varies slightly along the length of the hull. You can solve this problem by marking the first line and then either raising or dropping the laser by the required amount when you remark the second line.

🕐 **Approx. job time: 3 hours**

📖 **Skill level: Easy**

✂ **Tools you will need**

- Rotary laser
- Masking tape
- Spirit level
- Wax pencil

Finishing a Wooden Dinghy

Rita Barry

All the hard work and long hours pay off the first time you launch your home-built boat.

I t has long been said that the devil is in the details, and this is never truer than when painting a boat. The instructions that came from Chesapeake Light Craft with their East-port Pram kit claimed approximately 40 hours of building time, which I found to be fairly accurate. Estimating the paint-ing and varnishing time is more difficult as it depends on the level of finish you want. You could just slap on a few coats of paint and go off in your boat, but this would not do justice to the Eastport Pram.

The correct finishing techniques are the same whether you are painting a dinghy or a much larger boat. I chose to varnish the interior and paint the exte-rior, which I feel presents an attractive finish; the warm glow of the varnished ply and rubrails is offset nicely by the very pale yellow of the outside.

I used products from Interlux not only because I liked the color (a tasteful shade called Fighting Lady Yellow) but also because I was familiar with their working characteristics. You'd get good

Approx. job time: 35+ hours

Skill level: Intermediate

✂ Tools you will need

- **6" foam rollers and disposable paint trays**
- **2 badger-hair or good-quality paint brushes (the best you can afford)**
- **Masking tape**
- **120- and 240-grit sandpaper and 100-grit sanding sponges (3M)**
- **Plastic mixing tubs**
- **Disposable paint strainers**

- **Paint products. I used the following from Interlux:**
- **Perfection (Fighting Lady Yellow)**
- **2 quarts Interfill 813/815 Solvent 333**
- **2 quarts Solvent wash 216**
- **1 quart Primekote 404/414**
- **2 quarts Goldspar clear varnish**

results with products from any other reputable paint company.

Don't be in a rush to start slapping on paint and varnish. The smoother the surface prior to application, the better the result will be. Be especially vigilant when it comes to dust. Clean the work area prior to applying paint. Dampening the floor helps too, especially if you're working in a garage. Close the door when you're finished and avoid disturbing the air until the paint or varnish has hardened.

1. To do a first-rate job you need an array of paint products. I used a two-part polyurethane, which provides excellent durability and superb gloss. Make sure to get the correct thinners and solvents for the type of paint you buy.

2. Before any paint or varnish can be applied, the whole boat needs to be thoroughly sanded. Use 120-grit paper to start and then switch to 240 grit for a super-smooth finish. Electric sanders take much of the hard work out of sanding, but you'll still have to work into all the corners with a hand-held piece of sandpaper.

3. The prepared hull should look like this. Run your hands over each and every part, as you can feel rough spots and indentations far better with your fingertips than you can see them by eye.

TOP TIP

Before applying any finish, read the can and follow the instructions. Most paint manufacturers have excellent Web sites that provide all the information you need. Interlux's is www.yachtpaint.com

Finishing a Wooden Dinghy

4. Dust off the surface using a soft brush, and then vacuum. Avoid wetting the surface at this stage as moisture raises the grain and will spoil the smooth sanded finish.

5. Mix up a batch of unthickened epoxy and use a foam or short-nap roller to roll on a coat over the entire surface of the boat. Watch for runs, and use a cheap brush to coat those areas you can't reach with the roller. Do the inside one day, and turn the boat and do the exterior the following day.

6. Ideally, leave the epoxy to cure for one week before preparing it for painting and varnishing. I found that 3M 100-grit sanding sponges worked well. Used wet, they cut reasonably fast without clogging. Wet-sanding the epoxy also removes any surface blush, a waxy residue that can be a by-product of the curing process.

7. Warm the can of varnish in hot water to make it flow better. While it's heating up, wipe the boat with a solvent recommended by the paint manufacturer to remove any final traces of surface contamination.

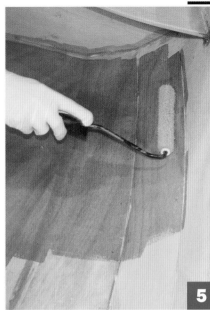

PAINT AND VARNISH

8. Never use paint or varnish straight from the can. After stirring, put several ounces through a disposable paint strainer into a plastic cup—about as much as can be used in 15 minutes. This will ensure that any bits in the can are removed and will not mar your finish.

9. Use the best bristle brush you can to apply the varnish. Use a tack rag to wipe a small area just in front of the area you are about to varnish to pick up any small specks of dirt and debris. Do not overbrush. I find it helpful to think in terms of laying on the varnish rather than brushing it on.

10. To do the job properly and provide adequate protection, apply at least five coats and sand lightly with 240-grit paper between coats. This is how my boat looked before the penultimate coat of varnish.

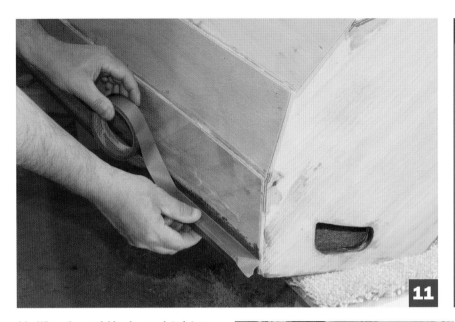

11

11. When the varnishing is completed, turn the boat over onto padded trestles. Now it's time for the paint. Mask off the varnished gunwales to protect the bright finish from damage as you work on the exterior of the boat.

12 & 13. To fill small holes and imperfections left over from the wiring-up process, mix up some epoxy surface filler and, using a plastic squeegee, spread a thin layer over the boat. Don't leave large lumps that will be hard to sand down later.

14. Avoid using a rotary sander, which is too aggressive for sanding the filler. A quarter-sheet sander is far better. If you don't have an electric sander, use sandpaper wrapped around a wood block. Pay special attention to the corners where planks abut one another.

15. If you're using a two-part primer undercoat, you have to mix the contents and allow them to stand for 15 to 20 minutes before adding the special thinners. The paint is then ready for application.

12

13

14

15

RESOURCES

Interlux
www.yachtpaint.com
800-468-7589

Epifanes
www.epifanes.com
800-269-0961

Pettit Paint
www.pettitpaint.com
800-221-4466

Chesapeake Light Craft
www.clcboats.com
410-267-0137

16

17

16. Paint is best applied using the roll-and-tip method. One person applies the paint with a roller, and a second immediately tips off the paint with a dry brush to relax the orange-peel effect left by the roller and smooth the paint surface.

17. When the primer dried after a couple of days, I sanded it lightly with 240-grit paper before applying the first of three finish coats. I applied these coats with the roll-and-tip method described above. To get the ultimate finish, make sure the work area is as dust free as you can make it by vacuuming and then damping down the floor around the boat.

18. The completed boat after the third and final topcoat. I sanded between each gloss coat with 400-grit wet-and-dry paper used wet. The shine is a reflection of the hard work. Leave the paint to harden for several days. Then you can turn the boat over and install the oarlocks and other hardware before launching the completed dinghy.

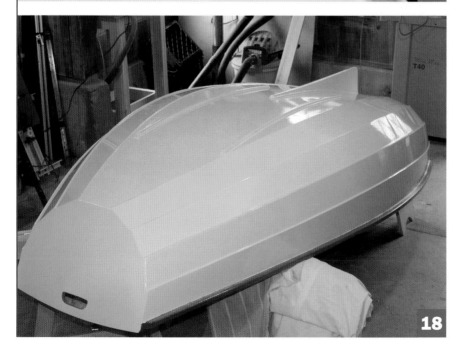

18

Finishing a Wooden Dinghy

Sails and Rigging

loth, string, and wire are the heart and soul of a sailing boat. When you get them all working together, life is sweet. If something is not quite right, however, the faulty component will be a constant source of irritation until you get it fixed.

One *BoatWorks* contributor told us that his wife loves the fact that sailors like to sew. While that's not true of every sailor, it's more common than you might think. Running repairs are a fact of life for all long-distance sailors, and even those of us who never get more than a few miles from home will benefit from being able to look after our own sails and rigging. In fact, you can't truly

call yourself a sailor unless you're on intimate terms with every aspect of your boat's rig.

With a little practice, you'll find out how satisfying it is to do useful jobs like fitting compression terminals and splicing lines. With this book at hand you can fit a furling gear or an inner forestay, or even build yourself a mast.

Despite its mystique, even sailmaking is not beyond you. If you can teach yourself to sew, you can make your own sails, as one of our contributors did. Unless you have two left thumbs, basic rigging and canvas work are perfect ways to sharpen your practical skills.

Peter Nielsen

Mainsail Choices

Lazybags—lazyjacks combined with an integral sail cover—are increasingly common on modern boats like this Hanse 311.

There are two kinds of sailors—those who love lazyjacks and those who think they're a damned nuisance. There's no doubt that a well-designed and properly installed lazyjack system is a boon aboard any cruising boat, but it's a fact that poorly planned systems outnumber the good ones. This is what accounts for their bad reputation among performance-minded sailors.

The primary task of lazyjacks is to keep the mainsail from spilling over the cabintop when it's doused. A well-set-up system will catch and hold the sail securely as it drops onto the boom so there is no need for you to do more than a minimal tidying-up afterward. It should allow you to hoist or drop your mainsail without the battens or leech catching in

the lines and without bringing the boat head-to-wind. It won't chafe the seams of your mainsail, pinch its cloth, or vibrate annoyingly when the wind gets up.

A poorly designed system, on the other hand, will snag the headboard or a batten every time you try to raise sail. It will rub against your expensive sailcloth and put sharp creases in your sail. In short, it will irk you so much that eventually you'll get rid of it altogether.

Secrets of success

Most lazyjack systems, whether supplied commercially as kits or made up by individual boatowners or riggers, consist of light lines running from somewhere around spreader height down to 6 feet or so above the boom, where they

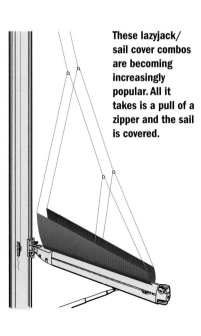

These lazyjack/ sail cover combos are becoming increasingly popular. All it takes is a pull of a zipper and the sail is covered.

split into two, three, or four legs. It is generally accepted that three legs are better than two. Two-leg systems, except on smaller boats or shorter booms, always allow some part of the sail to spill out of their grasp, which defeats the point of having lazyjacks in the first place.

With a three- or four-leg system the lines can be spaced so that all parts of the sail are well contained. This matters most for singlehanded sailors and shorthanded crews who don't want to spend time fussing with the sail after it is dropped.

There are no hard-and-fast rules for rigging lazyjacks. Walk down any dock and you'll see any number of variations, ranging from ingenious simplicity to macramé-like complexity. But whether you're buying a kit off the shelf or designing your own rig, one thing should be high on your list of priorities: It should not be possible for the headboard, battens, or leech of the sail to snag in the lines when you're raising sail.

There are various way of achieving this. Instead of fixing the top of the lazyjack lines to the mast above the spreaders, you could secure them to the underside of the spreaders, no more than a foot out from the mast. The extra space between the lines makes it harder to snag a batten, but you need to make sure that spreaders don't have too much strain put on them. Also, you will still have to be head-to-wind or nearly so when you raise the sail, or the shorter battens will blow inside the lines. Gener-

ally, lazyjacks are most effective when used with full-batten sails.

Or you could decide you want to clear the lazyjacks out of the way while you're setting sail. Instead of tying off the lines to eye straps on the mast or spreaders, you might want to install small cheek blocks and lead the lines down to the deck. This will allow you to ease the lazyjack lines and pull them forward to the mast so they lie along the boom when not needed. Some commercial kits are designed to do this, and most others can be adapted. There's a catch, though. One of the best things about lazyjacks is that they keep the excess cloth of a reefed sail out of your line of sight; if they're stowed away, you'll have to redeploy them after you reef.

A wide variety of lines and hardware is used for lazyjacks. The consensus is that ¼″ or (for bigger boats) ⅜″ polyester braid is superior to nylon, which stretches when it's wet so that the lines flop around and don't hold the bunt of the sail so well. Blocks can be used to connect the various lines in the system, but these can chafe the sail unless they're sheathed in plastic or leather. Stainless-steel rings serve just as well, at least on smaller boats, and they're a lot cheaper. Kits will come with all hardware needed, sometimes right down to the drill bits and taps, which will save you a few trips to the store. Whichever method you choose, you want be able to adjust the lines so that they are slack when the sail is raised and taut when it is dropped. You'll also want to ease the lines when you're flaking and covering

the sail so you don't force sharp creases into the sailcloth.

Drop it and bag it

It's increasingly common for lazyjacks to be combined with a cloth bag for covering the sail. Doyle Sails's StackPack was the first of these, and the concept has since spread worldwide. These systems are now ubiquitous on multihulls, which usually have their booms set so high it's hard to put a sail cover on, and they are also finding plenty of fans among monohull owners.

Various sailmakers market different versions of these lazybags, as they are called, but it's also possible for you to make your own. There is a page on the Sailrite Web site that explains how to do this. Usually, the bag has a boltrope at the bottom so that it can be fastened to the boom; the StackPack is sewn to the sail itself. The upper part of the bag will have horizontal battens to keep it rigid, and the lazyjacks are secured above the battens. Typically, a full-length zipper is used to close the bag over the flaked sail.

I've heard plenty of arguments for and against the lazybag concept. It does take a lot of the work out of sail stowage, and many people—especially those with bigger boats with high-set booms—wouldn't be without one. But if it's poorly designed or made, a lazybag can flop around annoyingly when you're under sail and make a hellacious racket when the breeze gets up. Because all of the sail is stacked atop the boom, as opposed to having its folds flaked over either side, windage can be a problem too, especially if you have a light boat that's already prone to sailing around its anchor. I've heard lazybags referred to as the "fourth reef."

A better mousetrap?

The Dutchman system is the most efficient way of controlling a falling mainsail so that it flakes itself evenly along a boom. It employs two or three vertical lines, depending on the length of the boom. The lower ends of the lines are secured to the boom, the upper ends to the topping lift. The lines are threaded through plastic grommets in the sailcloth; as the sail is dropped, they guide it onto the boom. Put the sail cover on, and you're done.

Unlike lazyjacks, Dutchman lines can't foul the sail's leech or batten ends, and you don't need to be head-to-wind to raise or lower the sail. The lines go slack when the main is raised and

---

Lazyjack Technique

I came across the following tip on the Jasper & Bailey Sailmakers Web site (www.jasperandbailey.com) for preventing battens from fouling on lazyjacks. It makes a lot of sense and can be adapted according to halyard location.

"Slack off the lee-side lazyjacks, or both lazyjacks, and carry them forward to the shrouds or mast while hoisting. For example: If the main halyard leads down the starboard side as it does on most boats, slack the port lazyjack and hook it on a cleat on the port side of the mast. Head the boat so that the wind is about 10 to 20 degrees on the starboard bow and start hoisting the mainsail.

"By keeping the wind on the starboard bow as the main goes up, you will also keep the sail off the person pulling on the halyard and keep the boom away from the crew in the middle of the cockpit. Once the main is set, the lazyjacks may be moved forward out of the way so they cannot chafe the main or simply left up at the predetermined correct tension."

Topping Lifts or Lazyjacks?

Lazyjacks have been around for centuries. On gaff-rigged boats they're called topping lifts and perform two roles—guiding and controlling the fall of the mainsail, and preventing the boom and gaff from falling onto the deck. It's rare to find them used to support the boom on a Bermuda-rigged boat, but you do occasionally see cruising and racing boats equipped with them.

After sailing a big bluewater boat with twin topping lifts, I can see the attraction. They are easy to rig, easy to repair, and cheaper to purchase than a spring-loaded or hydraulic boomvang. The hardware needs to be stronger, and there is a bit more fiddling to do—they need to be slacked off when the sail is raised, and the windward lift needs to be hardened up when reefing, then slacked off again afterward.

There is enough slack on the falls to enable the lifts to be taken forward and hooked out of the way, though the crew of the boat I sailed on had not found chafe to be a problem and so left the lifts in place when sailing.

the boat is sailing, and when the main is dropped and a bit of weight comes on the boom, the lines come taut again. It's a simple, logical system, and very effective. It makes for the tidiest-looking reefed sails I've seen, and is the closest there is to a "set and forget" sail-containment system. And unlike most lazyjack systems, using a Dutchman does not require that you drill holes

in your mast or boom for blocks or eye straps, though it does require you to put holes in your sail.

So what's the catch? The monofilament lines do chafe the sail seams, though arguably not as much as a typical lazyjack setup. Also, airborne dirt can be attracted to dew on the lines and will then rub off on your sail;

how much of a problem this is depends on where you sail. I have read of instances where the monofilament lines get trapped around spreader tips when the main is squared off on a run, but this has not been an issue on the Dutchman-equipped boats I've sailed on. (It would also be possible for lazy-jack lines to do this, but I've never seen it happen.) You'll also need to

RESOURCES

Dutchman
www.mvbinfo.com
203-838-0375

Sailrite
www.sailrite.com
800-348-2769

Lazyjack Kits
  Barton
  www.bartonmarine.com,
  U.S. distributor: www.sailnet.com
  800-597-1781

  E-Z-JAX
  www.ezjax.com
  877-585-9162

  Harken
  www.harken.com
  262-691-3320

  Sail Cradle
  www.sailcare.com
  800-433-7245

  Schaefer Marine
  www.schaefermarine.com
  508-995-9511

  Wichard
  www.wichard-usa.com
  401-683-5055

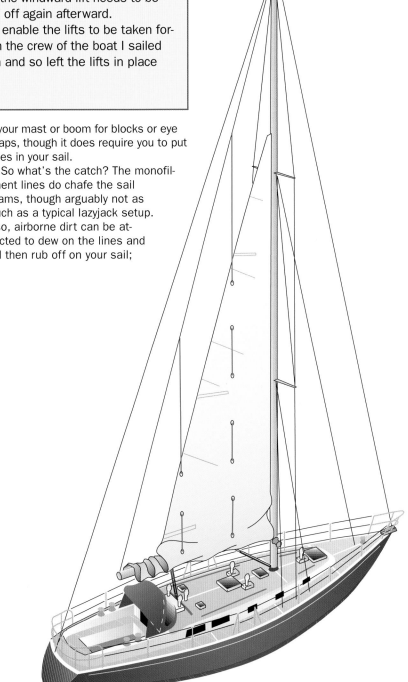

The Dutchman employs two or three vertical lines running through grommets in the sail to guide the sail as it drops.

have your sail cover remade to fit around the lines. Plus you have to buy the Dutchman system as a kit and can't really make one up yourself. The sail must be modified by a sailmaker, so the total cost is typically a couple of hundred dollars more than a set of professionally installed lazyjacks.

Conclusion

Dutchman or lazyjack, lazybag or not? It all boils down to personal preference. If it's important to you that your sail stacks itself neatly when doused, and you cruise rather than race, invest in a Dutchman. If economy is important, or if you don't want to have holes punched in your sails, lazyjacks would be a better bet. Either way, you won't have the hassle of dealing with a sail draped all over the cabintop at the end of a day on the water. If you don't think having to bundle up the sailcloth and flake the main is that big a deal, by all means keep your sail and rig uncluttered by extraneous lines and don't bother with either system.

Unlike lazyjacks, the Dutchman flakes the sail neatly.

Lazyjack Options

Basic (2-leg system)

The simplest possible system involves having the risers of the lazyjacks (¼" prestretched line) secured to padeyes about 50 to 60 percent up the mast, or just above the spreaders. The legs are secured to the boom about two-thirds of the way abaft the gooseneck, taken up a few feet, through small blocks or stainless steel rings on the falls, and forward to jammers or cleats on the boom about one-third of the way back from the gooseneck. You should mock up the installation before drilling holes in your boom. Make sure there is enough spare line to allow the lazyjacks to be eased and pulled forward where they can be secured clear of the sail.

Better (3-leg system)

There are any number of variants on 3-leg rigs. It is common to see the risers taken up to cheek blocks on either side of the mast, then back down to the gooseneck, where they are cleated off or run through jammers so they can be adjusted. The legs are usually secured to eye straps, evenly spaced along the boom starting at 15 to 20 percent of the way forward of the clew. The legs may be run through 1" (stainless rings or small blocks so they can be pulled flat along the boom when you want to hoist sail or put the sail cover on; or you can simply seize the legs to the rings and either leave the lazyjacks permanently rigged or secure the legs with snap hooks so you can easily unclip them from the boom and tie them out of the way.

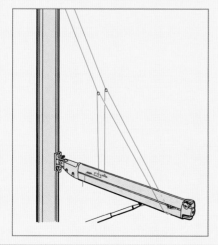

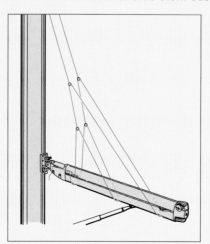

Charles J. Doane

Assembling Compression Terminals

Do-it-yourself sailors have long been attracted to the concept of swageless rigging terminals, also known as compression terminals. Unlike swaged terminals, which require expensive dedicated machinery to create, compression fittings can be assembled with simple hand tools. They can also be reopened and inspected periodically, and their proponents claim they can be reused. In fact, once a terminal has been well and truly loaded, it can be difficult to take apart.

Assembling the terminals is fairly easy. The first time may seem difficult, but a little practice makes it routine. At present there are three different types of terminals available, each of which goes together differently. The most common types by far are the Norseman and

Sta-Lok terminals, which are very similar. More recently, Suncor Stainless has introduced Quick Attach terminals, from Denmark, and Petersen, from the U.K., has offered its Hi-Mod terminals on the U.S. market.

TIP

Be sure to tape stainless wire before cutting it with a hacksaw. Or try clamping the wire between two blocks of soft pine in a vise, and mark the wood where you need to cut. The wood will adapt to the wire's shape and stop the ends from unlaying while you're cutting.

A couple of tips apply to all these types: First, make sure you get a clean cut at the end of the wire to which you want to fit your terminal. Cable cutters work quickest, but usually yield a lop-sided cut that can make putting the terminal on the wire much harder. It is best to cut the wire with a hacksaw (be sure to use a fresh blade) or with a grinding disk so you get a clean, square cut. Second, be sure you are using the right size terminal and appropriate parts for the type and size of wire you are working with.

A1. Slip the terminal head onto the wire nose first, then carefully unlay the outer strands of the wire with a small screwdriver. The hands doing the job here belong to Loric Weymouth, of Lyman Morse Boatbuilding, and you can see he's quite good at doing it neatly. Keep a firm grip on the wire a couple of inches down to keep it from unlaying more than you want. Also, be sure you are using wire with a left-hand lay.

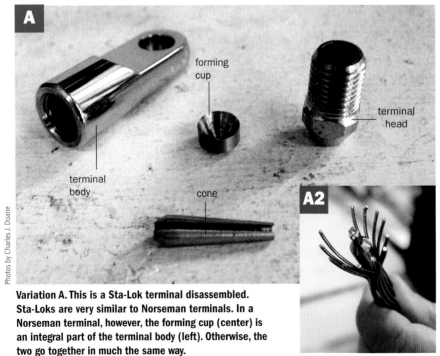

Variation A. This is a Sta-Lok terminal disassembled. Sta-Loks are very similar to Norseman terminals. In a Norseman terminal, however, the forming cup (center) is an integral part of the terminal body (left). Otherwise, the two go together in much the same way.

A2. Next, slip the slotted cone over the wire core, narrow end first. You'll probably need to tap it a bit with a hammer to get it to slide up the core. When you've got the cone all the way on, there should be about 2mm of core sticking out the end, like this. It's not a bad idea to measure to be sure.

forming cup

terminal head

terminal body

cone

Photos by Charles J. Doane

A3. Now re-lay the outer wire strands around the cone, and then slide the terminal head down the wire over the cone. The key here is to make very sure that none of the wire strands fall into the slot on the cone. The slot must stay open so the cone can compress around the wire core.

A4. Note that it is possible to get the cone on the core without unlaying the wire. If you cut the wire very cleanly, you should be able to carefully work the leading edge of the cone's narrow end between the core and the outer strands. Then you can slip the cone up the core. Again, you need 2mm of core sticking out the end, and no strands should fall in the slot on the cone.

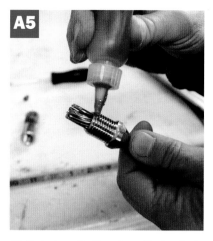

A5. Next, dress the threads on the terminal head with some Loctite, which helps to prevent galling. If the threads gall, the terminal will be ruined and you'll have to start over again with a new one. With a Sta-Lok terminal, you must also remember to drop the forming cup into the terminal body before threading it onto the head.

A6. Now carefully tighten up the terminal with a wrench (or two wrenches if you can't use a vise). If you feel any hint of galling, immediately stop, open the terminal, and add more Loctite.

A7. After you've tightened up the terminal all the way, immediately open it again to check that the outer strands of wire have properly formed around the base of the cone, as shown. Again, be sure no strands have fallen in the slot. Here you also see why you must use wire with a left-hand lay—the outer strands must lay around the cone in the same direction as the terminal body screws on the head.

A8. The final step is to drop a marble-size dab of sealant into the terminal body. Then screw the body back on the head, tighten it all up nice and snug, and you're done. Do not tighten it up as hard as you can! Overtightening the terminal will damage the wire and cone inside.

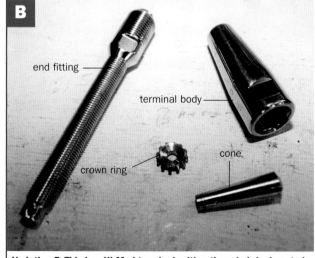

end fitting

terminal body

crown ring

cone

Variation B. This is a Hi-Mod terminal, with a threaded rigging stud instead of an eye. It has a slotted cone, like a Sta-Lok, but the cone has thin twin slots instead of one big one, so you don't have to worry about strands of wire getting caught in them. Note the toothed crown ring (center), which captures the wire strands when the terminal is assembled.

B1. Unlike the Sta-Lok, the main body of the terminal with female threads is the part you slip over the wire first. Then, as with the Sta-Lok, you unlay the outer strands of the wire and slip the cone over the core, as shown. Unlike the Sta-Lok, the leading edge of the cone is beveled outward rather than inward. This means it isn't possible to take the shortcut of working the end of the cone onto the core without unlaying the wire.

B2. The terminal's end fitting with male threads has a recessed cup into which the end of the wire core fits. After you slide the cone up the core, slip on the crown ring, then mate the end fitting over the core. The recessed cup makes it unnecessary to measure the protruding bit of core.

B3. The tricky part of assembling a Hi-Mod terminal is re-laying the outer strands of wire so that the ends of each bit of wire fit into their respective slots in the crown ring. We found a third hand was helpful here. Keeping all the bits in place while re-laying the wire is a little fiddly. The advantage of the crown ring is that you can use either right- or left-hand-lay wire with the terminal.

B4. The finished terminal, after the end fitting has been screwed into the body. You'll need Loctite on the threads, but Hi-Mod claims sealant is not necessary because the crown ring keeps the wire strands separated enough that moisture cannot get trapped in the terminal.

Variation C. This is a Suncor Quick Attach terminal disassembled. Of the three terminals we worked with, this one was by far the easiest to assemble.

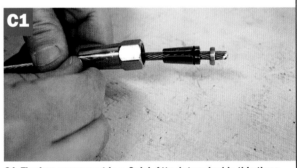

C1. The key component in a Quick Attach terminal is this three-piece gripping jaw, which has serrated teeth on the inside and a small rubber O-ring on the end holding the three pieces together.

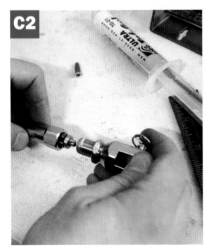

C2. To assemble the Quick Attach, all you do is slip the terminal body, gripping jaw, and pressure ring over the entire wire. There is no need to unlay the wire or otherwise separate the core from the outer strands. You do need to measure to make sure the proper amount of wire (5mm) is sticking out the end, but then you just screw the end fitting into the body.

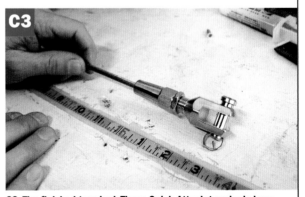

C3. The finished terminal. These Quick Attach terminals have performed well in tests with static steady loads, but Suncor's competitors question whether the teeth in the gripping jaw will stand up to dynamic cyclical loads, as are experienced in working sailboat rigs. Suncor believes this is not a problem and claims there are no reports of any of these terminals failing in service. Because they are so easy to assemble, the terminals are ideal to use in temporary jury-rigging situations.

Charles Mason

Choosing and Installing a Headsail Furler

Elizabeth B. Wrightson

All non-hydraulic headsail-furling systems operate on the same general principle—an aluminum foil connected to a drum controlled by a furling line rotates around the forestay to increase or de-

crease headsail area. They differ in the bearings used, in the halyard and tack swivel fittings, how the foils and sleeves attach to each other, whether the bearing design allows the foil to rotate freely around the forestay, how the upper and

lower swivel units attach to the deck and forestay, and whether the furling drum is open or closed and how easily it can be removed for racing.

While a few manufacturers offer single-groove foils, most of today's foils have a double groove. The advantage of a double groove is that the racer avoids having to sail without a headsail when changing headsails and a cruiser can hoist two headsails wing-and-wing when sailing downwind.

To begin

Your first step in installing a new unit is to determine the *precise* distance from the center of the pin that holds the top of the forestay to the masthead toggle to the center of the pin that holds the bottom to the deck. Use a tape measure or other accurate measuring device to get the pin-to-pin measurement. The measurement can be made with the stay installed, but it's better to remove the stay and measure the distance when it is flat on the ground. Before you remove the stay, ease the backstay and pull the mast forward using spare halyards.

Don't attach these halyards to something with their shackles. Rather, tie them to a strong fitting or use a strong D-shackle with each one. After the halyards are secured and the forestay is slack, unpin the lower end of the stay and go up the mast in a bosun's chair to disconnect the upper end of the stay. It's safest to work with an assistant when you go aloft. Gently lower the forestay to the deck, take it ashore, and lay it out on the ground in a straight line.

You must also inspect the existing forestay. If it is over five years old (four if the boat is sailed in salt water) or if its swaged terminals show any sign of fraying or rust, replace it. Never install a new furler unit over a suspect stay. Some manufacturers include a new forestay as part of their installation package.

Furling systems generate significant sideways loads in addition to the fore-and-aft loads generated by a conventional sail. To handle these loads, the forestay must have an extra toggle at the upper and lower ends (some furling units do have an integral toggle at the lower end). The additional toggles allow the stay to move easily in all directions, minimizing the chances of a forestay that fails from metal fatigue. If a furler unit has never been installed over the

Photos 1 and 2. Check first to see whether the anchors or other gear at the bow could interfere with the furler unit (above). If so, use a link in addition to the extra toggle (shown on the unit at right) to raise the furler unit.

Photo 3. Make sure the furler drum has plenty of room to move laterally; this installation is quite marginal.

existing forestay (assuming it passes your inspection), the forestay will probably need to be shortened to accommodate the extra toggle links.

All installation manuals describe exactly how much an existing forestay needs to be shortened to accommodate the extra toggle/links needed for that system's furler. A rigger can swage the old or new forestay to the proper length; if you shorten the stay yourself, use a Norseman or Sta-Lok compression terminal.

Furler drum height

Next, check the area on the deck where the forestay attaches to see whether the bow anchor, hatch, windlass system, or other installation will interfere with the furler drum. If there is an obstruction, you'll have to raise the furler drum to clear it (Photos 1 and 2).

All furler units come with links of various lengths so you can position the drum above any obstruction. If you are shortening the wire, you'll have to subtract the length of the toggles and link plates from the pin-to-pin measurement. (Profurl units are designed a little differently and may not require the stay to be shortened.)

Finally, make sure there is enough room inside the bow pulpit for the furler drum to operate without hitting a stanchion or part of the bow pulpit (Photo

3). Several inches of clearance are required. If there isn't room to comfortably accommodate the drum, you may need to modify the pulpit.

Installation

Collect all the tools suggested by the installation manual; any specialty tools

Photo 4. Note how the two toggles underneath the furler let it move in all directions. The lead furling block has been placed on the deck at a location that allows the furling line to run from the drum to the block at a 90-degree angle to the forestay.

needed for the specific installation should be supplied with the unit. With most installations, the hardest part of the job is installing the Norseman or Sta-Lok compression terminal on the forestay.

Once you've cut the forestay to account for the toggles and link plates, you're ready to assemble the furler and foils over the wire and turnbuckle. Make sure that the forestay is lying flat on the ground and that the area underneath it is as clean as possible. This minimizes the chance of getting dirt or grit into the bearings or foil connections. If possible,

TECHNICAL NOTE

Some furler swivels use stainless or hardened carbon-steel balls in sealed housings; others use Torlon 4301 balls. Torlon is a polyamide-imide (PAI) plastic whose surface is almost as hard as aluminum. Because it doesn't gall or corrode, it excels as a nonlubricated bearing and is easy to clean. Delrin is a tough, lightweight, heat-resistant, low-friction material. Its surface is softer than Torlon, and it cannot take the same loadings as Torlon in most furling applications.

Harken MKIII jib reefing and furling system

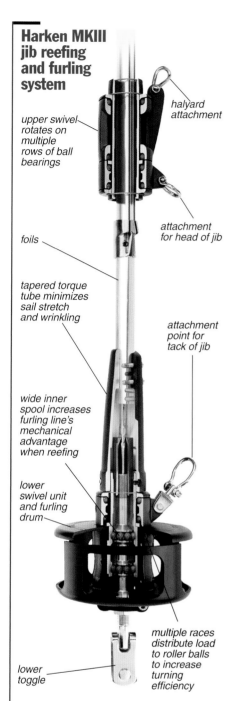

upper swivel rotates on multiple rows of ball bearings

halyard attachment

attachment for head of jib

foils

tapered torque tube minimizes sail stretch and wrinkling

attachment point for tack of jib

wide inner spool increases furling line's mechanical advantage when reefing

lower swivel unit and furling drum

multiple races distribute load to roller balls to increase turning efficiency

lower toggle

keep all the components in their shipping covers until they are needed.

The installation can be done from the bottom up or the top down; follow the method outlined in your installation manual. In almost every case the topmost foil will need to be cut with a hacksaw so the foil (again clearly described in the installation manual) fits properly below the upper stay's end fitting. When the unit has been assembled and all components have been checked for tightness, carefully rehoist the stay and foils aloft on a spare halyard. Be careful

not to bend the foils, and have an assistant to help stabilize them.

Then go aloft in a bosun's chair and install the pin that attaches the upper set of toggles/links to the mast tang. Insert a cotter pin or equivalent and cover it with tape. Return to the deck and attach the lower end of the furling unit to the deck fitting. Insert the pin that attaches the toggle/links to the stemhead fitting, put in the cotter pin, spread it, and cover it with tape. Finally, release the halyards that have been holding the mast forward and return them either to the base of the mast or to their regular position.

Assuming your measurements are correct, the last step in the installation process is to run the furling line. The lead blocks for the furling line are usually attached to the stanchions to keep them off the deck. To prevent snagging and overrides, place the forwardmost block aft of the furler at a spot that allows the furler line to come off the drum at a 90-degree angle to the forestay (Photo 4). If there is no restraining device in the system for the furling line, consider mounting a ratchet block as the aftermost lead block. This will help tension the furling line when the sail is being let out and minimize further the possibility of an override on the furling drum.

Checkout

Is your installation correctly done? It's time to find out. Attach the headsail to the upper swivel unit and hoist the sail up the foil. When the halyard is all the way up, walk away from the boat and look up (binoculars can help here) to see whether the jib halyard is angled back from the forestay. Most furlers need a minimum 5-degree angle to keep the halyard from wrapping around the foil; a 10-degree angle is even better. If the angle is too small, you'll need to install a halyard restrainer below the halyard's exit point on the mast. That will drop the halyard down and create a wider angle. Check the installation manual for clear guidance on how to proceed. (Note that Profurl units do not require a minimum halyard angle; Photo 5).

Fine-tuning. For most units the headsail's luff length has the primary effect on the angle the halyard makes with the forestay. If the luff is short, the swivel will be located farther down the foil, which could make the angle too small. The solution is to position the upper swivel higher on the foil by using a pennant.

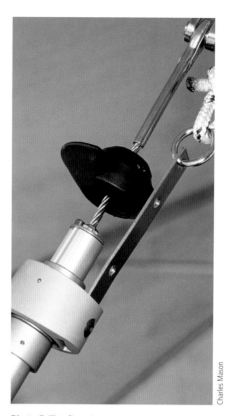

Charles Mason

Photo 5. The flat plate and restrainer above the upper swivel of a Profurl unit eliminates the need to have a minimum halyard/forestay angle.

To get the correct pennant length, attach the head of the sail to the upper-swivel shackle (leave the tack unattached) and hoist the sail until the upper swivel is high enough on the foil to get a forestay/halyard angle that will keep the halyard from wrapping around the swivel and stay. When the upper swivel is at the correct height, secure the halyard and measure the distance from the tack of the sail to the tack shackle on the lower swivel. This measurement is the length of the pennant—either wire or Spectra—you need to install. Always put the pennant between the head of the sail and the upper swivel, never between the tack and the lower swivel.

Final check. If the sail doesn't furl easily around the newly installed foil and there isn't excess halyard tension, check the following: there may not be enough forestay tension and the turnbuckle needs to be adjusted; the backstay may need more tension, or the bearings may have gotten dirty during the installation process. Re-tension the forestay and backstay and clean the unit according to the manufacturer's instructions. You should allow 4 to 6 hours for the project.

Choosing and Installing a Headsail Furler

93

Step by Step

The exact procedures for installing furlers are unique to each manufacturer. Here's a look at the key steps in installing a Schaefer System 1100 on a Catalina 30. The new unit replaced an older Schaefer model, and the boat's two owners decided to also replace the existing forestay. The new stay was professionally swaged to the length required by the installation manual for the new unit.

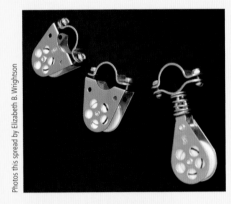

1. First inventory all the parts in the shipping container and check them against the inventory sheet. The items shown here include (from left to right) polyethlyene liners, a machined aluminum foil, the base of the furling unit with link, and (above) blocks for the furling line. Keep all tools and loose parts in buckets or boxes so they won't get lost or misplaced during the assembly.

Photos this spread by Elizabeth B. Wrightson

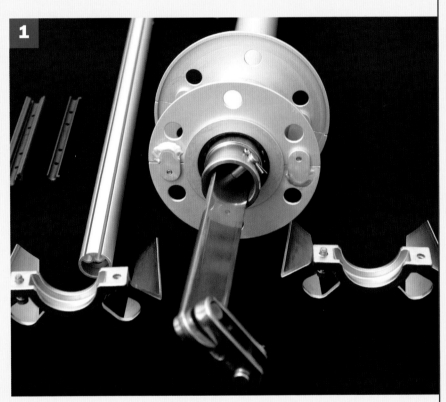

Furling systems at a glance

	Cruising Design	Facnor	FaMet	Furlex
Foil section length	open	6'	3'	8'
Foil material	PVC	aluminum	aluminum	aluminum
Ball bearing	Torlon	stainless	—	stainless
Bearing construction	open	sealed	—	sealed
Furler housing	plastic	aluminum	plastic/stainless	stainless
Furler profile	open	open	open	closed
Warranty*	6 years	7 years	lifetime	5 years
Contact	607-749-4599	704-597-1502	913-757-3167	843-760-6278
	sailcdi.com	facnor.com	fametmarine.com	seldenmast.com

* Warranties vary considerably in their specifics.

SAILS AND RIGGING

2. Lay the furler, torque tube, foils, and foil liners alongside the forestay to see how many foil sections will be needed to properly cover the forestay. Because the lower integral link/toggles (inset) come in different lengths, that measurement must be included when calculating the proper forestay length.

4. Insert the bottom joint into the top of the bottom foil and attach the two-part stainless feeder over the bottom joint (see 5a). Make sure to install the feeder right side up.

3. Remove the stainless cage from around the drum and its top and bottom plates. Remove the drum and loosen the clamp at the top of the torque tube. Remove the stop pin from the torque tube, and slide the tube down over the threaded swage stud and lower extrusion.

Harken	Hood	Profurl/Wichard	Reckmann	Schaefer
8'	6'	6'	10'	6'
aluminum	aluminum	aluminum	aluminum	aluminum
Torlon	Torlon	carbon	steel	stainless/Torlon, Torlon
open	open	sealed	sealed	open
plastic	plastic	plastic/stainless	aluminum	stainless
open	open	open	closed	open
7 years	5 years	10 years	10 years	5 years
262-291-3320	813-885-2182	401-683-5055	800-222-7712	508-995-9511
harken.com	**pompanette.com/hood**	**profurl.com; wichard-usa.com**	**euromarinetrading.com**	**schaefermarine.com**

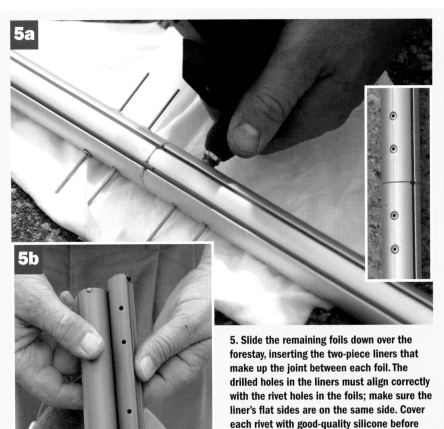

5a

5b

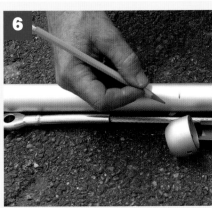

6

5. Slide the remaining foils down over the forestay, inserting the two-piece liners that make up the joint between each foil. The drilled holes in the liners must align correctly with the rivet holes in the foils; make sure the liner's flat sides are on the same side. Cover each rivet with good-quality silicone before inserting them in the foils, and make sure the rivets are completely inserted. To prevent distortions in the foil groove, always insert all eight rivets into the foil before starting to rivet. Photo 5b shows two foils that are properly aligned.

6. This system requires that the top foil be no less than 18" long and that the top of the foil must stop 2" below the top of the forestay. Measure the two upper foils carefully; the short foil included in the installation package can be trimmed to the proper length if necessary. If trimming is required, measure and mark the point where the foil needs to be cut. Use a hacksaw. To avoid confusion, mark the section to be discarded with an "X."

8

8. Slide the lower swivel and drum over the toggle link. Reassemble the torque tube, and refasten the bottom foil to the tube. When the system is fully assembled, check that all components are secure. Then hoist the system aloft on a halyard. Be careful not to bend the foils in the process. Go aloft in a bosun's chair and install the clevis pin that attaches the top of the forestay to the upper toggle/link. Put in the cotter pins and cover them with tape. Return to the deck and attach the lower toggle/link to the fitting at the stemhead.

7

7. Slide the upper swivel onto the foils and down to the feeder mechanism, making sure the large portion of the swivel is up. Put the upper liner into the top foil; the liner has a nub at one end that prevents it from sliding into the foil. Rivet the cap in place over the upper liner.

9

9. To adjust the lower turnbuckle to the proper tension, first loosen the clamp at the top of the torque tube and remove the stop pin and fasteners attaching the drum to the tube. Tension the turnbuckle to the proper tension; then insert cotter pins into turnbuckle and tape the pins. Reattach the torque tube to drum and retighten the assembly.

10

10. Attach the furling-line lead blocks to the stanchions, then lead the furling line from the drum aft through the blocks to the trimming station near the helm. Position the block nearest the drum so the line runs off the drum at a 90-degree angle to the forestay.

11

11. Attach the halyard and the head of the sail to the two attachment points on the upper swivel, and attach the tack of the sail to the tack shackle located on the drum. Attach the clew of the sail to the genoa sheets. If wind conditions are suitable, hoist the sail.

12. If the installation has been done correctly, the furling line will make the headsail roll in and out with no resistance or friction.

12

Peter Nielsen

Preventing Halyard Wrap in a Furling Gear

The last thing you want from your furling gear is for it to jam up in a rising breeze—or at any other time, come to that. I must be some kind of roller-reefing Jonah, because it's happened a few times on boats I've been sailing aboard. On two of those occasions, halyard wrap was the culprit.

Halyard wrap sounds like something you'd tear off a new piece of rope, but it's actually the most common cause of furling problems. It occurs when the angle between the genoa halyard and the headstay is too shallow. Instead of the two halves of the top furler swivel turning independently as the headfoil extrusion turns, the upper part of the swivel wants to turn together with the lower part, wrapping the halyard around the top of the headstay.

This usually occurs when the sail is being furled and there is tension on the halyard swivel. If the increasing reluctance of the swivel to turn is then greeted with extra exertion on the part of the person trying to furl the sail, the wrap will get ever tighter until the swivel will jam and the gear will refuse to turn at all.

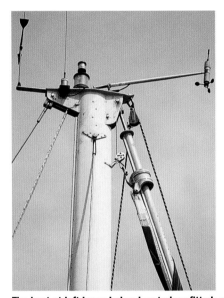 

The boat at left has a halyard restrainer fitted; at right, the disk above the foil may be enough to avoid a wrap.

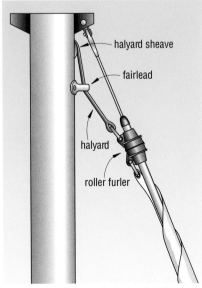

A restrainer will keep the halyard at the correct angle to avoid a wrap.

- halyard sheave
- fairlead
- halyard
- roller furler

If you're lucky, you'll be able to unwrap the halyard by reversing the direction of pull. It is not unknown, however, for a stainless wire halyard to cut so deeply into the alloy extrusion that it becomes caught in it. If this happens, there's usually no alternative to a trip up the mast. Nor is it unheard of for the headstay to begin to unlay as the halyard is forced in between the strands of wire or after it has been twisted back and forth a few times. Riggers will scare you witless with tales of masts falling down after repeated halyard wraps have weakened the headstay.

There are two ways to cure halyard wrap. One is to fit a bull's-eye fairlead 2″ to 3″ below the sheave box and lead the halyard through that before making it fast to the swivel. This will open up the angle the halyard makes with the headstay to 10 degrees or more and prevent it from wrapping around it (see figure). When you fit a bull's-eye fairlead you'll need to unreeve the halyard and then rethread it through the bull's-eye, over the sheave, and down through the mast, using a messenger line. This is a time-consuming affair, and it is possible to buy open-backed halyard restrainers that can be riveted on over the halyard.

This solution is usually the only one possible if the headsail is significantly short in the luff or if the furling extrusion finishes short of the top of the headstay. Another approach is to get the top swivel so close to the halyard sheave that there is not enough exposed halyard to wrap around the headstay. If the sail is not long enough in the luff to permit this, you can make up a pennant (wire or Spectra to avoid stretch) between the top swivel and the head of the sail. Don't add the pennant between the tack of the sail and the furling drum, as this increases the chances of the luff rope coming away from the headfoil.

The latter option is best for club racers or performance-oriented cruisers who use a range of headsails, as a halyard restrainer may restrict the use of full-hoist genoas. Or, if you have two headsail halyards, you could lead the secondary halyard through the restrainer for the cruising sail and leave the primary halyard in reserve for the full-hoist sails.

Scott Roberts

Installing an Inner Forestay

Several months ago I met a fellow sailor who had fitted an inner forestay on his boat to create a cutter-rigged sloop. It struck me that I could install an inner forestay on my Nordic 40, and I couldn't get the idea out of my head. I wanted to have the added benefit of a staysail in my sailplan for future offshore sailing.

At first, it seemed there were so many reasons for doing this modification that it only made sense. In many ways, the cutter rig is much more versatile than the sloop rig. Although there is more work involved in sailing a boat with two headsails because there is an additional sail to tack, stow, and trim, the rig offers more options for sail balancing and sail-area adjustment. And in some situations, it allows you to carry smaller, more manageable headsails without compromising overall sail area. But the installation is a major undertaking.

Getting started

Before you get started on a project like this, find out whether the builder of your boat offered an inner forestay as an option. If so, some of the ground work will have been done. Also, ask your sailmaker if a staysail will be a practical addition to your rig. Look carefully at your boat from every angle, and walk the docks looking at cutter rigs to see how boats with inner forestays are set up. Since the services of a rigger or a yacht designer will probably cost money, answer what questions you can before you consult an expert.

In order to optimize the double headsails' upwind performance, a traditional cutter has the mast farther aft in the boat than a sloop. You will also often find cutters with long overhanging bows or with a bowsprit to maximize the size of the foretriangle. There will need to be enough room for the new sail to work properly as well as for installing the

Installing an inner forestay allows you to carry more sails in favorable conditions and offers options for shortening sail when the wind picks up.

mast tang and deck fitting for the inner forestay.

Some advocate that the inner forestay should be as parallel to the headstay as possible. You may prefer having enough clearance between the stays for the easy passage of the head-sail during a tack. Make sure there is a place for running backstays if they will be needed. The staysail-sheet leads should be located on a dedicated track to create the proper sheeting angle.

The new track will be inboard of your primary headsail track. A good place on many boats is along the outside edge of the cabintop, where the house top is in effect stiffened by the house sides. Remember that if the staysail clew is cut fairly high, the sheet leads will run quite far back, so you'll have to make sure there is room for the leads. Finally, check that the sheets can be run to a winch.

You will also need to find a good place to add a halyard. Many masts have internal halyards, and there is often a spinnaker topping-lift block or halyard in place that can be used for a staysail halyard. If this is not the case, it is almost always possible to install an exterior block for a new staysail halyard. My mast came with an internal sheave just below the upper spreaders, which I used for my halyard.

After the preliminary planning stage, the first step in adding an inner forestay is to choose locations for the mast tang and the deck fitting. You will need to get help from a professional designer or rigger to do this properly. There can be very high loads at these points, and some reinforcements may be needed to ensure that these forces do not damage the mast or the deck. For example, my Nordic 40 needed a set of running back-stays to resist the staysail's tendency to bow the mast forward.

The boat's designer can determine the best places to make all of the connections as well as the best way to install them. One deck might require a tie rod, while another might call for a heavily backed padeye. Making the wrong decision could result in a damaged mast, a delaminated deck, or even personal injury.

Making the inner stay removable

You might want to consider making the inner forestay removable so that it can be pulled back out of the way when not in use. This is an advantage when you need to tack in close quarters, get into and out of harbors, or make space on deck for your inflatable.

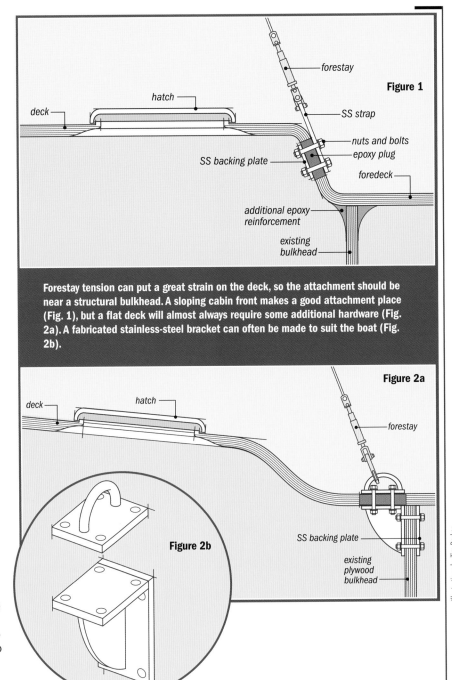

Forestay tension can put a great strain on the deck, so the attachment should be near a structural bulkhead. A sloping cabin front makes a good attachment place (Fig. 1), but a flat deck will almost always require some additional hardware (Fig. 2a). A fabricated stainless-steel bracket can often be made to suit the boat (Fig. 2b).

Illustrations by Tim Barker

There are several ways to set up a removable stay. The simplest way is to rig a release lever on the end of the stay that will detach it from the deck fitting. The setup you ultimately choose should allow you to both take up the slack in the forestay and run the stay down the mast to keep it out of the way.

Once you have chosen the appropriate deck location, the connection aloft is simple. There are several terminal fittings available, including swaged, Sta-Lok, Castlok, and Norseman. Choose the fitting, either a fork or an eye, that mates with the mast tang on your boat. You should be able to find a selection of

wire terminals at a good marine-supply store. Once you have measured the stay wire and cut it to length (with the fitting

TOP TIP

To check sheeting angles and get an idea of how the boat will look as a cutter, it is often possible to jury-rig a temporary inner forestay with a spare halyard. A line over the crosstrees with the end weighted down on deck will provide an excellent visual reference.

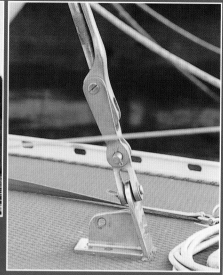

Above: A babystay is set farther aft than an inner forestay; it can sometimes be used for hanking on a storm jib. Right: The lower end of an inner forestay is attached to a lever fitting that clips the stay in place and tensions it.

lengths and release lever accounted for), you might want to take the parts to a rigger for assembly, especially if you're going to use swaged terminals.

Installing tracks

Installing the tracks was the most stressful part of the job for me be-cause I hate to drill holes in my deck. I had figured out the positioning of the tracks long before, and I knew I had done it accurately, but still it made me nervous. I started by laying the track on the deck and marking the through-bolt locations; then I went below and removed the cabin headliner. I carefully measured where the through-bolts

would come through and double-checked that they would not interfere with anything.

Next I drilled the holes and bolted down the tracks. Be careful to use the proper washers and backing, and make sure everything is sealed up watertight. I installed the cars on the new tracks and, after hanking on my new staysail,

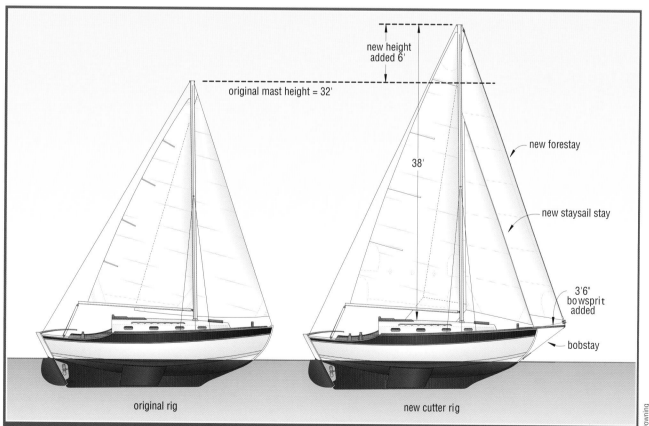

new height added 6'

original mast height = 32'

38'

new forestay

new staysail stay

3'6" bowsprit added

bobstay

original rig

new cutter rig

Not all boats can easily have an inner forestay fitted and still provide useful extra sail area. One option is to add a bowsprit and use the existing stay as the inner one. This will not work for all boats, but is an ideal solution on the Golden Hind shown above. However, in this case a new mast was fitted to make a useful foretriangle.

Illustrations by Kim Downing

Installing an Inner Forestay

led the sheets. Finally I was ready for action.

The boat sails beautifully with the new inner forestay. I like the way the rig looks, and I think the boat is more stable in heavy seas. There was always a bit of weather helm, and the staysail has helped reduce that—especially in high winds. Now I have no excuses not to start building up my offshore experience.

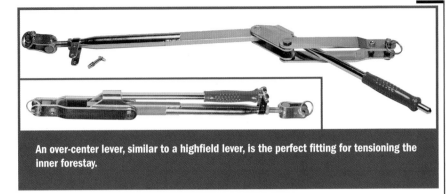

An over-center lever, similar to a highfield lever, is the perfect fitting for tensioning the inner forestay.

Robert Leach

Build Your Own Spinnaker

This past summer my family and I decided we needed an asymmetrical cruising spinnaker on *Time Out,* our Catalina 22. This is because we sail mainly on Midwestern lakes, where conditions tend to be light and shifty. Not only would a spinnaker help improve our performance, but we figured we could also show off our colors and aerodynamic shapes to all those motorheads.

The only problem was our tight budget. Being the pennypincher that I am, I asked myself, "How much could the materials cost?" Then I went online to search for "rip-stop nylon."

Sailrite (www.sailrite.com) seemed a dream come true. Not only did they sell all the materials I needed to build my own sail, they had the skill, technology, and experience necessary to design a sail for me and assemble a kit so I could build it myself.

I could have placed the order online, but since Sailrite is based only 30 miles from my house, I made an appointment and drove up for a visit. I sat down with designer Jeff Frank and began designing and plotting my spinnaker on his computer. Within minutes the sail was coming to 3D life on the screen. The software then broke the sail down into panels, which Jeff began arranging (he called it "nesting") by color on a simulated plotting table. After the printer spit out my design, we hiked across the warehouse to the plotter room. Stretched out in front of me was a 30-foot-long computerized robotic plotting and cutting table.

Jeff rolled out 10 yards of crisp crimson ¾-ounce rip-stop nylon, calibrated the plotter/cutter, turned on the vacuum

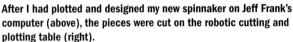
After I had plotted and designed my new spinnaker on Jeff Frank's computer (above), the pieces were cut on the robotic cutting and plotting table (right).

system to hold the fabric in place, then hit the "Go" button. At his command the plotter/cutter began traversing the fabric, marking the seam lines and cutting the panels to our exact specifications.

After we cut the fabric, we discussed construction. I was concerned about having to sew the entire sail myself. Not being the Martha Stewart type, I was relieved and amazed to discover that the bulk of panel assembly is now done with high-tech double-sided tape. The short of it is that if you can gift-wrap a present, you can build a spinnaker. The rest of the construction can be done on a standard home sewing machine.

At home, I scouted for a place to begin assembly. Luckily, my house has hardwood floors. I pushed the dining table out of the way, cleaned the floor carefully, and rolled out panel number 1. If you don't have a hard flat surface readily available, consider looking for a gym, racquetball court, or dance floor where you could work. The panels have seam lines printed right on them, so all you need to do is stick the tape between the edge of the panel and the seam line. The tape is ½″ wide and the seam allowance is ⁶⁄₁₀″, so you do have some room for error. I found it is important when applying the tape to gently stretch the fabric to remove all wrinkles. This takes some getting used to, so it's a good idea to practice on some scraps before tackling a big panel.

After sticking the tape onto the first panel, I peeled the backing off the adhesive on the tape's exposed side. Starting at the wide end of the panel, I care-

fully overlaid panel number 2 on panel number 1. Again, it is important to gently tension both layers of fabric as you line them up and press them together. Sailrite has a video clip on its Web site demonstrating in detail how to do this. Once I got the technique down, I was able to assemble the entire sail in just a few hours. At this point I stood back and admired my handiwork. My new sail had fit together with the precision of a jigsaw puzzle. Jeff's design was exact and each panel had lined up and intersected perfectly.

Once the entire sail was taped together, I used my home sewing machine. to zigzag-stitch the main vertical and horizontal seams. Practice with your machine before attempting to stitch the seams. It is important to get the thread tension just right to produce professional-looking stitches. The massive sail was hard to manage, so I recruited my kids to help me roll the beast right up to the seam I needed to sew. The rolled section was fed into the arm of the sewing machine. Putting the sewing machine on the floor made it much easier to stitch the long seams.

Each corner of the sail, including the head, then needed to be reinforced with three layers of 4-ounce Dacron, plus an additional layer of rip-stop nylon colored to match the rest of the sail. These sections were also precut by Sailrite, but I needed to trim them to fit exactly. I first tried taping them together, but found this didn't hold well enough to sew all the layers together. I ended up using spray-on adhesive, which you can buy at

most hardware stores, to sandwich the patches onto the sail. The spray adhesive worked much better. A few times I needed to peel and reglue the layers to remove the wrinkles, but the spray adhesive did not set quickly, so this wasn't a problem. Finally, I stitched up all three layers of Dacron, plus the outer layer of rip-stop nylon.

The sail kit came with 1″ nylon strips (called "tape," though they have no adhesive) to protect and strengthen the edges of the spinnaker. Using a warm iron, I creased the tape in half before basting it to the sail. You don't need to use expensive C3 spinnaker tape for the edges. Instead, use cheaper double-sided basting tape to attach the edge tape before sewing. It works far better than pins or staples for holding the fabric together. In fact, my wife now uses it for all her sewing projects. After I taped the nylon strips on the edges of the

What you need

- Sewing machine that zigzags
- Pair of sharp scissors
- Large, smooth floor (about 100 square feet)
- Spray adhesive
- Do-it-yourself attitude

What you don't need

- PhD in aerodynamics
- Large paycheck

The first step was to tape together the individual sail panels (left). The trick is to stretch the fabric of each panel slightly as it is overlaid along the seam (above).

sail, I secured them with more zigzag stitches. I put white tape on the foot, red on the luff, and green on the leech to help identify which side is which when wrestling with it on deck.

The final step was to attach the corner D-rings where the halyard, sheets, and tack downhaul would be bent on. Each D-ring was attached with nylon webbing. First I cut nine 15″ lengths of webbing with an old knife I heated on

the kitchen stove. Working on one corner at a time, I taped the first piece of webbing along one edge of a corner, ran it through the D-ring, then taped it on the opposite side. The second piece of webbing was installed on the edge opposite the first. The last piece went right through the center. Make sure that all the webbing is taped back onto itself, as the idea is to stitch the two halves together for maximum strength.

Sailrite recommends that you whipstitch the D-ring to the patch for added stability and then add a section of leather to protect each corner from chafing. Honestly, I was far too anxious to fly my kite to complete these last two details and decided to save this final chore for some cold winter night. Meanwhile, I'm enjoying my new asymmetrical spinnaker. It is spectacular, and I am the envy of the lake.

The Power of New Sails

When lost in a maelstrom of renovation and maintenance work it is easy to forget one very important fact about sailboats. You may spend untold hours and buckets of money bringing your old boat up to snuff structurally, mechanically, and cosmetically, and it may well be very gratifying, but none of this effort will translate into improved sailing performance. If actually sailing your boat is what you most enjoy about owning a sailboat, then the single most dramatic improvement you can make is to get it a new suit of sails.

Sails are expensive—a new set of working sails even for a boat as small as 30 feet will cost thousands of dollars—and even dedicated do-it-yourselfers may be unwilling to follow the intrepid Mr. Leach's example and build their own. But still it is money well

spent. The increase in performance will not be as noticeable while sailing off the wind, when a sail's efficiency is as much or more a function of its area than its shape. But the improvement will be startling when sailing with the wind on or forward of the beam, as this is when a sail's shape is absolutely critical. Even old sails that appear to be in very good condition are apt to have stretched and deformed over the years, and this greatly reduces their aerodynamic efficiency.

New sails are particularly handy when the wind starts to build. Because they stretch more, old sails get baggier when the wind blows harder, thus increasing their power just when you want to decrease it by flattening their shape. Because new sails stretch much less, it is easy to flatten them

out with boom vangs, outhauls, cunninghams, and halyards, thus allowing you to fly more sail in more wind. While your buddies are busy reefing down their old mainsails a bit earlier than they'd like to keep from being overwhelmed, you'll be able to play your new main like a fiddle, tensioning the vang and outhaul to tighten it up and easing the sheet just a tad as gusts go through to throw a little luff in the back. All these elements of fine control are lost once your sail gets too old and baggy.

So if you're a serious sailor, don't put new sails at the bottom of the list when planning out your rehab budget. Put them right at the top and let the cosmetic stuff hang fire for a while.

Charles J. Doane

My new sail reduced to its major components (above). The corners were reinforced with three layers of 4-ounce Dacron (right), which I fastened in place with spray adhesive before stitching them together.

After getting everything taped together, I stitched the seams on a sewing machine (above). Maintaining thread tension is important here.

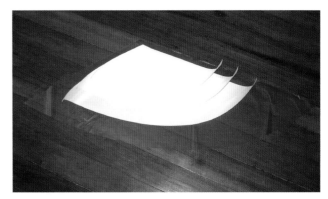

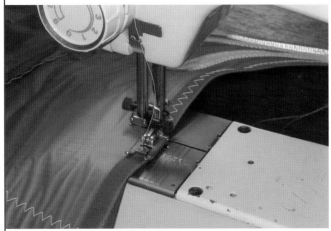

The edges of the spinnaker were trimmed with strips of 1" nylon tape (above). I used double-sided basting tape to hold the nylon tape in place before doing the final stitching.

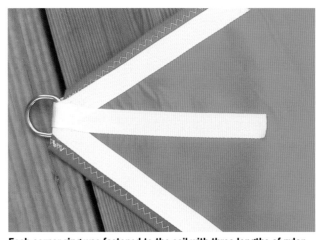

Each corner ring was fastened to the sail with three lengths of nylon webbing folded back onto themselves (above). The stitching went through both layers, providing maximum strength.

BUILDING TIME

Task	Time
Seam taping	6–8 hours
Seam sewing	1–2 hours
Corner patches	2 hours
Nylon edge tape	2 hours
D-ring installations	2 hours
TOTAL	13–16 hours

Combating Sail Wear

Sun, salt, high loads, and unforgiving rigging all combine to sap your sail's strength and performance. Here's what you need to look for and what your need to know to fight back.

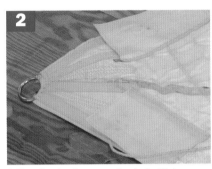

1. Overlapping genoas will inevitably chafe on spreaders and shrouds, even if there is chafe gear (spreader boots) on the spreader ends and reinforced spreader patches on the sail. Two good ways to reduce a headsail's life expectancy are oversheeting and not releasing the sail quickly enough during a tack. This headsail was reinforced with extra cloth but still chafed against the spreader end enough to weaken the cloth; the owner attached temporary spot patches to stop the small tears that occurred. If you keep a close eye on spreader patches and repair them before they start to show excessive wear, you can limit the damage to the sail.

2. The clew is also prone to chafe. Make sure that the stitching on reinforcing patches is unbroken and the clew ring has not deformed. The broken stitching on this clew's reinforcing webbing shows signs of chafe and may need to be resewn.

4. The bow pulpit is another source of chafing. Many headsails have sacrificial patches sewn into the foot of the sail to minimize damage caused by the pulpit. Keep an eye on the foot of the sail near the tack, and have the patches replaced it they start to show excessive wear or discoloration.

5. Furling headsails are subject to excessive strain when flown partially furled. Loads are concentrated along the upper leech and along the foot aft of the tack. Over time the cloth in these areas will stretch and deform. Deep creases show that this sail has stretched and been damaged because of excessive use while partially furled. Setting a smaller headsail in high winds will increase the life span of the genoa. It will also present a better shape than a partially furled headsail.

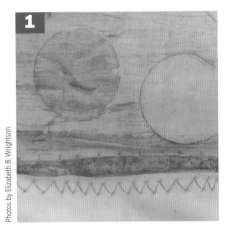

3. Hardware on the front of the mast can be just as damaging as the spreaders and shrouds. Radomes, foredeck lights, and spinnaker-pole tracks will chafe against the leech during tacks and jibes. Placing metal cages over these units will minimize chafe, but the leech is still a high-stress area that should be watched closely. It's a good idea before and after the season to lay the sail flat on a floor or in the yard and examine it for any signs or wear or discoloration.

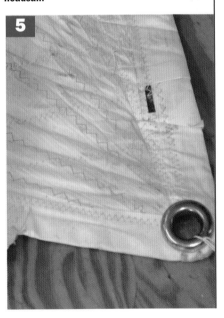

TIP

Sticky-back Dacron is often used for chafe patches, but after a while the edges tend to curl up and the patch can come adrift. If the patch has been doubled over around the leech, it could catch on a shroud or a spreader end. If using sticky-back as a temporary chafe patch, don't double it around the sail. Better still, stitch it on.

Photos by Elizabeth B. Wrightson

6

6. Batten pockets can be trouble areas, especially on older mainsails. Battens flex continually and stress the area around the pocket, especially the pocket ends. This batten pocket had insufficient reinforcement, which allowed the batten to chafe in the pocket under load until it finally poked through the weakened sailcloth. Look for excessive wear at the forward and aft ends of the pocket before things get this bad. Make sure your batten pockets are sufficiently reinforced and the battens are properly sized. Installing an undersized batten in a batten pocket will increase chafe dramatically.

7

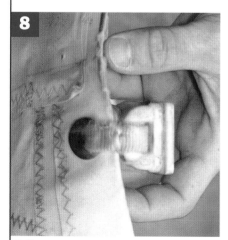

7. Batten cars and slugs can be another source of chafing. Well-installed batten cars will minimize chafing along the luff but still can cause excessive wear at the sail's attachment point.

8

8. The most common sail-slide system—slugs attached to grommets on the luff with nylon webbing—is also the most prone to chafing.

9

9. A misaligned slug will increase wear dramatically. The slug on this mainsail is placed too close to the batten pocket. Under pressure the batten pushes into the mast at a bad angle and results in increased chafe. A simple solution is to locate the slug in-line with or farther away from the batten pocket.

11. Reef points on the boom are a prime trouble spot. The luff of the sail tends to wear and chafe at the reef rings and the sailcloth under the reef rings tends to be crushed by the boom when a reef is tucked in.

10

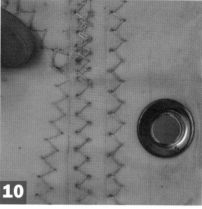

10. Mainsail grommets and slug webbing will be affected by high loads rather than chafe. Deformed grommets get progressively weaker and should be replaced.

11

12

12. In general, laminated sails suffer the same maladies as Dacron sails, with one addition— delamination. All laminated sails are only as strong as the glue that holds their layers together. And while huge advances have been made in adhesives, these sails are still subject to UV degradation that can eventually cause the glue to break down. Keep a close eye out for the first signs of delamination. If a sail gets as bad as this one, it's too far gone to save.

Building a Mast

Masts for everyone: Whatever the size and shape you need, most spar makers should have an extrusion to fit your boat.

Building your own mast might sound like a job better left to professionals. But truth be told, it's easier than you might think and involves little more than drilling a few holes and securing some hardware. More surprising than the level of difficulty, though, is the amount of money you can save by doing it yourself rather than buying a ready-to-step mast. The savings can be substantial, perhaps as much as 30 percent, according to some manufacturers.

Mind you, we're not talking about making the actual extrusion of aluminum or carbon fiber—that's hardly a project for the average DIYer to attempt in his or her garage. What we're discussing is assembling a mast from individual parts and/or a kit that includes everything you'll need—the extrusion, rigging hardware and fittings, tools, and an assembly guide.

The level of difficulty and amount of time required depends on the size of the mast and amount of hardware involved, but for daysailers or small cruisers under 26 feet—probably the largest boat for which you should build a mast—you're looking at a 1-hour job. The trickiest part may be finding a location in your garage or house long enough to contain the new extrusion while you do the work.

The first step is to accurately measure the length and diameter and identify the shape of your current mast. Many spar makers have a database of specifications and dimensions for most boats (drawings are often available online). But if your boat is unique, it may be helpful to make a sketch.

Now you have two options: (a) order an extrusion and simply remove and refit the existing cleats, tangs, and blocks; or (b) order a ready-to-assemble spar kit

that includes all the parts. If you choose this option, be sure to keep your old hardware as spares.

From there, it's as easy as assembling a child's toy. We had Mike Ammann of Dwyer Aluminum walk us through building a simple spar for a daysailer.

🕐 **Approx. job time: 1 hour**

📖 **Skill level: Easy**

✂ **Tools you will need**

- Drill
- Riveting tongs
- Screwdriver
- File
- Hard rubber mallet or hammer

1. Using the old mast (or a sketch/CAD drawing of it) as a guide, measure and mark all drill points for hardware on the new extrusion. To make the installation easier, place the hardware next to its appropriate location on the mast.

2. You can work from either the bottom up, the top down, or—if you have an assistant—in both directions at once. On this mast, Mike worked from the bottom up, first positioning the halyard cleat on the mast tube and drilling holes through the mast wall.

3. Using a screwdriver, fasten the first halyard cleat to the mast with stainless-steel screws. Repeat for the other cleat.

4. Slide the downhaul cleat into the sail slot and secure it with screws.

RESOURCES

Ballenger Spar Systems
www.ballengerspars.com
831-763-1196

Dwyer Aluminum
www.dwyermast.com
203-484-0419

Glen-L Marine Designs
www.glen-l.com
562-630 6258

Hall Spars
www.hallspars.com
401-253-4858, ext. 1533

LeFiell Marine Products
www.lefiell.com
800-451-5971

Offshore Spars
www.offshorespars.com
586-598-4700

Proctor Masts and Rigging
www.proctormasts.com
714-979-7820

Rig-Rite, Inc.
www.rigrite.com
401-739-1140

U.S. Spars, Inc.
www.usspars.com
800-928-0786

TOP TIP

- If the masthead won't fit into the top of the mast, file it down and gently tap on it with a hard rubber mallet.
- Secure the rigging hardware to the mast tube using stainless-steel—not aluminum—pop rivets. While aluminum rivets may be more readily available at your local hardware store, they are not strong enough to do the job.
- To prevent corrosion, coat all screws with Tef-Gel—or other anti-corrosive lubricant—before securing.

Building a Mast

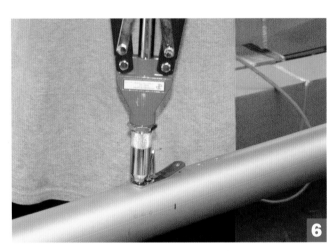

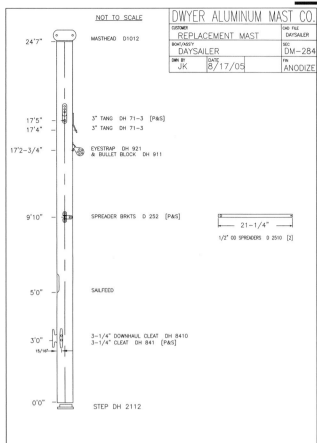

A sketch or CAD drawing of your mast will help ensure that hardware is attached in the right places. The drawing shown here comes with the spar kit we put together.

5. Moving up the mast, position the spreader brackets on the extrusion and drill corresponding holes through the mast wall. Now insert and attach stainless-steel rivets using riveting tongs or gun. Repeat the process for the other spreader bracket. Remember—measure twice, drill once!

6. Position the shroud tangs and the halyard block on the extrusion. As with the spreader brackets, drill holes through the fittings and the mast tube and secure pop rivets with riveting tongs.

7. After filing any burrs from the end of the extrusion, insert the masthead into the mast. Drill holes on each side of the fitting and attach the masthead with pop rivets.

Thanks to **Dwyer Aluminum** for their help.

Clarence Jones

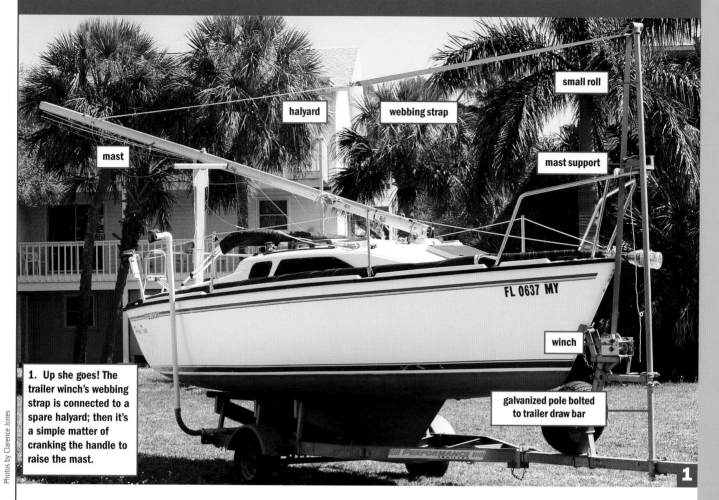

mast

halyard

webbing strap

small roll

mast support

winch

galvanized pole bolted to trailer draw bar

FL 0637 MY

1. Up she goes! The trailer winch's webbing strap is connected to a spare halyard; then it's a simple matter of cranking the handle to raise the mast.

Mast-Raising System

When launching and recovering my first trailerable sailboat, I always muscled the mast up and down at the boat ramp. But I was a lot younger then, and that mast was not nearly as heavy as the one on my current boat, a Precision 21. I'm not physically able to step or unstep this mast without help, so I designed and built a system that makes it really easy. So easy you can do it with your fingers.

I first created this system for a Precision 18. It worked so well that I built another when I moved up to my Precision 21. It's now in its fourth incarnation, and I'm sure the design can be easily adapted to other boats of the same type. The primary component is a 10′ length of 1¼″ galvanized plumbing pipe. I use this to create a high fulcrum point to raise and lower the mast using the trailer winch and its nylon strap. With a

small adaptation, stepping and lowering the mast with the trailer winch can be accomplished without a helper.

First, you need a crutch to elevate the mast at the transom. This will make stepping the mast simpler. It gives you a head start and also gets the mast up and out of the way when you need to work in the cockpit or cabin with the boat on its trailer. I made my crutch about head-high and put the roller on top to make it easy to move the mast forward or aft. The higher the crutch is, the easier it is to raise the mast.

Don't tow the boat with the mast in the crutch. It's not stable enough to stand up to a hard turn or a pothole, and the mast could bounce out into the street. The mast should always be tied to the sternrail and bow pulpit for stability when you're traveling. And however you design it, stability when the crutch is in place is critical. If the mast should

fall, it could cause you serious injury and/or damage your boat.

Mast cradles

I built cradles of synthetic wood to support the mast front and rear while trailering. The transom cradle does double duty; it also holds the mast crutch and keeps it stable. A similar cradle is strapped to the bow pulpit. The cradles are lined with carpet and are attached to the bow pulpit and transom rail with plastic clamps used to bolt electrical conduit to a flat surface.

On one side of each mast cradle, I drilled a hole near the bottom, knotted a short piece of line, threaded it through the wall of the cradle, and installed a cleat on the other side to secure the mast in the cradle. I always use either stainless-steel or weatherproof deck screws to avoid rust problems.

Approx. job time: 6 hours

Skill level: Easy

Tools you will need

- **Hammer**
- **Saw**
- **Wrenches**
- **Tape measure**
- **Screwdrivers**
- **Pliers**

Materials

- **One 10' length of 1¼" threaded galvanized pipe**
- **One approx. 2' length of 1¼" threaded galvanized pipe (for pole brace)**
- **Three 1¼" galvanized tees**
- **Six galvanized U-bolts, backing plates, and nuts (to attach pole and brace to trailer)**
- **Two 4" stainless ⅜" hex bolts and nuts**
- **One small piece of ½" PVC pipe (pulley roller)**
- **One 6' length of 2 × 4 lumber (main crutch upright)**
- **Short lengths of 2 × 4 lumber (lengths depend on boat dimensions) for crutch arm and foot**
- **Two 10" lengths of 1 × 2 hardwood (for roller hubs)**
- **Trailer roller slightly wider than your mast**
- **One 6" stainless ⅜" hex bolt, nut, and washer for roller axle**
- **One small piece of ½" PVC pipe (for axle bushing)**
- **Small cleat and length of ¼" line**
- **About 3' of 1 × 6 wood or synthetic deck planking**
- **Twelve 2½" deck screws**
- **Carpet scraps and SS screws to fasten them to cradles**
- **¾" plastic electrical conduit clamps**
- **Small cleat and length of ¼" line**

2. The stern mast cradle is similar in design to the one at the bow. The carpet padding prevents damage to the mast's finish coating.

The crutch

The crutch is made of 2 × 4 lumber with a crosspiece at the bottom. The base rests in the floor of the cockpit at the transom. The base has two slices of 1″ doweling screwed into the bottom, spaced to fit in the Precision's cockpit drain holes. These keep the crutch very stable. If your boat doesn't have drain holes, you'll need to find another way to anchor the crutch to both the sternrail and the transom. The base of the crutch should be as wide as the cockpit floor to help prevent its leaning to port or starboard.

You'll need to screw a horizontal piece of 2 × 4 lumber into the crutch to tie it to the sternrail. You may also need to screw a piece of wood to the crutch as a spacer between the rail and the rear of the cockpit to keep the crutch vertical. I placed my horizontal arm so it slides into the aft cradle. I tie the crutch into the cradle so the crutch can't rise or move forward. Another way to secure the crutch to the sternrail is to screw a piece of 2 × 4 to the crutch upright, with a notch to fit the rail.

At the top of my crutch I installed a rubber roller to make moving the mast forward or aft much easier. To do this I screwed two pieces of 1 × 2 oak (chosen for strength) to the top of the crutch to support the roller's axle; I had to shim them out slightly to fit the 4″ roller in place between them. The axle is a ⅜″ stainless-steel bolt running through a short piece of ½″ (O.D.) PVC pipe. You won't need the PVC if you buy a larger

bolt, but stainless bolts are expensive and a larger one is not necessary for strength.

I had to cut the two side pieces of oak shorter than I would have liked, to allow the shroud fittings on the mast to roll past. If your shroud fittings will allow it, leave the oak pieces longer. This will help to support the roller and to keep the mast centered on it.

In most states the legal vertical road clearance under overhead wires or bridges is 13½'. Power lines are supposed to be higher. The 10' mast-raising pole, which is clamped perpendicular to the trailer tongue, will be about 11' high when the trailer is being towed. At first I cringed each time I drove under a telephone wire strung across a street, but the wires always seem lower than they really are. If a semi-trailer can go down the street without snagging a wire, so too can your mast-raiser.

I attached the 10' pole to the tongue on my trailer with standard galvanized U-bolts. It needs to be braced to the winch pedestal to make it stable. I use a short piece of 1¼″ pipe with a tee on each end to do this. Notice how the ridges at each edge of the galvanized tees form a slot to keep the U-bolts in place. You'll need to experiment to determine how far ahead of the winch pedestal you should mount the pole. (It needs to be just ahead of the bow pulpit on your boat when it is on the trailer.) Also check the lead for the winch strap, which will run to the top of the pole and then aft to hook onto a line that runs to a point near the top of the mast.

3. To support the end of the mast when it is in a semi-raised position, I made a crutch from 2 × 4 lumber with a roller on the top (inset). You can just make out the pushpit mast support that secures the mast when the boat is being towed.

4. With the mast in the horizontal position, a piece of rope is all that is required to hold the spar firmly in place. Make sure that the mast is well secured so that it can't slide forward when the towing vehicle brakes.

From the point where the pole is braced against the winch pedestal to the top of the pole is about 8′. This creates a lot of leverage on the pole when the mast is being raised or lowered—enough to bend the pole—so you'll need to find a way to lean the pole against the bow pulpit to decrease the leverage.

To reduce the leverage on the pole, I padded the mast cradle at the bow by bolting a short piece of 2 × 4 and a slightly longer piece of planking to the side of the cradle. Since the pole is bolted to the trailer off-center, this padding is in exactly the right place to provide a support point. The lip on the slightly longer piece of planking prevents the pole from slipping off the support point. From there to the top of the pole is only about 3 feet.

To create a smooth surface for the winch strap to slide over, I installed a length of ½″ (I.D.) PVC pipe on the bow mast cradle. This may not be necessary, depending on the angle between your winch and the top of the pole.

At the top of the pole, I also made a roller where the winch strap turns toward the boat's stern. I made this with

a galvanized pipe tee, two backing plates, a ⅜″ stainless-steel bolt as the axle, and a piece of ½″ (O.D.) PVC pipe as the roller wheel. Notice the piece of doweling placed inside the tee to maintain the angle for the backing plates.

My boat has a CDI Flexible Furler, but the original jib halyard is still in place. I use that halyard to raise and lower the mast. The winch strap comes up through the roller at the top of the pole, and then hooks into the halyard shackle.

If you can't use a jib halyard, you'll need to install a bridle of some kind near the top of the mast with a line attached. Make sure both the bridle and the line are strong enough to support the mast as it is raised or lowered.

With this system, it is extremely easy to raise and lower the mast. My wife cranks the trailer winch while I stand on top of the cabin to keep the mast centered and to make sure none of the rigging gets snagged on the way up. Crank very gently. The winch is very powerful, and you could easily break something if some standing rigging is snagged on the way up. Make sure the turnbuckles at the bases of the shrouds are not stuck

at an angle as the mast gets near the vertical position. They will bend easily if they're not swiveling freely.

I found that the base of my furler had a tendency to hang up as the mast is raised, so I built a protective boot from a plastic Gatorade bottle slit down one side to cover the fitting. The boot snaps on and off easily and is held in place with Velcro straps.

Make sure the sliding companionway hatch is closed when you lower the mast. If it's open, the mast may come down on the forward edge and crack it.

My 18-footer had small stainless eye straps on each side of the mast, about 6 feet from the base. Tying a line from each eye strap to a lifeline stanchion on either side keeps the mast centered as it is raised or lowered, making it possible to perform either task singlehanded. If a piece of standing rigging gets stuck, you can lock the winch, go release the snagged rigging, then return to the winch to finish the job.

In the photos you will notice that the roller-furler is not attached. I removed it for photographic purposes. You'll also see that the furler boot is in place.

5. With the base of the mast in the tabernacle, I place a wood block into the bow chock to give the mast-raising pole something to bear against.

6. A close-up of the roller pole attached to the trailer drawbar; (inset) the U-bolt attachment to the winch support and the pole top.

7. The top end of the pipe for the mast raiser has a small roller made from a piece of plastic pipe slipped over a bolt. The webbing strap rides effortlessly over this when the winch is operated.

Mark Corke

Splicing Three-Strand Rope

Splicing three-strand rope is a fairly straightforward process and a useful skill. Splicing joins together two ropes of equal diameter and does not weaken the rope to the same extent that tying a knot does. When done well, the finished product looks neat, though the extra bulk may prevent the rope from running through sheaves and around blocks. Practice on nylon rope that is soft and easy on the hands. For your first attempt use a larger-diameter rope (¾″ is ideal); small-diameter ropes are harder. Using ropes of different colors for practice work makes it easier to spot mistakes and keep track of the developing splice. Aim to keep the splice tidy, and take your time—speed will come with practice.

1. Unlay about 12 times the diameter of the rope and tie a piece of whipping twine around the rope to prevent further unraveling. Place the two ends of the rope together, alternating the strands.

2. Working against the lay of the rope, tuck one end over an opposing strand and under the next strand.

3. Rotate the rope and continue to tuck the first strand and under the next, as shown.

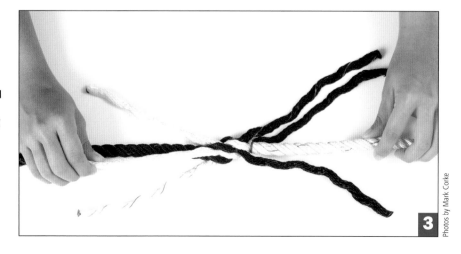

Photos by Mark Corke

4. Continue with one rope until you have four complete tucks. Make sure to pull the ends up tight—a slack splice will kink and is more likely to fail. When you have finished with half the splice, repeat the procedure with the three strands of the other rope.

5. Don't be in a rush to trim off protruding ends. Use firm hand pressure, or roll the rope under your foot, to get the tucks to sit comfortably.

6. Use a sharp knife to cut the temporary whipping from the center of the splice.

7. Trim the ends of the strands back flush to the rope. The splice is now complete.

TOP TIP

A small marlinespike is helpful for opening up the strands of small-diameter traditional hemp or polypropylene rope prior to tucking. To prevent individual strands from unraveling, wrap a small piece of masking or electrical tape around each of the ends.

EYE SPLICE
An eye splice is formed exactly the same way as a short splice except that the rope is spliced back on itself. This is a particularly useful splice for attaching fenders to lengths of rope.

RESOURCES

New England Ropes
www.neropes.com
800-333-6679

R&W Rope Warehouse
www.rwrope.com
800-260-8599

Samson
www.samsonrope.com
360-384-4669

Yale Cordage
www.yalecordage.com
207-282-3396

Rope Care

Overworked and often over-looked, ropes and lines need as much care as other on-board equipment. Rope is expensive, so it makes good sense to get the best and longest use possible out of it. Without proper care, any rope is more likely to break. Remember that your dream boat is attached to your mooring or dock with just a few lengths of nylon.

Dirt and salt shorten the life of ropes; both are abrasive and will wear away at the fibers, weakening the rope and making it stiff and unpleasant to handle. Salt is hygroscopic, so a rope that contains salt will always feel damp

to the touch and will attract more dirt. To prolong rope life, clean them at the end of the season. Wash them, dry them, and hang them up in a dry place—not in a damp locker—during the off-season. Most ropes are made from either nylon or polyester (Dacron) and are easy to care for. If you have any high-tech ropes, consult with the manufacturer before subjecting them to a dunking in the washing machine.

Note: There was some heated debate here at BW as to whether the correct term is "ropes" or "lines." The verdict? Unless it's performing a specific job, it's a rope. So there.

1. This jumble of rope came off a small daysailer and is about half of the total inventory of ropes and lines used aboard. The amount of rope used on a larger boat represents a considerable investment.

2. Check each rope for chafe and general wear and tear, and untie all knots. This braided rope is well worn and should be discarded.

⏱ **Approx job time: 3 hours**

📖 **Skill level: Easy**

✂ **Tools you will need**

- Washing machine
- Bucket
- Mild detergent
- Magic Marker
- Masking tape
- Lingerie bags

Photos by Mark Corke

Rope Care

117

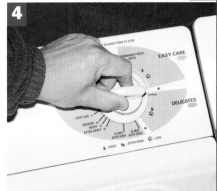

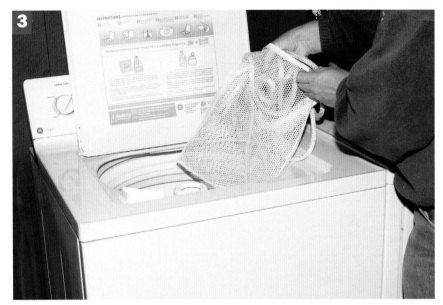

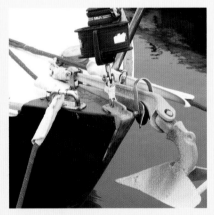

3. I like to wash small ropes in string lingerie bags. Use a bag that can be closed tightly with zippers to prevent the ropes from becoming tangled in the washing machine. For large rope, use a pillowcase.

4. Wash ropes in cool water, and set the machine for an extra rinse cycle if possible. Use a little mild detergent—about a third of the normal amount for a load of this size.

5. Ropes can be air-dried or dried in a machine on low heat. Remove the ropes from the bags first to cut down on drying time.

6. One or two ropes can be washed in a bucket. Change the water frequently after the soapy wash until all traces of detergent have vanished.

Chafe Protection

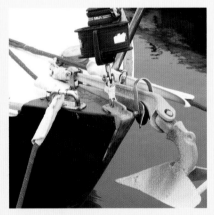

Protecting ropes from wear caused by chafe is probably one of the best things that you can do to extend their lifespan. For a permanent mooring pennant, a length of canvas stitched to the line works well.

Another favorite for chafe protection is a length of plastic pipe slipped over the rope. This is simple and cheap, but prevents the rope from bending and can cause hard spots.

Modern chocks are often undersized and may have sharp edges that can shred a rope in a matter of hours. Three-strand nylon rope stretches easily and is ideal for mooring lines and anchor rodes.

Coiling and storing ropes

1. With the rope on the ground at your feet, hold one end of the rope in one hand and make a loop about 3 feet in circumference with the other hand.

2. Continue to make loops and transfer them from one hand to the other as you do so. Twisting the rope slightly between thumb and forefinger helps the coils to lie neatly against each other.

3. When there is about 4 feet of rope remaining, put three neat, tight wraps around the coil.

4. Pass the bunt of the working end through the top of the coil. Make sure that the end of the rope is not pulled through, but hangs in a loop as shown.

5. Pass the loop over the top of the coil as you transfer the coil from one hand to the other.

6. Pull on the loose end of the rope to tighten up the loop. As you do this, work the loop down so that it sits snug against the three wraps.

7. This neatly coiled rope can be tossed into a locker without fear of tangling. It is instantly ready to use when you push the loop back over the top of the coil and undo the three turns.

8. If a rope will be stored for an extended period, use a tag of masking tape to note its function.

9. To keep ropes in top condition in the off-season, store them out of direct sunlight and hang them on individual pegs.

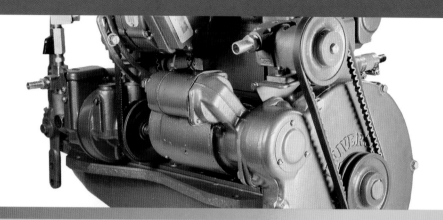

Engines

The oily beast lurking in the bilge can be the source of much soul-searching for the modern boater. On the one hand we have an automobile culture in which machinery has grown so complex that owner maintenance is not only discouraged but, in many cases, next to impossible. A whole generation is growing up without ever having known the joys of tinkering with cars or motorcycles.

On the other hand, we have the knowledge that at sea, our safety and that of the people who sail with us can depend on our ability to perform basic maintenance and troubleshooting of our engines and their related systems. You can't just pull over to the side of the road and call AAA, and even if you call a marine towing service, there's no guarantee that it will get to you before your lack of engine power puts you in

serious trouble. Sure, sailors have an advantage here, but not if there is no wind.

We've assembled a wide variety of topics in this section. There's a look at the venerable Atomic 4 gasoline engine—once almost universal aboard production fiberglass sailboats. There are many Atomic 4s still out there and giving great service. Who knows—maybe this information will encourage you to buy that 30-footer no one else will touch, even for a song, due to the gas engine in its bilge. You'll also find in this section guides to inspecting and maintaining such essentials as the cutless bearing, the stuffing box, and the cooling system. We have a bit of fun showing you how to service your fuel injectors. And we show you how to upgrade your engine controls and tell you why oil changes are so important.

Pamper Your Old Atomic 4

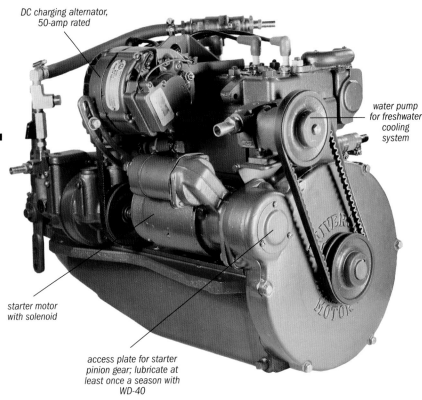

DC charging alternator, 50-amp rated

water pump for freshwater cooling system

starter motor with solenoid

access plate for starter pinion gear; lubricate at least once a season with WD-40

Photos courtesy of Moyer Marine/Stephen Moyer

All photographs show an early Atomic 4 UJ model that has been modified for a freshwater cooling system. Replacement parts for all Atomic 4 engines available through authorized Westerbeke/Universal dealers and distributors (www.westerbeke.com).

Although diesel auxiliary engines are now the norm in modern sailboats, there are still many boats out there with old gasoline auxiliaries, mostly Universal Atomic 4s. Between 1947 and 1985 some 40,000 of these 350-pound, 30-horsepower engines were installed in U.S.-built boats. An estimated 20,000 are still in use today.

In fact, there are more Atomic 4s in running condition now than there were 20 years ago. While parts for most old gas auxiliaries, such as the one-lung, two-stroke Vire 7, the bigger Vire 12, and the Atomic 2, have become difficult to find, parts for the Atomic 4 are still widely available. Moreover, there is a lively market for the old engines, which are not only cannibalized for parts but are frequently rebuilt and upgraded.

Though most sailors these days prefer diesels for their greater reliability, safety, and simplicity, many sailors who have purchased older boats with Atomic

4s have elected to keep and maintain them rather than endure the great expense and trouble of repowering. Safety is, of course, a key concern, as gasoline is much more volatile than diesel. But if the engine and its fuel lines are regularly inspected and well maintained, and if the engine space is properly ventilated with a blower fan, a prudent sailor can safely operate a gas auxiliary.

Common problems

Problems with gas engines typically result from humidity, salty air, and sharply fluctuating engine-compartment temperatures. Infrequent use of the engine and poor maintenance are contributing factors. In the marine environment condensation easily forms on the engine and in the fuel tank; corrosion and electrolysis attack metal parts. The seawater circulating through the cooling system harms the metal and leaves salt deposits. Occasionally it may penetrate into the

cylinders and carburetor, wreaking havoc. Pollution, salt, and grease can interfere with ignition.

The most commonly encountered problems are ignition failure, a malfunctioning carburetor, sticking valves, and overheating. Fortunately, these can be addressed with preventive measures that are well within the expertise of the most mechanically challenged sailor. Many are applicable to diesels and outboard engines as well.

Your first line of defense is to be familiar with the engine. Open its compartment and inspect everything regularly. Sniff carefully for gas fumes. Check for dripping fuel and oil. Examine all hose clamps, hoses, and wires. Feel the tension of the alternator belt. Check the engine-oil level. If something is not right, fix it at once.

Next, run the engine regularly—don't just start it and shut it down. Run it under load long enough for it to reach its normal operating temperature. Twenty minutes to half an hour is a good ballpark figure. If the engine is not to be restarted that same day, don't shut it down by turning off the ignition, but by allowing it to run out of fuel. (Never do this to a diesel!) If the boat does not have a shut-off valve in the fuel line, install one. It is an important safety feature. Carburetors in particular develop problems when left inactive with gasoline inside.

One good way to damage the carburetor on a balky engine is to spray it with starting fluid. Starting problems are often the result of the choke not fully closing. Merely tapping the carburetor may cure the problem. Spraying in a whiff of Marvel's Mystery Oil or WD-40 is not harmful and may help.

A nasty problem sometimes encountered with older installations is that water may back up the exhaust into the cylinders and carburetor. The Achilles' heel of marine engines is the cooling jacket where the exhaust gas and cooling water mix. This opens up a path for water to back up or be sucked into the engine. There are a variety of ways to prevent this; the most common is to

add a vented loop or other anti-backflow device.

Water in the carburetor may come from contaminated fuel or from the exhaust. If found in the carburetor bowl, it will be the former. If it is in the carburetor throat, it will probably be the latter. This can be a two-edged sword. A hard-starting engine invites excessive cranking. During cranking the water pump pushes water into the exhaust system, but because the engine has not fired and no gas has been blown out of the exhaust, water is able to collect there. Eventually it starts flowing back into the manifold and the cylinders. Never keep cranking an engine that won't start.

Problems associated with sticky valves can be prevented by adding Marvel's Mystery Oil to your fuel. At the risk of sounding like a pitchman, I feel obliged to mention Mystery Oil by name because I have found such a strong preference for it among those who work with Atomic 4s. Presumably some other additive may function equally well. It is also agreed that you should double the recommended amount when adding Mystery Oil to your fuel. If your valves

are already sticking, go ahead and squirt some through the spark-plug holes straight into the cylinders. A pint in your crankcase oil is also a good idea.

Even though Atomic 4s were not designed to run on unleaded gasoline, mechanics report that there are no problems when Mystery Oil is added. It is also recommended that you use high-octane premium gas for more even combustion.

Cooling-system issues

Most Atomic 4s have no heat exchanger or freshwater cooling system. Many do not even have thermostats, which jeopardizes the engine when operating temperatures fall below 100°F because of carbon residue on valves and rings. A number of Atomic 4s have been converted to closed freshwater-cooling systems that use a 50/50 mix of coolant and water. This is a good idea, as freshwater cooling can add several years to an engine's life.

Later models came with thermostats, and if you convert one of these from

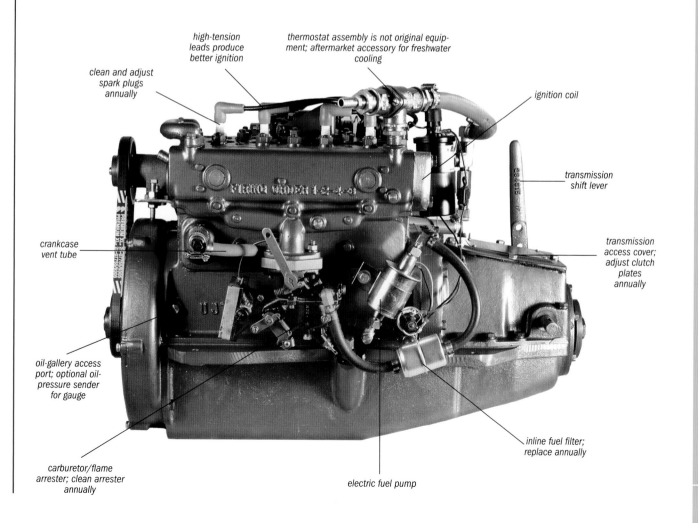

high-tension leads produce better ignition

thermostat assembly is not original equipment; aftermarket accessory for freshwater cooling

clean and adjust spark plugs annually

ignition coil

transmission shift lever

transmission access cover; adjust clutch plates annually

crankcase vent tube

oil-gallery access port; optional oil-pressure sender for gauge

inline fuel filter; replace annually

carburetor/flame arrester; clean arrester annually

electric fuel pump

raw-water to freshwater cooling, you should change to a thermostat set for 170°F. The factory-installed thermostats for raw-water cooling are set for 140°F, because salt precipitates faster at higher temperatures and causes deposits to form in the engine. If the engine still has a raw-water system but operates in fresh water, it is also a good idea to install a 170° thermostat. The higher operating temperature improves combustion.

In raw-water-cooled engines, the same stuff on which the boat floats is flowing through the delicate engine. Even with freshwater-cooled engines, raw water still flows through the pump, hoses, heat exchanger, and exhaust, so always be sure there is an in-line strainer on the raw-water line. When starting the engine, check to see there is good raw-water flow. In my experience, impellers have an unpredictable life span, so inspect the impeller periodically (see Impeller Pumps, page 148) and monitor the pump's output. Replacing an impeller is usually a simple task. To make it even easier, clamp a partially tightened hose clamp around the back side of the impeller blades. Making sure the blades are oriented in the right direction, you can then push the front

side of the impeller easily into the pump housing. Remove the clamp and seat the impeller by pushing it in all the way. Be sure to lightly grease the housing to avert damage to the impeller while the pump is priming.

Adequate cooling is, of course, crucial to your engine's longevity and performance, and over time salt deposits will restrict the flow of water, particularly in the cooling jacket. A simple way to periodically flush the system with fresh water to prevent this is by installing a Y-valve that allows you to toggle the engine's water feed between the raw-water intake and the boat's freshwater tank. Frequent quick flushes are very beneficial to the engine, and occasionally it should be flushed for a prolonged period of time. Also, every five years or so you should circulate a solution of muriatic acid (1 part acid to 15 parts water) through the system.

If your engine is freshwater-cooled, be sure to replace the water and coolant on the freshwater side every few years. Coolant left in the system too long may form a coating that fragments into minuscule slivers of solid debris that can clog the thermostat's pinhole and cause overheating. If this occurs, have a radiator shop boil out the heat exchanger.

Corrosion and condensation

Salt water is antagonistic to metal, causing corrosion and electrolysis. Unlike diesel engines, Atomic 4s and other marine gasoline engines do not have sacrificial zincs installed on the engine itself. The special alloys used in older Atomic 4s are allegedly nearly impervious to electrolytic corrosion, implying that later models are less so. It is a good idea in any event to connect a zinc guppy to the engine and hang it overboard if the boat is in an electrically hot marina. If you add a heat exchanger, be sure to install a zinc on the raw-water side.

The marine environment encourages condensation on and in the engine and fuel tanks. The engine space must be kept as dry as possible. Usually this can be accomplished by leaving hatches open when the boat is not in use, but if the boat is hooked up to shore power you can use a dryer-humidifier. Install it permanently on a bulkhead low in the engine compartment where bilgewater will not reach it. Be aware, however, that a less-than-perfect shore-power system will greatly aggravate electrolysis problems.

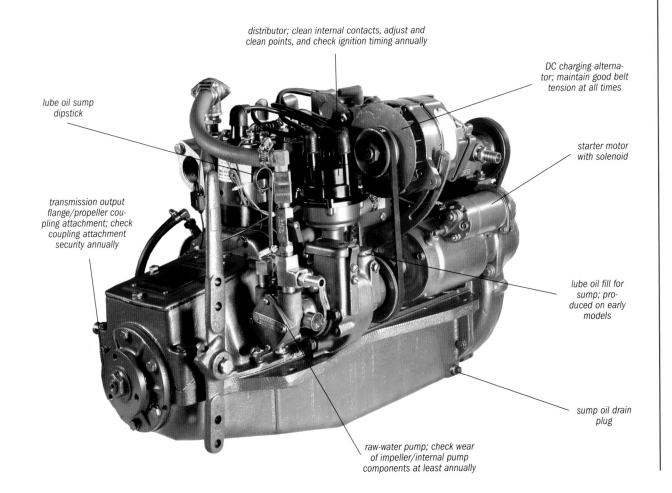

distributor; clean internal contacts, adjust and clean points, and check ignition timing annually

DC charging alternator; maintain good belt tension at all times

lube oil sump dipstick

starter motor with solenoid

transmission output flange/propeller coupling attachment; check coupling attachment security annually

lube oil fill for sump; produced on early models

sump oil drain plug

raw-water pump; check wear of impeller/internal pump components at least annually

It is best not to ventilate the engine compartment with air from outside the boat, as it tends to be moist. It is better to suck air into the engine compartment from the boat's interior, then expel it with a blower to the outside. This will help keep the compartment dry and cool.

To fight condensation in the fuel tank, which often results in water and algae contamination, it is wise to keep the tank topped off. (This is even more important for diesels than for gas engines.) Circulating cabin air over the tank by opening floorboards when the boat is not in use will help. Adding a heater with a built-in fan, perhaps in combination with a timer, will help even more.

Ignition problems seem endemic to some Atomic 4s. Keeping the engine dry and clean are good ways to combat them. Regularly replacing the spark plugs (use Champion RJ12C plugs), the points, and the condenser is also good idea. The spark-plug wires, distributor cap, and rotor should be replaced on a less frequent basis.

Finally, many problems are aggravated or are not detected early because engines are not kept clean. Grease, dirt, salt, and moisture facilitate electrolysis and corrosion and interfere with the ignition and other electrical systems. A disposable long-handled brush, an ample supply of rags, some sandpaper, a wire brush, and cleaning solvents, such as Grease Away or Grez-Off, will help keep your engine clean.

Otherwise, the best way to prevent rust on your engine is to keep it painted. Use a paint that can withstand high temperatures. Remove rust with sandpaper or a wire brush, or with Duro Naval Jelly in extreme cases. Parts that must not be painted can be sprayed with corrosion inhibitors, such as Boeshield T-9, Corrosion-X, or Lanocote. Rust is not merely unsightly, but will eventually damage the engine.

Pampering your Atomic 4 will forestall much frustration and wasted time. Even though the proper maintenance and care of an engine may seem more like work than play, ultimately you'll enjoy more time on the water and greater peace of mind as well.

Quentin Kinderman

To Repower or Not?

Fiberglass sailboats don't wear out quickly—at least, the hulls don't. Many of them are still afloat more than 40 years after they were built, with their original power plants. Thus, many owners have to choose between laying out money to repower with a new engine or limping along with an old, presumably difficult-to-maintain and unreliable power plant. At what point should you bite the bullet and spend 20 to 50 percent of the value of your boat to repower? Are there any other, less expensive options?

For many sailors, the decision is as much emotional as it is mechanical. It is comforting to know, or at least to believe, that Old Thumper will rumble to life with the turn of a key so that you can simply motor away from a lee shore in a gale or, perhaps more realistically, out of the path of a container ship in a shipping channel.

Most people considering repowering are tired of mechanics' bills, are frustrated by their current engine's poor reliability, and worry that it will fail at an inconvenient or perhaps even dangerous moment. They talk themselves into an expensive engine replacement.

Some engine manufacturers have successfully promoted two seemingly contradictory concepts—that marine

Photos by Mark Corke

The Perkins engine is a popular choice for many boats—and with good reason. Based on an industrial engine, it will run for years, parts are readily available, and almost every yard is familiar with it.

engines should cost significantly more than industrial engines and that they should be replaced after a short life span. Many sailors believe this and are quite prepared to spend many dollars replacing a diesel with relatively low hours on it.

Common wisdom has it that a new engine is always more reliable than an old one. Common wisdom has some merit. Unless it is really badly installed, a new engine will be more reliable—at least for several years. But is laying out $15,000 your best option?

Even a new engine can quickly become unreliable if not properly cared for. For many, the engine is a mystifying machine of enormous complexity. For others, it is a mechanism with both predictable and unpredictable vulnerabilities, to be understood and mastered.

One of my friends has an old Perkins 4-108 diesel with well over 5,000 hours. It runs fine until it develops a problem, and then he fixes it. Rarely does it surprise him. He knows the engine well and can tell when a problem is developing. For him, this is easier than dealing with a new but strange engine. His cost per hour of running time is quite reasonable. It is likely that he will continue to replace only worn parts—pumps, fuel injectors, and the like—until the internal parts exceed their wear limits. At that point, he will probably repower with a rebuilt engine of the same model.

What does it mean to repower?

Repowering usually means a custom installation with sometimes radical modifications to accommodate the new power plant. Even a new model of the same brand is rarely a drop-in replacement for a 20-year-old engine. You'll need to consider the fuel tank, transmission, shaft, and other components. The engine beds and fuel and exhaust systems will probably have to be altered.

Instead of focusing only on a new engine, buy the factory manuals for the old engine and learn all you can about it. These books are meant to be read; they use simple language and have pictures. You need to understand the engine you have to make a good decision about replacing it.

Should you replace Old Thumper?

The best reason to repower is that the engine is severely broken and cannot be repaired. Throw a rod through the block? Fill the boat with salt water for a couple of weeks? You certainly need another engine, but do you need a new one? An engine of the same model rebuilt using parts from your old engine might be the best deal. Then fitting your new engine is not a problem, labor and boat modifications will be minimal, and the performance of the new propulsion system is predictable.

Some other reasons are not quite as good.

- **Parts for my old engine are expensive and hard to find.** What is it you need? Most recent marine engines

have a lot of aluminum parts. These can corrode or freeze in place. Sometimes they are repairable; sometimes a superior cast-iron replacement is available. These parts often provoke the demise of otherwise functional engines, as well as virtually all outboard motors. If your old engine is based on an industrial engine, parts for the base engine will be available from many sources, including the Internet, for many years.

- **It leaks oil.** This is a simple but annoying problem; just don't pump the oil overboard. Replacing engine seals is labor-intensive. It might involve lifting the engine off its mounts and removing the transmission and bell housing and flywheel to reach the seal that is most likely leaking. The good news is that while you're in there, you can replace the engine mounts and the flywheel damper and send the transmission out to be "rebuilt." This makes the whole back end of the engine trustworthy, for a lot less money than a repowering job.

- **It's not going to fail me again.** This is my wife's favorite reason. It is why tires and batteries only get one chance to betray her on the road. Luckily, we sail together, or it would be an expensive process.

- **My wife/husband is nervous about the old engine.** Perhaps you should send him/her to weekend diesel school.

- **It has 3,000 hours on it.** So do you. Do you think you should be traded in on a newer model?

- **It costs too much to maintain.** You may think that the cost of maintaining the old engine is too high at today's mechanics' hourly rates and that a new engine will be cheaper. Is it really cheaper to spend $15,000? If you budgeted 5 percent of that per year over 20 years, you could spend $750 per year to defer repowering. If you need help, even at $75/hour, you can afford a mechanic for 10 hours a year.

There are some more good reasons not to replace your engine.

- **Diesels rarely ever wear out.** If it were in a forklift or truck, that engine would run three times the hours, be rebuilt, and run that long again.

- **The old one fits.** The factory saw to that. All the stuff hung on it— refrigeration compressor, alternator, propeller shaft, V-drive—actually works and has been proven for many thousands of hours in

If you choose to repower, many of the older ancillary parts, such as high-output alternators and fridge compressors, can be attached to the new motor before it is installed in the boat.

this boat as well as in many sisterships.

- **Reliability isn't just the engine.** The fuel system, wiring, and exhaust system will all need to be compatible with the new engine. If you get a new engine, these will be improvisations.

- **The engine has not been maintained.** Most diesels in commercial use are disassembled periodically. Sailboat engines rarely are, so minor engine problems compound into major reliability issues. With patience and a little study, you can fix the problems.

If you must repower, consider how you use your engine. For propulsion obviously, but for other things as well. Many sailors ask their engines to do more as they improve their boats. Heavy-duty alternators, often with double belt drives, are commonly added to engines, as are refrigeration compressors. Most boats with freshwater-cooled engines have hot-water heaters with heat exchangers run from the propulsion engine's cooling system. The geometry or design of a replacement engine may not lend itself to these applications. Shop wisely, because some popular engines can't tolerate side loads on their crankshafts and water-pump bearings. They may prove unreliable or, worse, may not be under warranty if you stress them with a big alternator.

Other components may need replacing. Transmissions and other drive components may not be suitable for a more powerful replacement engine or may not be compatible in terms of speed, torque range, or physical configuration.

Don't consider just the best-quality or cheapest marine engine. Go for the most commonly built engine in the industry if you want reliability and, even more important, the ability to get it repaired wherever you go.

One fundamental advantage of buying a new engine is that it can be disassembled before it encounters salt water. Engines live in hot, damp places—the worst possible environment. Literally anything threaded into aluminum or cast iron should be removed and coated with anti-seizing compound, and all hose clamps and wire should be replaced with marine-grade parts. You can do this yourself with the help of a service manual. Also replace any fasteners subject to stress with high-tensile-strength (GR-8) fasteners. A few years later, you might actually be able to mount that replacement circulation pump or alternator without having to shear off the bolts.

It helps to talk to other owners. Learning about pitfalls and hidden costs and getting referrals to knowledgeable mechanics will surely save you a lot of grief.

As you might suspect, as the owner of a 20-year-old, lightly used (1,500

Atomic 4

Thirty years old and still going strong, the Atomic 4 gas-powered engine has many fans. The side-valve engine might seem dated compared to many of today's products, but boatowners used to working on gasoline car engines will find it easy to maintain the Atomic 4 in serviceable condition. Concerns over the safety of having a gas engine on a boat have prompted many owners to swap the Atomic 4 for a small diesel.

hours), but somewhat neglected engine, I have opted not to repower—at least, not yet. Internally, the engine is in good shape. The engine is an early model, from the second year of production. It was built into the 1990s, so parts availability is not a problem. Although it still runs well, the catch-up maintenance has been considerable, and it is an object lesson in the unfortunate use of aluminum in marine engines. Refurbishing the engine has not only been an education in how to fix and maintain diesel engines, but also in what to look for should I ever buy a new one.

Was it the right decision? At about $700 to $800 per year to defer repowering, it will have been worth it. Most of the cost has been catch-up maintenance that I don't expect to repeat. The old starter and alternator are now the spares. With no sense of urgency, I have begun a search for a good rebuildable spare engine of the same make and model—an engine to recondition in the winter as a backup for Old Thumper. Should Thumper bite the dust, the backup engine could wear his shiny new parts.

Peter Caplen

Servicing Fuel Injectors

Mark Corke

Given a supply of clean fuel, injectors usually work without complaint for many years. But if at some point the performance of your engine begins to decline—particularly if it has difficulty starting, smoky exhaust, high fuel consumption, or runs rough, especially while idling—the injectors may be the cause. Though they have a long working life, they do eventually wear and need servicing. When problems arise, they can be dealt with quickly and cheaply by removing the injectors and taking them to a diesel-injection specialist.

Removing injectors is a do-it-yourself job, but servicing them is definitely not. The precise manufacturing specifica-

tions require specialized equipment and a clean working environment. You don't need a marine specialist. Check your local Yellow Pages for a service provider for diesel trucks.

Unless an engine's poor performance is clearly caused by some other factor, always consider servicing the injectors first. Injectors are the cheapest items to deal with and may solve the problem without further expense. Even if the problem is eventually found elsewhere, the overhaul is worth the few dollars it will cost you.

Most engine manufacturers offer specialized tools for removing injectors,

but you won't need one unless your engine is made by Volvo-Penta. Many Volvo engines use a sleeve, rather than the more common copper washer, to seal the injectors. With sleeved injectors, using a special tool that removes the injector while holding the sleeve in place is almost compulsory. If the sleeve has been disturbed, a new one must be installed—a costly job that requires a specialist. Removing sleeved injectors without a special tool is possible, but there is always the risk of disturbing the sleeve.

1. On this Volvo engine, first remove the high-pressure injector pipes that run from the injection pump to each injector. These are preformed steel and must not be distorted. It is possible to bend them out of the way, but on small engines with short pipe runs, this is bad practice and can ultimately lead to pipe failure. Loosen the pipe fitting on top of each injector and unscrew until free.

2. Do the same at the other end of each pipe, and then unbolt any supporting brackets along the length of the pipes. Once free, lift the pipes clear of the engine.

3. Next disconnect the fuel return pipes running from the side of each injector to the top of the fuel filter. Each connection consists of one bolt and two small sealing washers. Note the position of these washers on each side of the banjo joint (so-called for its vague similarity to the instrument) for subsequent refitting.

4. The injectors are normally fixed into position with one bolt that holds a securing bracket over the injector. Once the bolt and bracket have been removed, the injector-extraction tool is screwed onto the top of the injector. Tighten the nut on top of the tool; this draws the injector gently upward.

Photos by Peter Caplen

5. Once the injector is free, carefully lift it out. (Note the securing bracket held alongside the injector.)

6. With the injector removed, check for signs of blowby—gases leaking from the compression chamber—indicated by soot up the side of the injector, corrosion, or other damage. To replace the injector, reverse the removal procedure. Tighten the securing-bracket bolt firmly to the torque setting recommended by the manufacturer, but not too much. Once the engine is running again, check for blowby. If you find a problem, tighten the securing bolt some more.

7. Lucas/CAV-type injectors are fitted to most other makes of diesel engines. Regardless of the make of injector (Bosch, Stanadyne, and Denso are some brands), the procedures for removing and replacing them are the same.

As with the Volvo injectors, you must disconnect the associated fuel pipes before the injectors can be removed. The return pipes join all the injectors to the return connection on top of the fuel filter and then lead back to the top of the fuel tank where excess fuel and any small quantities of air are deposited. The connection to each injector is the same banjo joint seen on the Volvo.

8. During disassembly, carefully retain the soft aluminum or copper washers used to form a seal between the retaining bolt and the banjo joint (two per connection).

9. The preformed steel injector tubing must be distorted as little as possible while you disconnect it from the injector. On larger engines with much longer pipe runs, the pipes can be gently eased away from the injectors as the nuts are unscrewed rather than completely removed.

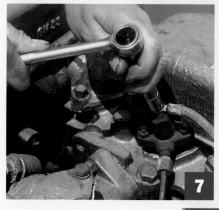

10

11

12

13

14

10. These injectors may be held in the cylinder head with two studs and nuts. Remove the nuts by slackening them equally a little at a time, to avoid distorting the injector. It is good practice to cover the end of the injector pipe once it's disconnected so no dirt can enter.

11. An injector that has not been disturbed for several years will probably be difficult to remove from its bore, as carbon deposits will have built up around the tip. Apply a generous portion of penetrating oil around the injector body and into the bore to break up any corrosion seal. Let it soak in for a few minutes (or a few hours, if it's really stubborn) before attempting to remove the injector.

12. A light tap with a soft-faced hammer—or light hammering against a block of wood—around the body is usually sufficient to free the injector. If it is particularly obstinate, you may need to lever it up with a bar under the securing flange while you gently tap around the body. Ensure that the leverage does not distort the securing studs, and do not exert excessive force in any one place. Patience and light tapping will eventually do the trick.

13. Once the injector begins to move, it can be lifted out of its bore.

14. With the injector removed, check that the copper sealing washer is still attached to the end of the injector body. If it isn't, you'll find it at the bottom of the injector bore. Hook it out with the end of a screwdriver or similar tool. Be particularly careful not to drop the tool inside the cylinder; you'll have to remove the cylinder head to retrieve it.

15. Wipe out the injector bore with a clean rag wrapped around a suitable rod; the handle of a socket wrench is ideal.

16. After servicing, refit the injectors. First replace the sealing washer. New ones are generally supplied when the injectors are overhauled. If for any reason new washers are not available, the old ones can be annealed to renew their sealing properties. Heat them cherry red over a stove burner or a blow lamp and then plunge them into cold water. Fit the new washer over the end of the injector body prior to replacing the injector into its bore in the head.

17. Run the retaining nuts down the studs until they are finger-tight, and tighten both equally with a socket or other wrench to ensure a gas-tight seal. Being careful not to distort the pipework, refit the injector pipe connections and firmly tighten the nuts. Also take care not to strip the fine threads through overtightening when refitting the tubing. Just nip them up enough to prevent leaks by lightly compressing the soft sealing washers on each side of the joint face.

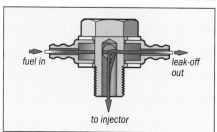

The Ins and Outs of Fuel Injectors

Banjo Unions
The retaining bolt on each banjo joint is drilled through the middle and also in the side to coincide with a channel around the inner edge of the banjo itself. This channel has one or two outlets that allow connection to the return pipes.

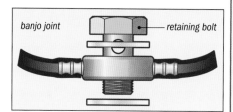

Injector Servicing
Once the injectors have been removed, wrap them up carefully, taking care to protect the small nipple on the end. If this is broken, a new end cap will be required, raising the price of the overhaul. The injectors can be taken to any diesel-injection specialist for overhaul. Costs vary, but truck dealers are usually the least expensive.

Starting the Engine
If there is evidence of blowby from an injector once the engine is started, the two most likely causes are that the sealing washer has been inadvertently omitted or the retaining nuts have been tightened unevenly. The cure for either problem is obvious.

Things to Remember
Bleeding the system should not be necessary if the injector pipes have not been removed. On small engines where the pipes were removed, simply loosen the pipe connections and turn the engine a couple of times on the starter to fill the injector pipes and clear the air. After the pipe connections are retightened, the engine should start normally. If it doesn't, repeat the pipe-bleeding procedure.

Thanks to **Mack Boring** for their help.

Servicing Fuel Injectors

Engine Spares to Have Aboard

Mark Corke

ENGINES

t's true that marine engines are very reliable—but not forever. And while on a boat, you can sometimes do the marine equivalent of pulling off the side of the road and waiting for help to arrive, it's best to be able to fix small problems yourself. That, of course, requires having the essential spares on hand. This *BoatWorks*-suggested list covers

many eventualities, but you should tailor it to suit your tastes and type of engine.

What you need

A Oil filters. Changing the filter every time you change the oil doesn't guarantee you'll never need to do it in mid-

cruise. As soon as you use the spare filter, order a replacement so you'll always have one in stock.

B Anode. Often overlooked and usually difficult to get at, pencil anodes should be changed every year. Change them more often if they show signs of being worn down to less than half of their original dimensions.

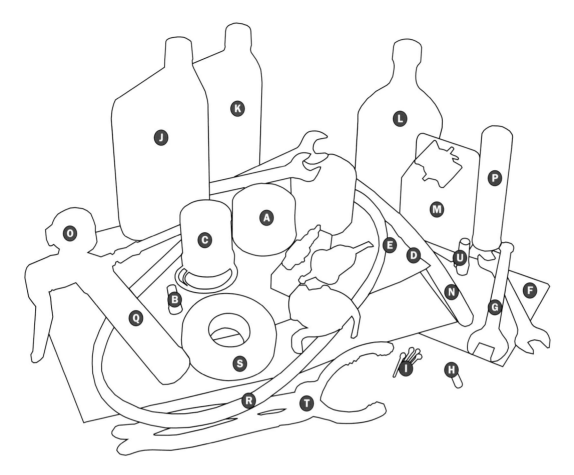

C Fuel filter. More engine failures are caused by dirty and contaminated fuel than anything else. Change the filters at least twice a season to ensure that water and other contaminants do not get in and block the injectors or carburetor jets.

D In-line fuel filter. Most often used on small outboards, this hides in the fuel line under the plastic motor-top cover. Thankfully, the plastic is clear so you can see when it needs changing. If yours is brown, it should have been changed ages ago.

E Spark plug. A fresh clean spark plug, correctly gapped, is often all that is required to get a reticent outboard to start. Make sure that you have a plug (or plugs, if you have a gas engine or your outboard needs more than one) of the correct reach and grade.

F Manuals. For basic troubleshooting you should at the very least carry the engine manuals in your engine-spares kit. A workshop manual might be better, especially if you are voyaging far.

G Basic engine tools. Carry the wrenches and other tools that came with the engine, but consider them a

supplement to, and not a substitute for, a proper onboard tool kit.

H Shear pins. Most outboards no longer use these, but always carry a couple if your outboard does.

I Cotter pins. These should be of the correct length and diameter for holding the castellated nut on the outboard prop.

J Engine oil. For topping up the engine and keeping it at the maximum mark on the dipstick. Use the correct grade as recommended by the manufacturer.

K Gear oil. The same principles that apply to engine oil apply here, except this is for the gearbox (obviously).

L Antifreeze. Even if you do not sail in an area subject to freezing, a good antifreeze mix keeps the heat exchanger on freshwater-cooled engines clean and free of corrosion.

M Impellers. Change these every season, and always carry a spare or two. Impeller failure is the prime cause of engine overheating.

N Fuel hose. For replacing leaky fuel lines. Diesel in the bilges smells horri-

ble, and a leak on the suction side of the fuel pump could prevent the motor from running.

O Pipe clamps. Useful for holding fuel and water hoses in place, although I did once use a couple of these and a beer can to repair an exhaust.

P Grease. Lubricates squeaking parts, but make sure that you use only waterproof grease.

Q Grease gun. Holds grease cartridges and forces grease into such hard-to-reach places as seacock nipples.

R Fan belts. Carry at least one spare of every type of fan belt you have aboard—alternator, fridge compressor, and any other engine-driven accessory.

S Self-amalgamating tape. In an emergency, this can even be used for sealing leaking pipes.

T Filter grips. These are essential, as filters are always in hard-to-reach places and tend to become tighter over time.

U Pipe connector. For joining spliced sections of fuel line together.

Engine Spares to Have Aboard

Peter Caplen

Replacing Cutless Bearings

Rubber-lined propeller-shaft bearings are now standard on most boats, and metal bearings are almost a thing of the past. Because the bearings are constantly immersed in water, the rate of wear is minimal, as the shaft actually revolves on a film of water between it and the bearing surface. But the bearings do eventually wear. The work involved in replacing worn shaft bearings is well within the scope of the experienced DIY owner. It is, however, quite time-consuming and needs to be performed with care if the shaft is to run smoothly.

While a boat is underway there are usually no clear indications of when shaft bearings need replacement, unless they have begun to break up. In that case the shaft will cause vibrations throughout the after part of the boat. Moving the shaft up and down to check for movement will give an indication of the amount of wear in the bearing and whether replacement is required. If the visible ends of the bearing show signs of detaching from the housing or there is more than about ¹⁄₁₆ inch of up-and-down play between the shaft and bearing, then the bearing should be replaced at the earliest opportunity.

A squeak from the bearing while idling, similar to that of a slipping fan belt, is not necessarily a sign of problems. Once rpms increase slightly the noise should stop as a film of water is established between the rubber flutes and the shaft. This is also likely to happen with new bearings, which are tight on the shaft.

Water-lubricated rubber-lined bearings are available with two types of liner, polyurethane or nitrile, depending on the area of operation. Both offer the same rate of wear, although polyurethane is far more abrasion-resistant and is specified for use in shallow-water areas where high levels of sand or grit are present. However, the softer nitrile bearing offers greater vibration and sound damping.

Materials

Two outer-shell materials are available, either brass or a non-metallic material, typically fiberglass. There is no difference in the performance of the two types. The latter is cheaper and avoids problems with corrosion, which is essential on aluminum- and steel-hulled vessels. Non-metallic types are also easier to remove for replacement as they can be split lengthwise with a sharp wood chisel, while brass-bodied types must be pulled, cut carefully with a hacksaw, or driven out. For this reason I always use the non-metallic shells.

Before starting the job, it is essential to check the shaft diameter and the inside diameter of the strut and/or propeller-shaft tube. It is also vital to determine whether these measurements are metric or English so you can order the correct bearings. (It may not be possible to measure the bearing length until the shaft has been pulled.) For example, a 25mm bearing cannot be used on a 1″ shaft, and vice versa. This step-by-step shows the shaft and bearing being removed from a powerboat, which has a double-ended shaft and flexible coupling. The basic methods pertain to both sail and power boats, no matter how the shaft is attached to the back of the transmission.

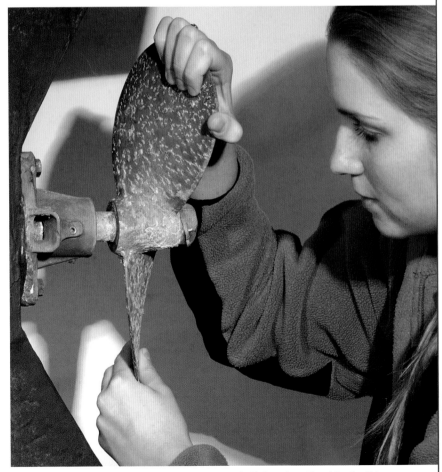

Grasp the propeller blades and try to wiggle the shaft. If there is noticeable play it is a sure sign of cutless bearing wear.

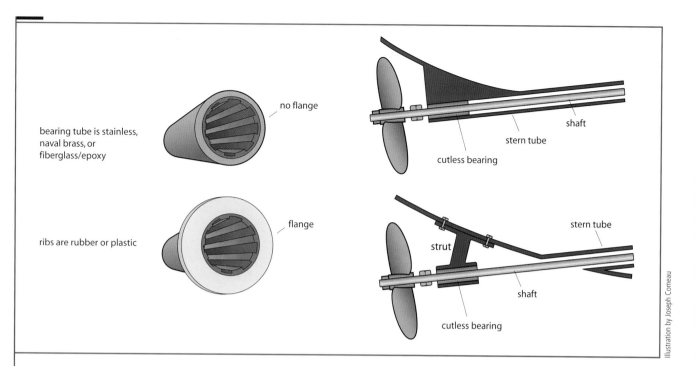

bearing tube is stainless, naval brass, or fiberglass/epoxy

no flange

ribs are rubber or plastic

flange

shaft

stern tube

cutless bearing

stern tube

strut

shaft

cutless bearing

Illustration by Joseph Comeau

1. Using a block of wood to keep the propeller from turning, undo the propeller nut using the biggest wrench you can find.

2. Leave the nut on the last few threads so the propeller doesn't fall off as it is pulled free of the shaft and attach the puller. Never try to hammer the propeller off the shaft; you'll damage it and affect its balance.

3. Sometimes the puller on its own is sufficient to break the seal between the shaft and the propeller. If not, apply heat to the propeller hub, which will expand and free itself from the shaft. A standard DIY blowtorch will eventually do the job. When the propeller comes free, it will remain hot for some time. Wear thick working gloves when handling it.

4. Once the propeller has been removed, screw the nut back on to ensure that the thread on the shaft has not been damaged. Then remove both the nut and the shaft key from the slot in the shaft and store them in a safe place.

Replacing Cutless Bearings

5. From inside the boat, disconnect the coupling between the transmission and the propeller shaft. The method will depend on the type of flexible coupling between the shaft and the box. This marine coupling requires undoing the six nuts and bolts that connect the shaft to the coupling.

6. Once all the nuts are removed, open the coupling by prying it apart while turning the shaft. Use a big screwdriver or a crowbar as a lever.

7. When the shaft has been drawn back about 6", you can get at the large securing nut, which attaches the coupling flange to the shaft. Here a locking bolt passes through the nut to prevent its coming lose. This must be removed before the nut can be undone.

8. Hexagonal securing nuts can be undone using a standard ½" drive socket. This one is circular and requires a special tool with two pins that fit into holes in the nut.

9. The nut and a removal tool.

10. The nut showing the locking arrangement. The split causes the nut to distort when the locking bolt is tightened and locks the nut onto the thread. If there is room, the propeller puller can be used to remove the coupling flange. If not, a simple puller can be made from a piece of thick steel plate with two holes corresponding to two of the holes in the coupling flange. By screwing on the securing nut a couple of turns so that it is just above the coupling face, the removal plate can be bolted into place where it will bear down on the nut and pull on the coupling flange. Heat may be needed to break it free.

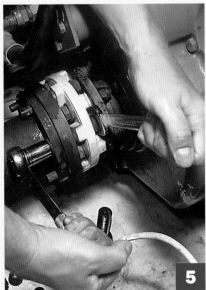

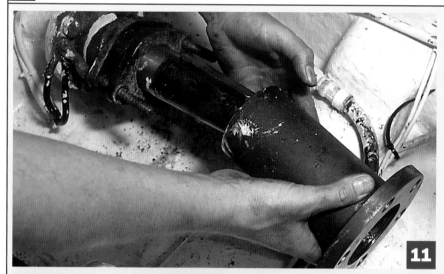

11. Remove the coupling flange once it is free of the shaft.

12. Once the coupling flange is off, remove the shaft key, dismantle the stuffing box, and rake out all the old packing to ease shaft removal. If a modern shaft seal is used, it will have to be removed.

13. The shaft can now be pulled out through the bearings and carefully stored on a flat surface. Some soapy water poured down the shaft can help with removal.

14. On most struts the bearings can be knocked straight out after the set screws that hold them in place have been removed, although those in the propeller-shaft tube will often need pulling. In this case a lip inside the forward end of the strut makes it impossible to knock the bearings through, so these must be pulled as well.

15. Graham, the boat's owner, devised a simple puller arrangement that is inserted from the pulling end. The piece that does the pulling is slotted to allow it to pass through the bearing, where it jams into the rubber when under tension and pulls the bearing away from the lip. A piece of threaded rod, some nuts, and a length of scrap aluminum tube form the rest of the puller.

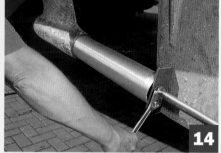

16. Once there is space between the lip and the bearing, the piece is pushed past the bearing where it fits on the front edge to provide a more substantial pull. The same procedure was used on the bearings within the propeller-shaft tube.

17. New (left) and old bearings. Although there was some wear in the old bearing, as shown by shaft movement, the main problem was that the rubber was delaminating from the shell.

18. The propeller shaft had suffered from crevice corrosion and wear in the bearing area. Crevice corrosion is unique to stainless steel, which is the only metal capable of setting up its own electrolytic reaction when the surface is shielded from oxygen. Rubber bearings can cause this if the shaft is not turned for many months, as the flutes shield the surface. Since the shaft has identical tapers at each end it was reversed so that the new bearings will run on unworn and unpitted sections of the shaft.

19. The new bearing shells were painted with soapy water to ease installation.

ENGINES

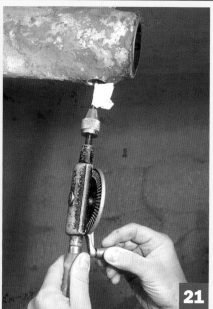

20. To avoid damaging the shell, each bearing was hammered home using a block of wood and a rubber mallet.

21. The bearing shells were carefully drilled for the conical-point set screws. A piece of tape on the drill bit ensured that the hole did not pass into the bearing.

22. Thread-locking compound was used to keep the set screws from vibrating out.

23. The screws were then carefully inserted and lightly tightened, again taking care not to screw them right through the bearing shell.

24. Reinstalling the shaft required extra "volunteers" as the new bearings were a lot tighter than the old ones. Again, soapy water was used to ease the shaft home.

25. A small modification was needed within the stuffing box because the packing did not have a proper shoulder to compress onto. Graham fabricated bronze rings that were set-screwed into place inside the stuffing box. All that had been previously installed was a short section of rubber bearing, which meant the first three rings were crushed into the rubber and distorted out of shape. It makes you wonder about the integrity of boatbuilders who can supply a several-hundred thousand-dollar boat with this sort of mess.

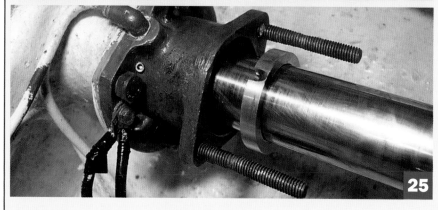

Peter Caplen

Stuffing Box Maintenance

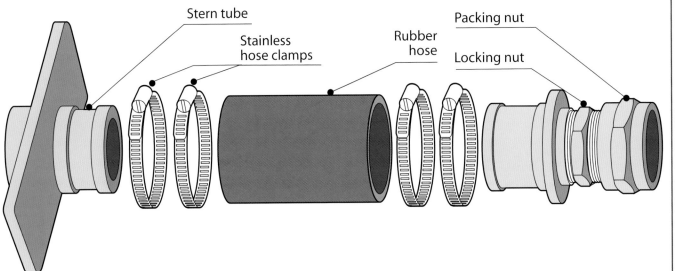

Stern tube

Stainless
hose clamps

Rubber
hose

Packing nut

Locking nut

Stuffing boxes have been around since the seventeenth century. They were originally developed by the Dutch to seal bearings on wind pumps. Despite their long history, they are still the most widely used form of seal for propeller shafts. Although more-modern alternatives are available, the vast majority of boats with engines still rely on the stuffing box because of its reliable and safe operation.

The stuffing box is a simple device that is easy to maintain. However, it can be somewhat messy and does require regular attention if it is to perform adequately. The only caveat with the stuffing box is that it must be allowed to drip very slightly to ensure that the packing remains moist. This requires not overtightening the assembly, as a stuffing box that does not drip is running dry and will need repacking more often. Perhaps more serious is the fact that a dry-running stuffing box will inevitably cause wear on the propeller shaft because of the friction between the metal shaft and dry packing. This wear may prevent a proper seal from being created even when the stuffing box is repacked. Ulti-

mately this leads to the propeller shaft having to be replaced or remetalled.

Many stuffing boxes have a grease nipple, either directly on top of the unit or remotely mounted and coupled via tubing. These make regular greasing more convenient. Some, however, have no way to inject grease externally and rely entirely on the grease in the packing to maintain their lubricating and sealing properties. It is particularly important that this type not be overtightened.

The principle of the stuffing box is that several rings of sealing material (or packing) are inserted into a housing through which the propeller shaft runs. A compression spacer then presses the packing and squeezes it onto the propeller shaft to form the seal. When the packing is squeezed too tightly, it rubs heavily on the turning shaft and causes wear on the shaft. The generated heat from the friction of the shaft rubbing on the packing in turn causes the grease to dry out and the packing to harden. At this stage the packing loses its sealing properties, and further tightening only increases shaft wear without improving the seal. This is why it is crucial not to overtighten the adjusting nuts.

Adjustments are generally made in one of two ways, depending on the design of the stuffing box. There are two main types. The most popular has nuts and studs on either side of the shaft, shown in the following photos. These must be tightened equally to ensure

🕐 **Approx. job time: 4 hours**

📖 **Skill level: Intermediate**

✂ **Tools you will need**

- **Wrenches**
- **Screwdrivers of differing sizes**
- **Rags**
- **Packing material of the correct dimensions**
- **Sharpened bent rod or corkscrew (for picking out old packing)**
- **Pliers**
- **Waterproof grease**
- **Kerosene**

that the assembly remains square with the shaft as the packing is squeezed. The other type consists of a large nut into which the packing is fitted; it screws onto the inboard end of the propeller shaft tube. Here the packing is squeezed as the nut is tightened.

One important point to note before starting the job: Use only packing designated for stern tubes. Commercial packing for industrial machinery uses graphite grease as the lubricating medium. Graphite is at the very top of the galvanic scale and will cause corrosion damage to every type of metal it makes contact with when immersed in salt water.

Packing comes in various sizes, and it is essential to use the correct size for your stuffing box. The packing material itself is square in section, and it is the thickness that gives it its size. To find the correct size for your stuffing box, measure the gap between the propeller shaft and the inside of the stuffing box. This measurement will also correspond with the thickness of the compression spacer that forms part of the stuffing-box cover.

1. The stuffing box shown here is a flexibly mounted unit and has no nipple for externally greasing the packing. It is crucial not to overtighten the finished job.

2. The first job is to remove the securing nuts and in this case the lock nuts, which keep the end cover from working loose. It is good practice to use lock nuts to ensure that the securing nuts can't vibrate loose. If this happens, the packing can shake loose and allow water into the boat.

3. Next pry off the end cover using a pair of levers, such as the large screwdrivers used here. (The rigid-type end-cover nut will be removed. Depending on its size, you may need a special wrench or a large pipe wrench to unscrew it.)

4. The most awkward part of the job is pulling out the old packing; you will need a variety of implements to hook the packing out. I find that a small sharpened screwdriver and a piece of sharpened bent rod generally do the trick—along with a little patience. Stab the packing with the screwdriver at an acute angle to get a grip for hauling it up the tube. A corkscrew is another useful tool if it is small enough to reach the packing.

Stuffing Box Maintenance

5

6

5. Once the packing comes loose, use the hook to pull it out.

6. When the packing appears out of the end of the tube, use a pair of pliers to grasp it and drag it out completely. You can use a variation on this method to suit the tools you have.

7. Once all the old packing is out, count the rings before making up the replacements. Five is about optimum; more will increase friction unnecessarily, but less than three will make the seal unreliable.

8. The shaft and stuffing box can now be cleaned of old hardened grease with a little kerosene or engine degreaser. Work the rag well into the packing recess.

7

8

ENGINES

9. Cut the new packing to length in separate rings. Do not simply wind the packing around the shaft in one length; the ends will not sit flush and a proper seal will not be made. To accurately cut the rings to length, wind the packing around the shaft the number of times required to provide the number of rings needed. Use a sharp knife and cut squarely *partway* into the packing.

10. Remove the packing and complete cutting it while it's off the shaft so you don't score the shaft. With the correct number of rings cut, check that each one will enter the stuffing box without being unduly tight. If any rings are too tight, trim the end(s) slightly to adjust the length. They are now ready for installation.

11. Insert the rings into the stuffing box one at a time and push them down inside. Orient the cut joints in the packing at approximately 120 degrees to each other. The end cover makes an ideal tool for pushing the packing down. Do not use the end of the screwdriver to push the rings in as it may damage the packing. However, the flat side of a large screwdriver blade is handy for pressing the packing in initially. Push each packing piece down as far as it will go before you insert the next. If you try to push the whole set down together, they may jam partway in. It is best to temporarily place the end cover and nuts to properly seat the last couple of rings. But be careful not to overtighten the packing.

With all the packing rings installed, leave the end cover loose and turn the propeller shaft through several revolutions to seat the packing comfortably in the stuffing box and make sure that it is not already too tight. At this stage the shaft should turn quite freely, although it may be a little tighter than before you began the job.

Loosely secure the end cover with the nuts and locking nuts, but don't tighten it up at this stage. Once the boat is afloat, run the engine in gear to turn the shaft and bed down the packing. A little water may enter up the shaft at this stage, and this will help with initial lubrication. You can now tighten the nuts—just a little over finger-tight. It is better for the end cover to be too loose than too tight. If there is a grease nipple, use it to add grease to the stuffing box.

Further adjustment will probably be needed after the first real run when the packing has had time to bed in properly. After that, an occasional greasing to keep the packing from drying out and a visual inspection to make sure that the seal is not leaking excessively is all you need to do.

Nigel Calder

What You Should Know About Engine Oil

It is essential to follow the manufacturer's recommendations when changing the oil. Oil changes should be carried out at the specified intervals using the specified oil type and grade.

Many boat engines have an arduous life. This is not necessarily from neglect (although all too often it is), but is frequently inherent in the way it's used. Most sailboat engines are operated intermittently and usually for a short time. The engine barely has time to warm up before it is shut down. Cruisers frequently compound problems by running their engines with very light loads for refrigeration and battery-charging at anchor. It's not unusual for a 50-horsepower engine to carry a ½- to 1-horsepower load. Without a decent load, the engine is slow to warm up and accumulates many of its operating hours below proper operating temperatures.

Engine damage

A major part of the wear on any engine occurs when starting and while warming up. Diesels in particular do not like to be run cold. Diesel fuels contain minute traces of sulfur (although this is much less the case than it used to be as a result of changed emissions standards in many countries), while water is a normal by-product of the combustion process. Some of the water will condense out in a cold engine and can then combine with the sulfur to form sulfuric acid, which is highly destructive to bearings and other engine surfaces.

At low speeds and loads and cool temperatures, wear on cylinder walls and piston rings is accelerated, frequently leading to a condition known as glazing in which the cylinder becomes highly polished. This in turn leads to rising oil consumption and declining compression, both of which are detrimental to engine life and performance. Carbon is formed from oil making its way up past poorly seated piston rings into the combustion chambers and from poor combustion of the fuel. The carbon tends to gum piston rings into their grooves, exacerbating the existing problems with high oil consumption and loss of compression. Additional carbon is washed down the cylinder walls into the sump by the lubricating oil. On a diesel engine, this suspended carbon is what gives the oil its characteristic black color after just a few hours of engine-running time. If sufficient carbon builds up, it forms a sludge that will eventually plug smaller and slower-moving oil passages.

Modern lightweight diesel and gasoline engines operate at higher loads and faster speeds than their forebears, but with a smaller volume of oil in the sump. Because less oil is doing more work, the oil is more highly stressed. Oils have to be specially formulated to deal with these tough operating conditions. Diesel oils, for example, contain detergents to keep the carbon in suspension and other additives to neutralize any acid buildup. As a result, many oils designed for gasoline-engine use are not suitable for a diesel engine. It is essential when adding to, or changing, any engine's oil to use a good grade of oil appropriate for that engine.

API classifications

The American Petroleum Institute (API) has developed a classification that is used in many parts of the world. The letter "C" (which stands for compression ignition, the fundamental process at work in a diesel engine) designates oils suitable for use in diesel engines, while the letter "S" (for spark ignition) desig-

TIGHT FILTERS
Many marine engines are not amenable to easy maintenance. This filter is tucked behind the dipstick, making it difficult to use a filter grip. To make matters worse, the horizontal mounting means that oil will run out as soon as the filter is loosened. Oil-absorbent pads and plenty of rags are essential to avoid a mess.

NEW FILTER
Before screwing on the new oil filter, smear a little fresh engine oil on the O-ring seal and screw it on hand-tight. When the engine has been run for a few minutes, check for leaks and retighten if necessary.

nates those rated for use in gasoline engines. The C or S is followed by another letter to indicate the complexity of the additive package in the oil, with the better packages being given a letter further into the alphabet. Thus any oil rated CC, CD, CE, CF-4, or CG-4 is suitable for use in diesel engines, with the CG-4 oil being the best at present (Detroit Diesels use CD-II). Cruisers who are planning to go to undeveloped countries should carry a good stock of the highest grade oil money can buy.

Oil is also given an SAE (Society of Automotive Engineers) number that describes its viscosity. Most diesels work well with SAE 30 oil, except in extreme climatic conditions, while gasoline-engine manufacturers tend to recommend multi-grade oils (these have additives that thin the oil at low temperatures, reducing its resistance during cranking, and then thicken it as the engine warms).

Regardless of the quality of the oil and the engines's operating conditions, if regular oil-change procedures are not followed, sooner or later the various contaminants forming in the engine will begin to overwhelm the additives in the oil. A carbon sludge will start to block oil passageways, eventually leading to a seizure of some critical engine part, while acids will start to corrode sensitive bearing surfaces. According to one major bearing manufacturer, 58 percent of all bearing failures arise from a lack of, or dirty, oil.

Preventive maintenance
So what can you do to avoid these problems? First of all, especially with a diesel, when the engine is used, give it

Changing Oil Filters

Whenever the engine oil is changed, the filter needs to be changed as well. Start by thoroughly cleaning the area around the old filter. Most filters are of the screw-on variety, which requires a special filter wrench to undo. This should be a part of the boat's basic tool kit; if you don't have one, a V-belt wrapped around the filter and gripped tightly will probably provide enough leverage to get it moving. Failing this, a screwdriver can always be hammered through the filter—this is messy but will give the necessary leverage.

There is no way to remove most filters without spilling at least some oil (it is particularly frustrating that many engine manufacturers still provide horizontally mounted filters, which inevitably lose half their oil into the engine pan while being unscrewed). I find that the best way to catch any spillage is to place a disposable diaper under the filter; it's amazing how much oil can be soaked up. The plastic backing keeps the oil from seeping through (unlike rags and paper towels), while the elasticized sides can be formed into a convenient bowl. Another way is to slip a plastic bag over the filter or a cut-off 2-liter soda bottle under it, although it is difficult to keep either of these in place while unscrewing a horizontal filter.

If the new filter has a sealing ring built into it, oil it lightly before installation. The filter housing on the engine needs to be checked to make sure the old ring is not still stuck to it. The new filter is screwed in hand-tight and then given an extra three-quarter turn. After the engine is started, the filter seal should be checked for leaks.

Turbocharged engines sometimes have an additional filter in the oil line to the turbocharger. This too must be changed every time you change the oil—the turbocharger will be the first thing to suffer from poor oil-change procedures.

some work to do and run it long enough to reach proper operating temperatures. This will help to cook condensates out of the oil and engine. If necessary, at dockside tie the boat off firmly and put it in gear to warm it up faster; at anchor, put it in reverse when refrigerating or battery-charging. Better yet, review the boat's energy systems and redesign them so that the main engine is not needed for these light loads.

Next, religiously follow the manufacturer's recommended oil and filter change intervals. If the engine unavoidably accumulates many of its hours at low temperatures and loads, or if it is operating in an area with high-sulfur-content diesel fuels (such as parts of the Caribbean), change the oil more frequently than recommended—it can never do any harm. Be sure to use only the very best grade of engine oil available.

Finally, whether it's time for a scheduled oil change or not, change the oil and filter at the end of the boating sea-

Changing Engine Oil

There isn't enough room under most boat engines to insert a pan to catch the oil when the drain plug is removed. Often there isn't enough room to even get at the drain plug. Oil changing becomes a messy and frustrating business, which is then postponed.

To make oil changing as clean and easy as possible, ideally a marine engine will have a sump, or oil-change, pump plumbed to it. The most effective installation has a hose fitting screwed into the drain hole in the pan with a hose running to a conveniently mounted hand or electric pump. Should the hose fail, there will be a catastrophic loss of engine oil, so the hose and all fittings must be designed for use with oil and installed to the highest standards.

A less-effective approach is to slip a thin tube over the dipstick hole and suck the oil out through the dipstick tube. The small bore of the dipstick tube tends to make this slow work.

Oil should be changed only when hot. This lowers its viscosity, making it easier to pump and encouraging all the old oil to drain out of the various engine passages. The area around the filler cap needs to be scrupulously cleaned before pouring in the new oil.

son, not the beginning of the next one, so that any contaminants already in the oil do not have all winter long to go to work on the engine.

There are few things that will do more to prolong the life of an engine than fanatical attention to these oil changes.

Peter Caplen

Raw-Water Strainers

There is a minor problem unique to some Volvo-Penta raw-water strainers. If you are aware of it, you can easily fix it when the engine is serviced.

The raw-water strainer basket sits inside the strainer, over the water inlet, allowing water to enter the basket from the sea. When sediment builds up under the basket around the inlet spigot, the strainer basket can't seat properly. Tightening the cap to remedy this problem will force the basket down, causing it to distort. This allows sediment to bypass the strainer basket and enter the engine cooling system. Eventually the basket remains permanently distorted—or even breaks—and sediment will continually pass into the cooling system.

If the basket is only distorted, placing it in near-boiling water for a few minutes can rejuvenate it. It will return to its proper shape and become fully functional once again.

🕐 **Approx. job time: 30 minutes**

📖 **Skill level: Easy**

✂ **Tools you will need**

■ **Very hot water**

1. The water strainer is located above the water pump on a Volvo-Penta engine.

ENGINES

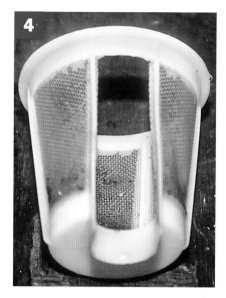

2. This badly distorted strainer basket shows clear signs of sediment bypass.

3. This basket is distorted but can be rejuvenated by soaking it in very hot water until it returns to its proper shape.

4. After soaking, the sides of the basket are fair and the basket can be reused.

5. This basket is split and must be replaced.

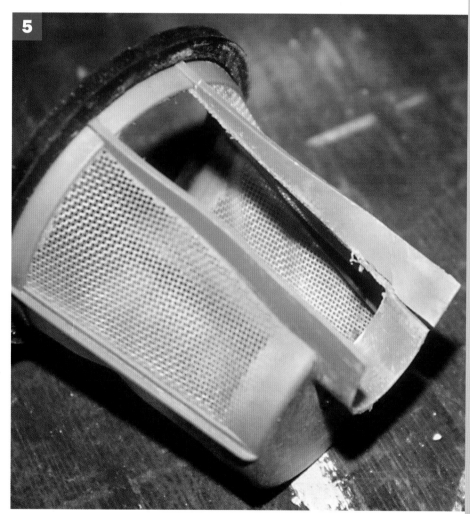

Conclusion

To avoid this problem, clean out all sediment (it doesn't take much to cause a problem) from the strainer body before replacing the basket. Before you put the lid on, lightly grease the seal to ensure it forms a proper seal.

If there are signs that some sediment has entered the cooling system, it is worthwhile checking the entire system for sediment buildup elsewhere. Add flushing this system to your annual-maintenance checklist.

Raw-Water Strainers

Impeller Pumps

Mark Corke

A raw-water-cooled engine is cooled by water drawn from outside the boat and circulated through its engine block and cylinder head.

On a freshwater-cooled engine, the "raw" water is pumped through a heat exchanger, where it draws the heat from the freshwater/antifreeze mix that cools the engine, and then is injected into the exhaust hose, where it cools the hot exhaust gas before being pumped overboard. In both cases an impeller-type pump circulates the raw water.

Impeller pumps are simple and robust, which is what you want such an essential item to be. The big flexible blades on the typical "rubber" (actually, it's a synthetic compound) impeller will gobble up leaves, twigs, grit, and other detritus with scarcely a hiccup. When they stop working, though, you're in trouble. When an impeller gives up the ghost it tends to disintegrate inside the pump body, and the shards from the vanes can cause some serious damage—for example, by blocking the tiny waterways inside a raw-water-cooled en-

gine, or by clogging up a vital artery inside a heat exchanger. With no cooling water getting to the exhaust, a fire is not beyond the realm of possibility.

Two things tend to finish off an impeller—owner negligence, or a lack of water. I managed to kill one by a combination of the two—I forgot to open the engine intake seacock. It took me all day to get the bits out of the heat exchanger. Often, impeller damage is caused by owners not bothering to drain water out of the pump body when winterizing the engine.

Some mechanics insist that you should change the impeller annually. Others say every second year should be enough, depending on where you sail (silty water wears impellers out more quickly) and the hours you put on the engine. I once had to replace an impeller at sea, an experience I'm not keen to repeat, so I figure an annual replacement at $20 or so is cheap insurance. At the very least, I will pull the impeller every spring and visually inspect it to make sure there are no cracks or splits in the blades. If it appears that the blades have taken a set, flip the impeller over when you replace it.

It only takes a minute of dry running to destroy an impeller; this doesn't give you long to respond to your cooling water alarm (assuming you have one) and shut down the engine before the impeller self-destructs. For around the same price as a regular black impeller you can get a handsome blue Globe Run-Dry impeller, which can survive for 15 minutes without water. That quarter-hour might just be enough to get you into a harbor or anchorage where you can change the impeller at your leisure.

On some marine engines, most notably smaller Yanmar diesels, the impellers are very hard to get to. I love my little Yanmar 2GM, but I have to remove the water pump in order to change the impeller, and that would be a hell of a job on a dark, rough night. So I've fitted a Speedseal kit ($60, www.speedseal. com) that does away with the half-dozen tiny screws securing the pump cover. This will make it much easier for me to change the impeller in a hurry.

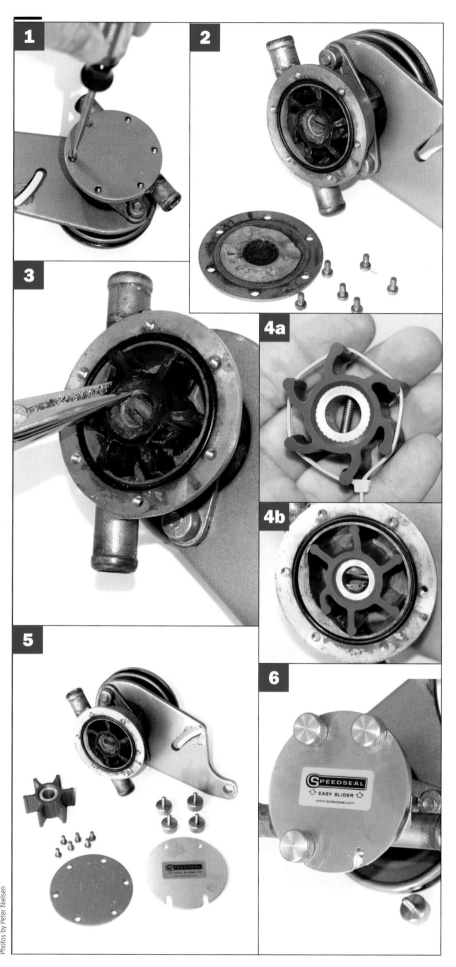

Changing an impeller

1. If the boat is in the water, be sure to close the inlet seacock. Impellers can be hard to access. On some engines you'll have to loosen the drive belt, remove the inlet and outlet hoses, and remove the pump. Then remove the screws holding the faceplate onto the pump. If you haven't tried to open the pump for a while, these little screws can often be the devil to undo.

2. You may have to use a screwdriver to pry the faceplate free from the body. Take care not to damage it. The plate will be sealed with a paper gasket or an O-ring. In either case, plan on replacing it. Check the plate for wear.

3. Most impellers are push-fitted onto the central spline, but some are fastened to it with a bolt or screw, which will need to be removed. You can usually get the impeller out by gripping its body (not the blades) with a pair of Channellock or needle-nose pliers. You could also buy a special impeller removal tool.

4. Make sure the vanes are facing in the right direction when you fit the new impeller (opposite to the "direction of rotation" mark on the pump faceplate). Sometimes it can be a bear to bend the stiff blades enough to fit them into the pump body, a job you need more than five fingers for. Use a plastic cable tie to hold the blades in the right position. When you push the impeller into the pump, the cable tie will slide off. Grease the pump body lightly with Vaseline or water pump grease; this will keep the impeller lubed until the water starts flowing.

5. Rather than fiddle about with those tiny screws again, I fitted a Speedseal cover (right).

6. This cover has just four screws, with knurled heads so there's no need to use tools to get the cover off. You just need to remove two of the screws, and loosen the other two; the cover is slotted, so it slides right off. If I have a spare impeller ready to go, I should be able to replace a ruined one without having to remove the pump. Since impellers never choose a convenient time to fall apart, I look on this as a safety feature. Speaking of which—don't forget to open the seacock!

Impeller Pumps

149

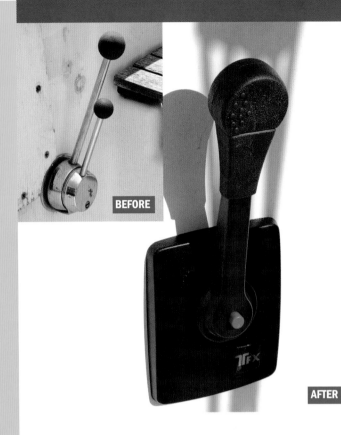

BEFORE

AFTER

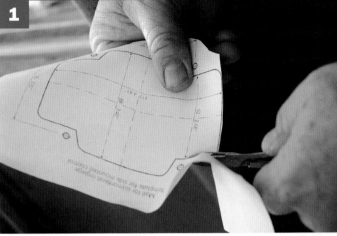

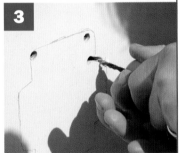

Photos by Peter Nielsen

1. The controls come with a template for the cutout in the cockpit side. Do not be tempted to do without this.

2. We traced around the template with a pencil and then tried the throttle lever in position to make sure we had full movement forward and astern.

3. Hmmm... My Dremel or RotoZip tools would have been ideal for this job, but we had no electricity. We used an excellent little tool called a Drillsaw ($8 from Sears), which made short work of the fiberglass.

Replacing Engine Controls

The twin-lever engine control on our Norlin 34, *Ostara*, had been annoying me for as long as we'd had the boat. The detent was so worn that it was sometimes not possible to tell if you were in neutral or reverse gear. More than once I had been alerted by yells from the neighboring boats as *Ostara* sidled crablike around her mooring, pulled by the prop walk of the engine ticking over in reverse. The need to juggle separate throttle and gear levers in the confines of a marina seemed silly and unseamanlike. In the heat of the moment, it was easy to try to change gears with the throttle still open—which is not good for the transmission.

The last straw came on launch day this year, when I tried to engage forward gear and nothing happened. We had to be ignominiously towed out to the mooring by the yard workboat. Once there, I discovered that the bracket securing the

cable to the twin-lever control had broken. It was all the excuse I needed to upgrade to a single-lever control. There are various makes of these, and they all work on the same principle, allowing seamless, one-handed throttle and gear operation. Most, like the Teleflex model I chose, also have a neutral button that when depressed allows the throttle to be opened for starting without engaging the gears.

Ostara's previous owner had installed a new Yanmar 2GM diesel but (I suspect because of sticker shock) had retained the old engine controls. The cables, however, looked as new as the engine. The existing controls were on the starboard side of the cockpit, as is traditional, but they were next to the large plywood-covered hole that had been left when the old engine instrument panel was removed. When this is filled in with a fiberglass sheet (next winter's project), there would be no access to that

part of the boat, which would make maintenance impossible. So I decided to install the new control on the port side, where we could access the cables easily via the cockpit locker.

Approx. job time: 2 hours
Skill level: Easy
Tools you will need

- Cordless drill
- Drillsaw
- File
- Needle-nose pliers
- Screwdriver

ENGINES

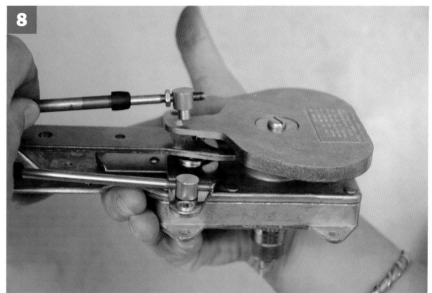

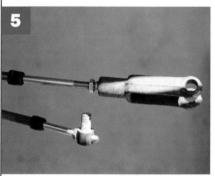

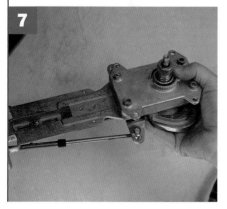

4. Once the hole was roughly cut out, we taped the template over it and drilled the holes for the mounting screws.

5. The cables as they came off the old controls. New end fittings were provided with the Teleflex control.

6. The instructions stressed that the cables had to be disconnected at the engine and transmission, but it didn't seem to make any difference.

7. The gear-shifter cable goes to the end of a bracket that pivots as the lever is moved backward and forward, thereby selecting forward-neutral-reverse. The instructions again proved confusing on this point, but logic carried the day. You just have to work out whether the cable is initially being pushed or pulled. We got it wrong the first time and had to reinstall the cable on the opposite arm. You also have to decide which of the two holes to use—this depends on the cable throw. We had to do some juggling to get the outer cable secured properly in the retainer.

8. Next we installed the throttle cable. This proved easy—it's retained by a cotter pin, and there's no way to get it wrong.

9. The control head is held in place by four self-tapping screws.

10. The cover plate is a push-fit, and the lever is retained by an Allen bolt, which must be tightened. Then the red neutral button is pushed into place, and we're ready to go. The new control is smooth and easy to use—all in all, a truly worthwhile upgrade.

Systems

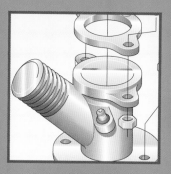

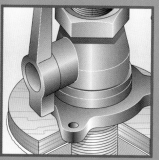

ow can a boat, which is so much smaller than a house, be so much more complex? For starters, a boat has to be self-sufficient once the shore-power umbilical cord is unplugged. There's limited room inside a boat, so everything has to be miniaturized or contorted into odd shapes to fit available spaces. And the marine environment is hard on machinery and raw materials.

A sailor needs to be as familiar with the operation and maintenance of his or her boat's essential systems as he is with the engine. Some of these systems are a good deal less complicated than others. Installing a flexible water tank, for instance, is a snap compared with installing a fuel tank or converting a boat from tiller to wheel steering, yet neither of the latter two projects would be beyond the scope of a competent amateur.

For this section we've chosen projects as diverse as installing a new propeller and overhauling seacocks. There's nothing here that is so complex as to absolutely require the services of a professional.

You do need to be prepared and patient, however. Installing the wheel steering system, for instance, took much longer than we'd anticipated simply because of the difficulty of access. Squeezing himself beneath the cockpit of a 30-footer was difficult for the slim, limber 30-something who did the job; it would have been impossible for someone older, heavier, and less flexible.

You need to know your limitations, and realize when it's time to get someone else to do the work.

Installing a Fuel Tank

Note the pipe fittings on the left side of the photo and the bulkhead on the right. Once the material is cut, inserting the fittings is easy. Be careful not to overtighten the flanges. As with many fasteners, compression is effective only to a point.

⏱ **Approx. job time: 40 hours**

📖 **Skill level: Intermediate**

I carried a fuel tank in the cockpit of my trailerable sailboat for years. Most small sailboats like mine don't have built-in tanks.

The tank was lashed at the transom because that's where it had to be, but the cleats on the tank around which the fuel hose was wound snagged things, and I wanted the cockpit sole to be clear. In nasty weather a tank like mine could bounce around and leak or break loose. Stepping back and forth into the cockpit with that 3-gallon, 20-pound portable tank was always a nuisance.

I thought there had to be a better way. The selection of ready-made tanks is huge, yet I couldn't find one that was exactly right. Ordering a custom tank was not an option—too complicated and expensive. My objective was simply to clear the cockpit and carry a five-day fuel supply.

I got the solution to my problem when I saw an ad for fuel bladders in a European yachting magazine and immediately thought that this could be just the thing for my boat. The rubberlike neoprene/nitrile material and the construction are reminiscent of inflatable dinghies with their overlapping seams and corner reinforcements. Water and waste versions are also available. After some searching, I found a 14-gallon version that seemed about right for my boat in my local chandlery.

I removed and saved the fuel hose, bulb, and vent screw from the old red can and ceremoniously tossed the can into a Dumpster.

The "bag" should be mounted under the V-berth, I decided, even though this location would involve considerable labor. There was nowhere to attach the tank; no bulkheads existed from the centerboard case forward to the stem, and I would be sleeping above the tank in a confined space with oil lamps, electrical switches, and a battery nearby.

My boat never had a chain locker. I figured that I could have one with very little extra labor. A much larger fuel capacity and a chain locker seemed to be about 40 hours away.

I cut a hole in the V-berth very close to the stem, glassed in a tiny bulkhead, and added two stainless-steel eyebolts. Positioning the tank well forward allowed me to retain the middle section (the forefoot area) of the bilge for other storage.

I cut a hole in the deck at the bow and ran a filler hose through what would become the new chain locker and then through a hole in the newly fashioned bulkhead to the filler connection on the tank. Hard-wall tanks are rigid forms; flexible tanks collapse as they empty. I routed the filler hose loosely to allow for movement so the bag wouldn't "hang" on the hose, stressing the hose fittings and clamps.

A thick bungee cord running through the corner grommets of the tank and tied off at the eyebolts holds the tank against the bulkhead but allows it to expand and contract. I put soft carpeting material behind it to prevent wear on the bag. The capacity of the tank is somewhat compromised because the bungee cord draws the corners up and because the tank I chose is rectangular and the space is triangular. Sailing at a large angle of heel, as I often do, would also affect the shape of the tank.

The fuel line to the engine meanders through chambers and bulkheads to the fuel filter/water separator unit mounted under a cockpit seat near the transom. I made sure that the hose was well clipped up and also installed grommets to protect the hose where it went through bulkheads. I attached the bulb and engine connector from the old fuel tank at the place where the hose exited the transom.

My carpal tunnels started howling after I squeezed the bulb for about 20 minutes trying to fill the empty 25' fuel line for the first time. I suspected that between engine runnings, the fuel might slide back to low points in the route. Installing a small automotive electric fuel pump brought the fuel quickly and ensured that the tank could be sucked down flat. I mounted the pump to pull, not push, through the filter/water separator. The electric pump and the bulb are operated momentarily and alternately, just enough to get the engine running. Now the 4-horsepower Suzuki supplies itself dependably. A fuel shut-off also went in at the tank.

All flexible tanks should carry their filler and supply connections on top of the bag. The directions stated that ". . . no vent is needed with the possible ex-

TIPS FOR FUEL TANKS

- My system is permanent, but a flexible tank need not be so elaborately mounted to be a great asset. Nauta makes a collapsible tank that can be lashed on deck to temporarily increase the motoring range of any vessel. The fuel is gravity-fed into the boat's tanks, and the fuel bladder is then rolled up and stowed away.
- A flexible tank should be secured where it will not shift, be struck by a sharp object, or impede foot traffic while being within a practical distance to the deck filler. The weight of a full bladder (they are available up to a massive 530 gallons) should not upset the boat's weight distribution.
- A filler hose should be installed and secured to a stanchion or similar solid post while fueling. A shut-off valve should be installed at the end of the supply hose, not underneath the tank. Be cautious when transferring fuel from the bladder to the boat's tank while under way; know the existing level in the tank. The flow rate from the Nauta portable tank should not be more than the deck-filler port will accommodate. Refueling should be done all at once and in mild weather; topping off periodically or repositioning the bladder while en route is unadvisable. Do not store the empty fuel bladder belowdecks.

ception for fuel and holding tanks" and that "there is no air in a flexible tank." However, I think that a joint or a coupling in a fuel line and all tank spaces should be vented, so I created a vent for the tank at the deck by drilling and tapping the filler cap and inserting the vent screw from the old tank cap. The vent is screwed down tight while underway.

The space under the V-berth where the new tank sits and the area under the cockpit seats where the fuel filter/water separator unit is located are

vented by a spark-proof 3″ inline fan in each compartment.

After five years my flexible tank has been concern free, other than superficial corrosion on the metal grommets. A fuel-vapor test proved the venting system to be effective, if not redundant.

The San Juan Islands of the Pacific Northwest are on my cruising wish list. Now I won't have a gasoline can sitting next to me in the cockpit in bad weather. Motoring time at moderate rpm is over 48 hours.

1. No chain locker or bulkhead existed in the V-berth to hold the tank, but with the plywood, the tools, and the fiberglass already on the bench, it was a good time to create them.

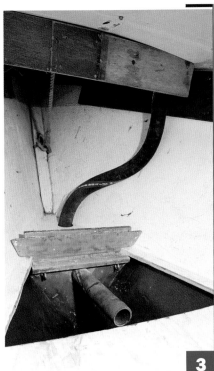

2. A tiny bulkhead, a kiss-fit to the hull, was glassed in place. The flange on the bulkhead right above the model's hand and the unfinished plywood piece running across overhead locate the chain locker.

3. I drilled a hole with a Forstner bit for the filler hose. Notice the eye bolts located on the left and right sides of the bulkhead. A bungee cord runs through the eye bolts and the grommets on the tank to hold the tank against the bulkhead.

TOP TIP

Drill Bits

There is more than one way to drill a hole, and sometimes only the best will do. Spade bits are cheap and readily available, but even when sharp they drill a hole by scraping their way through. The more expensive Forstner bits, available in a wide variety of sizes, produce a clean, splinter-free hole that requires no additional work. They must be used with an electric drill.

Mark Corke

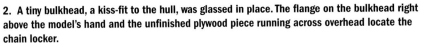

4. The removable chain locker goes into place to cap off the area. No problem has occurred with the fuel-filler hose and anchoring equipment locked up together.

SYSTEMS

156

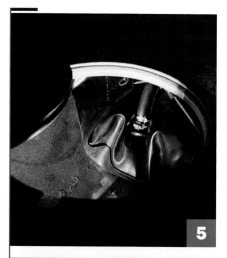

5

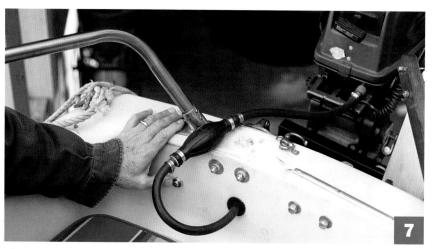

7

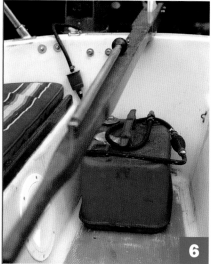

6

5. The tank can be monitored and, if necessary, removed through an inspection port. A bungee cord holds up the corners of the bag.

6. The "before" picture. The red can was lashed at the transom and occupied a space now used by a small food cooler—a net gain in safety, space utilization, and appearance. The entire cockpit was later resurfaced.

7. The "after" picture. The fuel line exits the transom near the engine. The electric fuel pump nearby brings the fuel up from underneath the V-berth. The standard fuel-pump bulb helps empty the fuel line of air.

RESOURCES

Imtra (Nauta flexible tanks)
www.imtra.com
508-995-7000

Vetus
www.vetus.com
410-712-0740

West Marine
www.westmarine.com
800-685-4838

Mark Corke

Installing a Water Tank

TOP TIP

Pilot Holes

It is often necessary to drill holes to run hoses through bulkheads. Although you should always take accurate measurements, it can be difficult to see where a hole will emerge. Drilling a ¹⁄₁₆" pilot hole enables you to verify the exact position before enlarging with a larger drill bit.

My boat is small, and space is definitely at a premium—especially space for a flexible 14-gallon water tank that, when full, would weigh almost 120 pounds. So for the past five years I have decanted drinking water from various portable containers while trying to decide where to install the tank.

I considered putting it in one of the cockpit lockers or under the cockpit sole behind the shaft log, but either place would have resulted in weight too far aft in the boat. I finally installed it under the chart table. This was not ideal in terms of the space that would be lost to the

⏱ Approx. job time: 8 hours

📖 Skill level: Easy/intermediate

Installing a Water Tank

tank, but it did place the weight near the center of the boat where it would have the least effect on trim.

There are many similarities in installing fuel and water tanks, but there is an important caveat: You must use only hoses and fittings made and specified for potable water. Anything else may make the water taste bad and/or contaminate it.

Hose comes in different grades, some with reinforcement built into the hose. Reinforced hose is less prone to kinking and collapse; unreinforced hose is able to bend to tighter radii and is somewhat cheaper. I used reinforced hose for the large 1½" filler pipe and clear unreinforced ¾" hose for the delivery hose from tank to faucet.

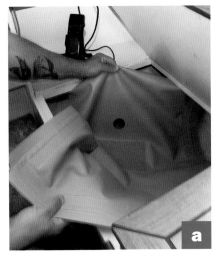

Flexible tanks often fit where rigid tanks would refuse to go. Even when the space is completely smooth, padding (such as a piece of carpet) helps prevent chafing the tank.

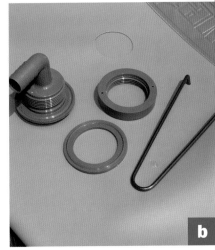

Deciding where to install the inlet and outlet connectors is up to the installer on almost all flexible tanks. A connector consists of three parts and a wire wrench.

After cutting holes of the size called for in the instructions, I fed the outlet elbow through the side of the bag.

The next step was to install the compression ring. This has a small V-shaped ridge that corresponds to a similarly shaped notch in the main flange on the elbow outlet. If you install the ring the wrong way up, the two parts will fail to align and the joint will leak.

Overtightening the nut risks damaging the tank and outlet. It is essential to only use the tools supplied with the tank; don't be tempted to use pliers or Vise-Grips.

SYSTEMS

Photos by Mark Corke

Pipe and Hose Clamps

Photos by Aussie Bray

Above left: Ear clamps are a neat and easily applied solution for fuel hoses.

Above top right: Double clamping may not improve the seal, but it does increase security on critical hose connections.

Above bottom right: Bolted clamps create high compression, and are good for holding stiff exhaust hose over a metal pipe.

A boat's fuel, cooling, and domestic water systems use numerous flexible hoses, all of which have to form a seal where they join rigid fittings. There are various options and techniques for achieving that seal.

Hose tails

The most common end fitting is a hose tail, which is tapered so it can be easily inserted into the hose and has one or more reentrant barbs that prevent slipping when the hose is clamped behind the barb. Metal and plastic hose tails are available in many sizes and a variety of forms, but most have a standard pipe thread on the other end. A tail can generally be used with hose bores—the hose can be stretched and larger bores, if they're not too big, will be gripped by the barbs. Any elasticity and stretching helps clamp the hose in place, but getting a thicker-walled hose to pass over a tail can be a struggle, although often some soapy water helps.

Tight fits

Thermoplastic (PVC and ABS) hoses soften when heated, making them easier to stretch. Steeping the hose end in a mug of recently boiled water usually warms it enough to noticeably soften it, but I prefer the judicious use of a hot-air gun or hair dryer. The very end of a reinforced or spiral hose can be stretched a bit, but not for very far along the hose.

In addition to using heat, it may help to cut the hose at an angle and perhaps to form a tag that can be pulled with pliers. A lubricant (even a bit of saliva) may also help, but grease or oil might make it easier for the hose to slip off again. Once the hose is completely over the tail, pushing is more effective than pulling.

Leaks

Leaks occur when fluid pressure is sufficient to separate the sealing surfaces, exceeding, for example, the preload pressure applied through the hose wall by a clamp. Softer hoses have a better

chance of deforming to seal scratches and corrosion pits in the underlying rigid fitting. The smaller the area a clamping force is distributed over, the higher the pressure it can resist. But the more it cuts into the hose, the more likely it is that subsequent plastic flow of the material will reduce the sealing pressure.

Sealants

A sealant isn't usually necessary when securing a hose over a pipe or hose tail. Exceptions may occur where corrosion or scratches would otherwise provide a leak path or where a heavily reinforced hose is too inflexible to be compressed. Sealant applied inside the hose will

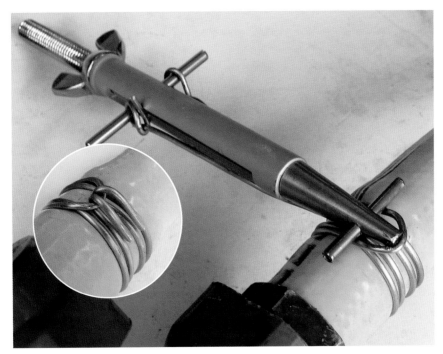

A ClampTite tool produces neat, lightweight wire clamps. Inset: The completed wire clamp.

accumulate in the bore as it is forced onto a tail, so unless this can later be cleared, sealant should be applied only to the tail. Silicone sealants are useful because they initially flow easily, are heat and fuel tolerant, and are permanently resilient after they cure. The slipperiness of uncured silicone can also be helpful when forcing a hose onto a tight tail, and since the final adhesion isn't very strong, usually it is not too difficult to later remove a hose that was clamped over silicone. Silicones also cure fairly quickly and, unlike polysulfides and polyurethanes, are compatible with most plastics. For rubber hoses over metal pipes, a polysulfide might be considered when adhesion is specifically desired, but don't use a polyurethane sealant if you might ever want to remove the hose.

Pipe tails

Threaded adapters that allow a hose tail to be connected to a pipe are available for the ends of most rigid plastic and metal pipes. In many situations, though, it is simpler, neater, and lighter to clamp the hose directly on to the pipe itself. Where pressures are small the hose can be simply stretched over the pipe end and secured with a clamp. But be careful. Internal pressure will tend to force the hose off the pipe if the clamping friction is insufficient.

Joining hoses

There are proprietary fittings for joining hoses or copper pipes of the same or differing diameters. In many same-bore situations a simple DIY solution is to use a length of rigid tube with a similar bore. Depending on the pressures, temperatures, and fluid involved, the tube might be rigid plastic, copper, stainless, or aluminum. The tube should be long enough to extend several diameters into each hose, and, if the working pressures are significant, the pipe ends should be flared slightly or the clamps on each hose should be tied to the other with wire.

Where pressures are low and the hose is flexible enough, it is possible to join hoses of different diameters in a similar manner, by first placing a length of intermediate-diameter hose over one-half of the rigid pipe. Copper pipe has fairly thin walls and is manufactured in standard outside diameters. In sizes below 1″ (25mm) there is usually a copper pipe that is also a good fit inside a standard-bore hose. Holes in most hoses can thus be repaired by simply cutting the hose, inserting a length of copper pipe (preferably slightly flared at the ends), and clamping it. Short pieces of copper pipe can be bought very cheaply from scrap dealers.

Hose clamps

Most boats contain scores of hose clamps. Worm-drive band clamps, with the worm engaging a rack cut or pressed into the band, are the most common. Racks that are cut are more inclined to damage the surface of softer hoses, but are satisfactory in practice.

Worm-drive clamps. These are easily installed with common tools and don't

have to be slid over the bitter end of a hose. They are easily slackened or removed for maintenance of pumps or other attached equipment. They do a satisfactory job in most boat plumbing applications, and the wide band minimizes hose damage. However, they do not generate very high clamping pressures and are quite vulnerable to failure through overtightening, or even through repeated retightening. Also, the design and quality of these clamps varies considerably, and most "stainless" models eventually seize with rust if exposed to seawater.

Oiling the worm box helps protect against corrosion and reduces the required torque, but overtightening will still either strip the rack or cause the worm to slip over it. The protruding band is notorious for injuring fingers and should be bound or covered when left exposed; plastic end caps are available for some brands. To avoid cutting your finger, select clamps with hexagon drive heads rather than just screwdriver slots and use a small ratchet socket driver to tighten them.

Two clamps do not necessarily improve the seal, but they do provide a backup against clamp failure and increase the friction between the hose and the pipe.

Worm-drive clamps are often the only

Most stainless worm-drive hose clamps eventully rust in a salty environment.

type stocked by chandlers; provided the correct size is used, and they're not overtightened, they generally do the job. However, there are alternatives that are stronger, more corrosion resistant, lighter, and sometimes cheaper.

Bolted clamps. Exhaust hoses are usually quite stiff and thick, and although worm-drive clamps are often used to secure them, bolted clamps are preferable. Those made of spot-welded stainless steel are usually very strong and can resist very high pressures.

Tie-wire clamps. Tie-wire hose clamps are not reusable and cannot be retightened, but they generate high sealing pressures and have the advantage of being able to be made on board quickly and very cheaply. Most people consider them a temporary replacement for failed worm-drive clamps, but an engineer friend of mine has used tie-wire clamps extensively on two boats over 30 years. Stainless wire is more durable than most worm-drive hose clamps when exposed to salt water, such as within a chain locker. Tie-wire clamps are also extremely light.

The wire should be wrapped around the hose in situ, tightened, and then secured. There are several ways of doing this.

- **Twisting ties.** The simplest way is directly pulled. Just pass the wire twice around the hose and then twist the ends of the wire around each other so that the joint is right over the underlying turn of wire. This can be done with an ordinary pair of pliers. Vise-Grips make the job easier and tighter because clamping pressure doesn't have to be maintained while twisting, and the wire can be pulled to apply pretension instead of relying only on the twisting action to progressively wind in the two ends. A screwdriver can even be inserted under the first couple of twists and levered up to help the wire bite into the hose before tightening down. The excess wire is cut off, and the tail should be bent down flat against the hose. If protruding dangerously, it can be held down with insulating tape or a cable tie. It's not uncommon to break the wire while attempting to twist it just a bit more—two ties provide some insurance.
- **ClampTite.** Where space permits, a tighter and neater job can be achieved (without risking broken wires) by using a ClampTite tool, which segregates the tensioning and securing tasks. The top photo-

tos on page 160 show just one of several ways it can be used. Here a loop of wire is passed around the hose and the free ends are twisted around opposite sides of the draw bar. The tool's grooved nose is placed on the loop, and the wing nut is used to pull the draw-bar wires tighter than can be achieved by twisting. When the draw-bar wires are tight enough, the tool is pivoted over the nose, putting sharp bends in the end wires and forming hooks that lock them in place over the loop. The end is normally cut off neatly and pushed down flat, but if the draw-bar loops are left attached the tie can later be tightened further. If several ties are to be made it's helpful to precut measured lengths of wire and form the draw-bar end loops before wrapping the wire around the pipe.

The same technique can also be used with a large number of turns of wire—for example, to bind a patch over a holed pipe. Or rope can be used instead to splint a spar or oar.
- **Tie wire.** Tie wires are soft; they combine adequate strength with a low "yield" point, so they deform easily and are relatively tolerant of severe bending and stretching. Hardware stores generally stock galvanized tie wire in a range of diameters. It is suitable for securing galvanized shackle pins and for making temporary hose clamps or jury repairs.

Stainless wire is usually preferable for longer-term applications, and a small coil may earn its place in your toolbox. Soft 304-grade stainless tie wire is made for the aviation industry, so if your hardware/chandler doesn't stock it, have a look on the Internet. Diameters between 1 and 1.25mm are best, but sizes slightly smaller and larger are suitable, too.

In an emergency, multistranded copper wire can be obtained by stripping the insulation from a piece of electrical wiring. The strands will probably be too small

PowerGrip heat-shrink clamps suit low-pressure applications, such as vent lines.

to be used individually, and copper is relatively weak, but a bundle of strands can be twisted together and might get you out of trouble. Wire coat hangers might be another last resort source.
- **Flared connectors.** Reusable clamps make sense when a hose will need to be detached for foreseeable maintenance, but it isn't always easy to pull a well-bedded hose off a hose tail. There are various two-part alternatives in which tapered flares and/or O-rings are forced together with a threaded nut. This allows the joint to be split open without detaching the hose from half of the fitting.
- **Quick connects.** Garden-hose fittings are readily available for $\frac{1}{2}''$ and $\frac{3}{4}''$ bore hoses, and larger diameters are available from irrigation-supply firms. Product ranges include various flare-type connectors and mating quick connectors that clamp on the hose end without requiring tools. Snap-together plastic fittings are useful in intermittently pressurized systems, such as a deck hose. Brass garden fittings can be tightened further using tools and may suit tougher hoses, but they shouldn't be used in critical saltwater plumbing.

Self-sealing quick connects are widely used in outboard fuel systems, and similar fittings can be used with diesel fuel. Be aware that compressed-air fittings may contain O-rings that are not fuel-compatible. Garden-hose versions can be useful when connecting a flexible solar-shower tank to a below-decks shower area.

Various factory-swaged hose-clamping systems are used on engine fuel or hydraulic lines. In some situations it may be well worth buying hoses from specialized firms with such fittings professionally applied.

- **Ear clamps.** Ear clamps have one, two, or more "ears" that are clenched to produce a clamping force. They are commonly found on new outboard fuel-hose systems. Each preformed ring fits only a narrow range of hose diameters (such as 7–9mm or 15–18mm) and must be slid over the hose from a bitter end. They're available from hose-fitting makers, and while special tools are available, smaller sizes can be applied with ordinary hand pliers. They are cheaper and tighter than small worm clamps when replacing, say, the squeeze bulb on a fuel hose. They can't be reused, but can be cut off with a hacksaw.
- **PowerGrip.** PowerGrip is a specialized product developed by Gates

Corporation for clamping soft-rubber or silicone hoses in engine-cooling systems. It exploits the same thermoplastic "memory" effect used in electrical heat-shrink insulation. The plastic rings are shrunk in place with a hot-air gun set to high (the label changes color when it's hot enough) and form a smooth, light, low-profile clamp. The clamp is tight enough for this application because the coolant-relief valve ("radiator cap") limits pressure to low values (typically between 4 and 7 psi). Because of differing rates of thermal expansion, metal clamps slacken their grip on plastic and rubber hoses at low temperatures, sometimes leading to loss of coolant through so-called cold leaks, but PowerGrips clamp tighter as the thermometer drops. They're not reusable, but a tool is available to cut off a PowerGrip without damaging the hose. They come in a variety of sizes and might be used on hoses connecting an engine with a water-heater calorifier or nonpressurized vent lines, for example. The weight saving is attractive, but don't be tempted to use them at higher pressures or with significantly harder hoses than they are designed for.

A socket drive is safer than a screwdriver when tightening worm-drive clamps.

Worm-drive hose clamps come in a plethora of sizes.

HOSE CLAMPS

Upgrading Deck Hardware

Photos by Mark Corke

After 4 days' work, *Castaway* wore new deck hardware.

Upgrading the deck gear on your boat can seriously enhance your sailing pleasure. Once you've sailed a boat set up with low-friction blocks, good rope clutches and jammers, and genoa-sheet cars that are quick and easy to adjust, it's hard to go back to the creaky, friction-riddled 30- or 40-year-old deck gear that so many older boats are still saddled with.

We had always planned to replace and upgrade deck hardware as part of the makeover of *Castaway*, an Ericson 34 and the *BoatWorks* Bailout boat. Much of the existing hardware was original, and some had been added over the years; some of it no longer worked. The refinishing of the deck presented a good

opportunity to bring *Castaway*'s deck gear up to date, and Lewmar generously offered to supply the new equipment.

The hardest part of the project was choosing the hardware we needed from Lewmar's extensive catalogue—and with new paint on the deck, the last thing we wanted was to make a bad choice and mess up the paint surface.

Owner John Smith and I had already removed the old hardware in preparation for painting. It took us four days to install the new gear, mostly because we followed the guidance of my old woodworking teacher: "Measure twice and drill once." We also spent a good deal of time with a length of rope making sure that the leads to winches, blocks, and clutches were positioned correctly.

Checklist

TOOLS
- ☑ Drill
- ☑ Tape measure
- ☑ Marker pen
- ☑ Vacuum
- ☑ Mastic gun
- ☑ Wrenches
- ☑ Screwdrivers
- ☑ Sockets

MATERIALS
- ☑ Caulking
- ☑ Epoxy
- ☑ SS nut washers and bolts to suit hardware
- ☑ Aluminum or fiberglass backing plates

1. Before the deck received its top coat of paint, we laid out the new hardware where we thought it should go to make sure we had everything we needed. Even a modest 34-footer like *Castaway* needs a considerable number of (expensive) items.

2. After the deck had been stripped and freshly painted, we placed the individual items in their final positions, checking the sketch of the original layout for position and checking leads with a length of line.

3. We first placed the winches (mounting instructions come with them). Before we could mount them, we had to remove the drums to access the mounting holes.

4. We traced the holes with a pencil. The marks showed up well on the light-colored deck; a Magic Marker of a contrasting color would work well on a dark deck.

5. Drilling through the deck requires a steady hand and the correct size drill bit; here we're using a $\frac{9}{32}$" bit for the $\frac{1}{4}$" bolts.

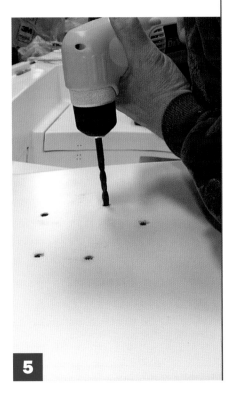

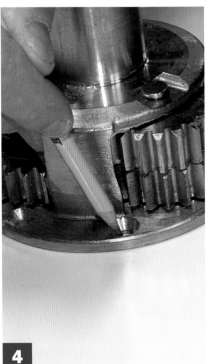

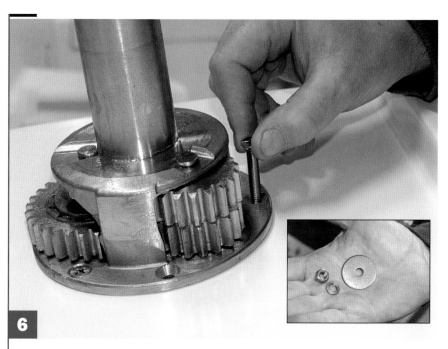

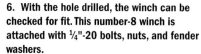

6. With the hole drilled, the winch can be checked for fit. This number-8 winch is attached with ¼"-20 bolts, nuts, and fender washers.

7. A good bead of waterproof caulk (we used Sikaflex 391) ensures that water cannot creep under the winch and into the deck. We did this for all the hardware and additionally sealed with epoxy any holes that penetrated the balsa core.

8. A backing plate is essential to spread the large load a winch puts on the deck. This backing plate is made from ¼" fiberglass; aluminum is another option. We used the winch base as a pattern for drilling the holes.

9. A socket is ideal for tightening the nuts on the underside of the deck. Placing a spring washer and a fender washer under each of the nuts ensures that the bolts stay put and don't eat into the fiberglass plate.

10. While John tightened the nuts, I held the countersunk machine screws steady with a properly sized screwdriver.

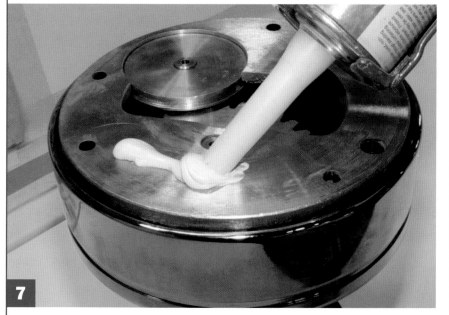

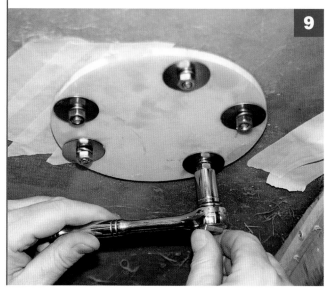

Upgrading Deck Hardware

11

Castaway's Deck Gear

Bringing *Castaway*'s deck gear up to modern standards meant that we had to replace everything. This represented a good opportunity to look at the layout as a whole and consider which elements of the original layout worked well and which could be improved. Interestingly, we ended up with less gear on the deck than before.

For example, the primary winches were originally placed on pedestals located port and starboard on the coaming adjacent to the wheel, and this was not the best location for efficient operation. We removed the pedestals and glassed, filled, and faired the coaming; now you'd never know that there were ever pedestals there. We moved the primaries forward by a couple of feet to the positions on the cabintop previously occupied by the small, non-self-tailing secondary winches and replaced those with the larger ST 40 self-tailers. These now do double duty as halyard and spinnaker winches. With the spinnaker guy led to the cabintop, the trimmer gets a good view of the spinnaker. This makes trimming easier and gets the crew out of the rear of the cockpit (and out of the helmsman's way).

Castaway's makeover involved top-of-the-line gear from Lewmar costing thousands of dollars. A project like this one starts with a wish list; depending on your budget and immediate needs, you can do it all at once or piecemeal. Keep in mind that it's a good idea to stick with gear from one manufacturer for the sake of uniformity and visual compatibility.

Here's what we chose:

Two ST 40 winches mounted on either side of the cabintop to control halyards and spinnaker lines

Two ST 50 winches on the cockpit coamings for genoa sheets

Two three-sheave deck organizers to lead the halyards around the saloon hatch to the clutches

Two triple clutches adjacent to the port and starboard cabintop winches for handling halyards

Six 60mm stand-up blocks for leading halyards from the base of the mast to the deck organizers

One triple-purchase mainsheet traveler mounted on the bridgedeck

Port and starboard genoa-sheet tracks and cars

Two low-profile hatches to replace the leaking (and ugly) wooden originals

12

11. The traveler track was too long, and one of the Waterline crew made short work of cutting it to length with a chop saw. A hacksaw would have worked just as well, if a little more slowly.

12. We positioned the end caps and traveler block before finishing the installation to make sure the block ran freely from side to side.

13. Four days, and the job is finished. The low-profile deck hatches replace the heavy (and leaky) originals and let light and air into the belowdecks spaces.

RESOURCES

LEWMAR
www.lewmar.com

TOP TIP

One of my best decisions was to have a helper document the placement of the original fittings before we removed them. His sketch was a tremendous help when the time came to install the new gear. For example, we were able to see at a glance that the tracks for the genoa-sheet blocks went inside the chainplates. In retrospect, we should have taken photos, too; you think you'll remember where everything goes, but you often don't.

13

Mark Corke

Installing Seacocks

Castaway, the *BoatWorks* Bail-out boat, needed new sea-cocks. The original bronze through-hull fittings and sea-cocks were nearly 30 years old. Most worked after a fashion, but some were seized in the open position, a potentially dangerous condition that in a worst case could result in the loss of the boat. The most deteriorated were the cockpit drains, which by necessity tend to get left open all the time; moreover, they were inaccessible and hard to service.

Before new through-hulls and ball valves could be installed, the old ones had to be removed, and this was no easy task. Many of the threads were corroded and had to be unscrewed with a large wrench or cut off with a reciprocating saw.

We chose ball valves with separate through-hull fittings. Proper seacocks with mushroom or countersunk through-hulls screwed into the base are best (especially if space is an issue), but the base must be screwed or bolted to the hull; never rely on the through-hull to hold it in place.

We installed Marelon ball valves from Forespar. They are lighter and cheaper than bronze seacocks, and since Marelon is a reinforced plastic rather than a metal, it is not subject to electrolysis.

Checklist

TOOLS
- ☑ Step wrench or home-built tool to hold through-hull fitting
- ☑ Reciprocating saw
- ☑ Wrenches
- ☑ Scraper
- ☑ Old chisel

MATERIALS
- ☑ Polysulfide sealant
- ☑ Teflon pipe-sealing tape
- ☑ Ball valves and through-hull fittings
- ☑ Rags
- ☑ Denatured alcohol
- ☑ ½" plywood

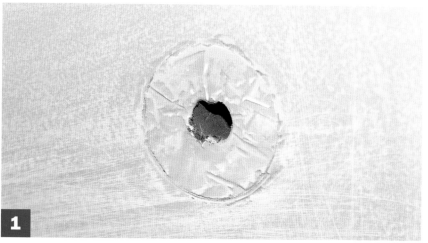

1. *Castaway* has pretensions of being a racing boat, so the through-hulls are recessed into the hull. This is the view from the outside of the ¾" sink drain.

2. The same through-hull on the inside of the boat after the valve was removed. The plywood backing plate has started to delaminate from water migration, and there appears to be insufficient bedding compound between the backing plate and the hull.

3. Space was tight, and the only tool we could get onto the retaining nut was a largish pair of Channellock pliers. A wrench is better, if space permits.

4. While I held the nut on the inside of the boat, owner John Smith unscrewed the fitting with an improvised tool made from a section of scrap aluminum that he turned with a large Stillson wrench.

5. With the through-hull pulled out of the boat and the backing nut removed, the plywood backing block came away easily. Had there been more polysulfide sealant, it would have been necessary to carefully pry off the block with a paint scraper or wood chisel.

6. Next clean off all traces of bedding compound both inside and outside the hull. An old wood chisel is ideal for this job, but be careful not to gouge the gelcoat. Periodically run your fingers over the area where the fitting will sit to feel for lumps. When you're sure the surface is fair, wipe it down with a solvent to clean off any grease and dirt.

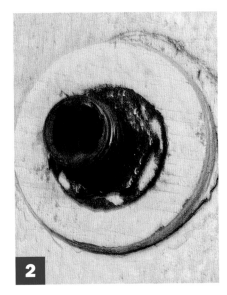

2

3

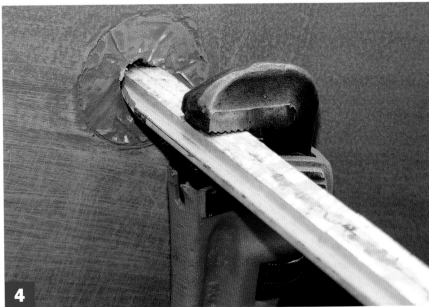

4

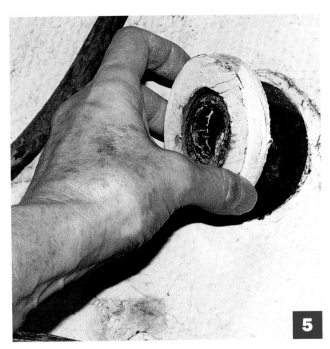

5

6

7. Apply a good bead of polysulfide sealant before sliding the through-hull into the hull for the last time. I used Sikaflex 291, which is ideal for this application. Don't use 3M 5200. It's a good product, but the through-hull will be permanently embedded and impossible to remove if this should become necessary.

8. When pushing the fitting into place, look for excess sealant to ooze out; this indicates that the mating surfaces are adequately covered.

9. With a helper holding the fitting in place, go inside the hull and coat the hull-to-block mating surfaces with sealant. Slip on a plywood backing block. The sealant should squeeze out as shown.

10. Twist the nut down the threads and then use a wrench to tighten it against the backing block.

11. Wrap three layers of Teflon tape around the top inch of thread. Wrap in a clockwise direction, pulling the tape tight as you go.

12. Scrape away sealant that has oozed out on the outside with a blunt tool. Be careful not to scrape the gelcoat or paint finish. Then wipe down the surface with alcohol to remove the last traces of goop and neatly finish the job.

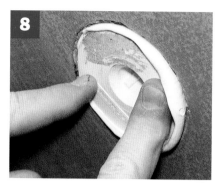

TOP TIP

Using alcohol rather than acetone to clean up is far safer. If it gets on your skin it will not strip oils from the epidermis like acetone will.

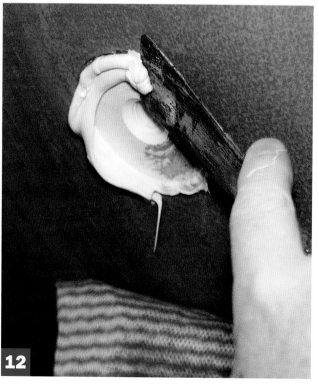

Installing Seacocks

13. Marelon seacocks and valves come in different sizes for different uses. The one shown here is a ¾" model, which we are using to close off the sink drain; it installs between the through-hull fitting and the discharge hose. Notice that the valve's handle is vertical in the open position and rotates a quarter-turn when closed. Unlike a gate valve, it is easy to see at a glance whether this valve is open.

14. The valve is screwed onto the through-hull fitting. Be careful not to cross threads or overtighten it. Hand-tighten the valve, then tighten a further half-turn with a wrench. Make sure the handle is easily accessible and can be turned without catching on any obstructions, such as joinery work or other pipes. The internal thread in the top of the valve will be used for a barbed tail piece to which the drain hose from the sink will later be connected.

13

14

TOP TIP

When installing the back nut on a through-hull fitting, tighten it, then leave it for 15 minutes before tightening it again. The sealant will compress a bit during those 15 minutes, and the nut will probably be a bit looser than it should be.

Seacock Smarts

Don Casey

Quick! How many seacocks are there on your boat? Do you know precisely where each one is located? Are you certain right now that none are frozen open or closed?

Stay clear of breaking waves, and the only thing that will sink your boat is a hole in its hull. So why in Neptune's name do we intentionally make holes in our otherwise watertight hulls? The question is rhetorical, but the point is not. No matter how bulletproof your hull may be, it is only as secure as the seacocks in it.

If you discover water rising inside a molded hull, odds are it is coming in through a drilled hole. Properly installed seacocks let you close all the big holes

(shaft and rudder logs excepted), but you have to be able to put your hand instantly on the handle of every valve, perhaps in the dark and under water, and the seacock must close freely and completely.

Is it a seacock?

Gate valves are not seacocks. A gate valve operates exactly like an overhead garage door. Anything solid in the way will prevent the door from closing. Rotating the wheel of a gate valve as far as it will go gives no assurance that something inside the valve is not preventing it from closing. In addition, nearly all gate valves are brass, which is unsuitable for immersion in seawater. It is the height

of folly to entrust the safety of your boat to a valve intended to keep fresh water from leaking onto the lawn.

Seacocks operate with a quarter-turn of a handle directly connected to the valve. If you turn the handle perpendicular to the hose attached to the seacock, the valve is closed. Period. Seacocks may have flanged bases that bolt onto the hull, taking the strength of the through-hull fitting out of the equation. And seacocks are made only from materials that can tolerate immersion in seawater, typically either bronze or glass-reinforced nylon (Marelon). If any of the valves keeping the ocean out of your boat are not real seacocks, change them.

Seaworthy installation

Except in an emergency, seacocks should be replaced or installed with the boat out of the water. Disconnect the hose and remove the old valve. Typically, the through-hull fitting itself is bonded to the hull with polyurethane sealant, so you can safely unscrew the attached valve with the aid of a pipe wrench without affecting the through-hull.

Now is a good time to think about replacing the through-hulls. Scratch a bronze through-hull with the corner of a screwdriver. If the scratch shows yellow, the fitting is still good. If the scratch has a pinkish hue, tin has leached out of the bronze and the through-hull needs replacing. If your through-hulls are plastic, and if you did not install them and cannot confirm that they are Marelon and not intended for above-the-waterline use, replace them. Also, if you are replacing a metal valve with a nylon one, ignore the manufacturer's assurance that nylon seacocks can be installed on bronze through-hulls. Differences in thread hardness and expansion coefficients aside, it simply makes better sense to install a corrosion-free seacock on a corrosion-free through-hull. Replace the through-hull. If the valve is bronze, the through-hull should be bronze, too.

When you remove an old through-hull, scrape away all sealant residue. To ensure you get a good bed of sealant

To prevent bilge water and other contaminants from rotting the marine plywood backing blocks, we sealed them with unthickened epoxy.

The traditional material for seacocks and through-hulls is bronze. Somewhat more compact than Marelon, bronze ball valves are installed in exactly the same way. The mushroom profiles (bottom) are ideal for all but the fastest racing hulls.

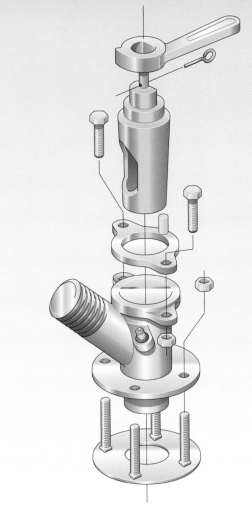

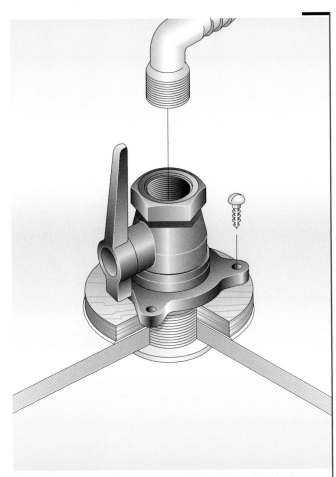

Blakes-style seacocks (left) have a taper instead of a ball valve. Made entirely of bronze, they are expensive, very reliable, and have the added advantage of being able to be greased without dismantling. Marelon ball valves (right) are made of reinforced nylon with stainless-steel ball valves.

under the head of the new through-hull, grind a small chamfer all the way around the hole outside. If you are installing a flush-head through-hull, now is the time to countersink it. Brush away grinding dust, and clean the area around the hole—both inside and outside the hull—with denatured alcohol.

The flange of the seacock must sit flush on a reinforced base. Traditionally this has been a plywood backing plate—a ring or square with a hole in the center to receive the through-hull. Plywood is perfectly acceptable provided you completely seal it in epoxy. Cut your backing plate from ¾" plywood and either shape it or fill and fair the curvature of the hull around the hole to get a full-contact fit between the plate and the hull. Drill the fastener holes before sealing the plate.

If the hull is cored, you must excavate the core at least to the diameter of the through-hull flange and replace it with epoxy thickened with colloidal silica. The epoxy provides a solid base for the through-hull and prevents water from entering the core.

Unless your hull is extraordinarily thick, you will need to shorten the through-hull so the seacock can be tight-

ened against the backer block. Remove the nut from the through-hull and thread on the seacock until it bottoms out. Mark the first visible thread. Disassemble the two parts and insert the through-hull into the hull. While an assistant holds it in place, seat the backing plate over the protruding threads inside the hull and again mark the first visible thread. Count the threads between your two marks and add two. Your shortening cut will be this many threads from the end. Thread the nut back on the through-hull just beyond the cut-off distance and use it as a guide to keep your saw straight. When you remove the nut after the cut, it will also dress the threads. Discard the nut.

Reinsert the shortened though-hull, put the backing plate in place, and screw on the seacock until it touches the backing plate. Position the seacock so its lever can turn without interference. If the seacock has one or more drain plugs, you need to orient it so that one of them is at or near the lowest side of the valve. When you are satisfied with handle clearance and drain-plug location, use the holes in the flange as

drill guides to drill mounting holes through the hull.

From outside the hull, countersink these holes. Dry-fit the fasteners for alignment and length and to make sure the heads are flush. On a bronze seacock, the bolts and nuts must be bronze. Stainless-steel fasteners are acceptable for securing nylon seacocks, but bronze is the better choice.

Dismantle everything and drill the fastener holes in the plywood backing plate a drill-size larger than they need to be. Then give the backing plate three coats of epoxy. Be sure to saturate the edges, including inside the holes. Let the epoxy cure fully before doing the final installation.

To screw the through-hull into the seacock, which is now fixed in place, you will need a step wrench—a special tool that grips the ears inside the through-hull. Hopefully your yard will have one you can borrow. If a step wrench is not available, a chisel or hardwood wedge can sometimes do the job. Or buy a cheap socket that fits snugly inside the through-hull and cut slots in its sides to convert it to a step wrench.

A hole saw is the best tool for drilling through the hull.

The best sealant to use for through-hull fittings is polyurethane. You want to bed the through-hull to the hull, the hull to the backing plate, and the plate to the seacock. Do not seal the seacock threads with polyurethane; removing it later will be exceedingly difficult. Instead, coat the threads with Teflon thread tape or thread sealant.

Put two or three concentric rings of polyurethane sealant on both sides of the plywood backing plate and twist it into position. Position the seacock on the plate, also with a small twisting motion to help distribute the sealant. Ring the top inch of the fasteners with sealant and insert them from outside the hull. Inside, put a washer over each and thread on a locking nut, but do not tighten it. First put a generous bead of polyurethane sealant around the underside of the head of the through-hull, then insert it through the hull and thread it into the seacock. Tighten it only enough so that the sealant starts to squeeze out. Check everything for alignment. Tighten the nuts on the flange bolts to secure the seacock, then turn the through-hull from outside to snug it against the hull. Use a bit of the sealant that squeezed out to fair over the heads of the screws.

When you fit your new seacock with a tailpiece, be sure you select the correct thread in addition to the correct material (bronze on bronze, nylon on nylon). Bronze seacocks sometimes have tapered top threads (NPT), while nylon seacocks have straight-top threads (NPS). Use thread sealant on the tailpiece to ensure that the connection will be watertight. If the barbs on the tailpiece are long enough to allow it, double-clamp the hose.

Maintaining seacocks

A new seacock, whether bronze or nylon, will be a ball valve. Some seacocks still in use are of the tapered-plug or expanded-rubber-plug varieties, with a smattering of piston styles. Because ball valves turn against Teflon seats, they need to be exercised religiously every three or four months to operate smoothly year after year. They can, however, benefit from an annual wipe of Teflon grease on each side of the ball. If you don't want to remove the hose and/or tailpiece, lubrication can be accomplished from outside the hull with a length of thin dowel or a wooden skewer. Put a pea-size blob of Teflon grease on the end of the dowel and smear this onto the closed ball of the valve through the through-hull. Now rotate the handle about 70 degrees and put a fresh blob of grease near the end of the dowel, but on the side this time. Carefully feed this through the less-than-fully-open valve, then rotate the dowel to allow raking the grease off on the upper lip of the ball. Remove the dowel, then close the valve and reopen it to spread out the grease.

Piston-style seacocks should be dismantled and greased annually, as should expanded-rubber-plug seacocks. The latter may need minor surgery. A permanent "bump" can develop on the rubber barrel when the valve is left in the closed position for a long time, and this needs to be shaved off. Parts are no longer available for these seacocks, so carefully trimming the barrel can extend the seacock's useful life. Except for this, and some susceptibility to chemicals, expanded-rubber-plug seacocks are dependable and watertight.

Seacocks that are properly installed and well maintained never fail, but sailors who do their own maintenance are not as reliable. A tapered plug of soft wood tied to each seacock is a smart backup.

Installing Seacocks

Upgrading to Wheel Steering

There are two kinds of sailors—those who like tillers and those who like wheels. When Bill Blazewicz and his wife, Tanya, bought *Secret Spirit,* a Pearson 30, three years ago, they got such a good deal on it that they thought they could live with the fact that it came with a tiller instead of the wheel they'd have preferred. A couple of seasons sailing the boat was enough to convince them otherwise. They didn't like the way the tiller dominated the cockpit while they were underway; it banged shins, guests tripped over it, and the family dog always seemed to get in the way during tense situations like maneuvering in marinas.

It was not surprising that of the many upgrades Bill wanted to lavish on the veteran P30, wheel steering was high on the list, hard on the heels of some roller-furling gear and new sails. But it was clear that it wouldn't be an easy upgrade. Retrofitting a wheel involves some pretty serious surgery—in most tiller-steered boats you have to cut the

✂ Tools you will need

- **Reciprocating saw**
- **Dremel tool**
- **Socket set**
- **Adjustable wrenches**
- **Open-ended wrenches**
- **Handsaw**
- **Hammer**
- **Allen wrenches**
- **Screwdriver set**
- **Power drill with a right-angle attachment**
- **Fiberglass mat and rovings**
- **Epoxy resin kit (including pumps and rollers)**
- **Loctite**
- **Bedding compound**
- **Advil and Band-Aids**

Manu the dog did not get along with the tiller—but the steering pedestal offers interesting possibilities . . .

For the tiller

- Simplicity—it has only a couple of moving parts
- Reliability—there's very little to go wrong
- Tiller autopilots are less expensive than wheel pilots
- Use of space—in port, the tiller lifts out of the way to clear the cockpit
- Feel—you can't get a more direct connection between hand and rudder, hence many people like the responsiveness of a tiller

Against the tiller

- Sweeps the cockpit when you're sailing
- Can be tiring to use in breezy conditions, especially when sailing downwind
- Awkward to steer with it while standing

- Tiller pilots take up room in cockpit
- The tiller can flop over and trap you against the cockpit sides when reversing under power
- Some people never adjust to having to push a tiller left to go right and vice versa

For the wheel

- A wheel is intuitive to use—there's no mental adjustment needed
- A wheel frees up more cockpit space when the boat is under way. And in port, the wheel can be removed from the pedestal
- A wheel is more comfortable to use when motoring or motor-sailing
- Wheels are easier to use when maneuvering in close quarters

- You can steer from the windward or leeward rail with equal ease
- A wheel is better for boats that carry excess weather helm

Against the wheel

- Wheel steering is more complex than a tiller
- Wheel systems need more maintenance
- You don't get the same "feel" under sail as with a tiller
- You usually won't be able to turn as sharply as with the tiller
- It takes up more room in the cockpit when you're at rest, especially on boats under 30 feet
- Wheel autopilots are more expensive than tiller pilots
- Connecting it to a windvane is more complicated, and the vane will not perform as well as with a tiller

---

rudder tube, and you'll have to make a big hole in your cockpit sole—so it pays to think out the pros and cons dispassionately.

Just like everything else to do with boats, the wheel/tiller debate is highly subjective. A diehard tiller fan is unlikely to find peace at the wheel, and the wheel lover will be reluctant to come to grips with a tiller, no matter how compelling the arguments.

Expense is another consideration; a tiller-to-wheel conversion will cost upward of $1,000 if you do the work yourself, much more if you have a professional install it. You'll never recoup this outlay on an older, smaller boat when it comes time to sell it. If, on the other hand, you intend to keep the boat for several years or more and you think a wheel would add to your sailing pleasure, then you can certainly justify spending the money.

Wheel steering systems

The wheel systems suitable for DIY retrofitting fall into two categories—chain-and-wire and rack-and-pinion. The latter has a pinion gear on the end of a horizontal wheel shaft, which acts on a toothed quadrant (the rack) mounted atop a vertical shaft. A lever fixed to the bottom of this shaft is connected to a metal rod, which in turn is connected to a steering arm bolted to the rudderstock. A variant of this system sometimes seen on older

boats has the rack mounted directly to the rudderpost. Island Packet Yachts used this system for many years, and it is extremely reliable, though not a suitable retrofit for most modern sailboats.

Rack-and-pinion steering provides excellent feel and is easy to maintain.

A chain-and-wire system employs a chain looped over a sprocket that turns with the wheel. Inside the pedestal, the

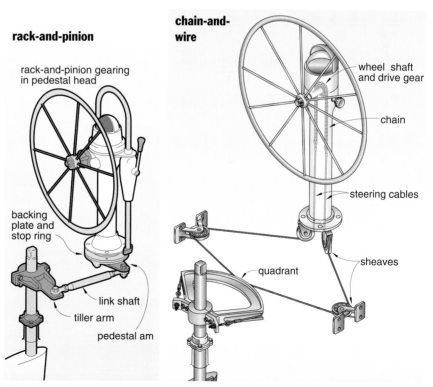

rack-and-pinion

rack-and-pinion gearing in pedestal head

backing plate and stop ring

link shaft

tiller arm

pedestal am

chain-and-wire

wheel shaft and drive gear

chain

steering cables

quadrant

sheaves

The two main types of steering systems suitable for owner installation are rack-and-pinion (left) and chain-and-wire (right). The latter looks complicated but is more versatile because the wires can be run around obstacles belowdecks. Rack-and-pinion steering requires a short, straight linkage between rudder and pedestal.

chain is connected to a pair of stainless-steel cables, which are led via one or more pairs of sheaves to a quadrant or radial-drive wheel bolted to the rudderstock. There are a number of variations on this basic arrangement—the cables can be led via flexible conduits to a steering arm fixed to the rudderstock, for instance—depending on how tortuous the route between the steering pedestal and rudderstock is.

Even though it has more moving parts than the rack-and-pinion system and therefore seems more complex, the chain-and-wire system is actually easier to repair and is generally better suited to older boats. A rack-and-pinion system ideally should have a short, straight connection between pedestal and rudderstock, which is not always possible. On the Blazewiczs' Pearson, three factors

conspired against the rack-and-pinion system, which, having fewer components, would otherwise have been easier to install. The first was the steep rake of the rudderpost—a rack-and-pinion system can cope with the Pearson's 20-degree angle, but it's borderline. The second was the gas tank under the cockpit sole, which prohibited a straight run between the pedestal and the rudderpost. The third was the size of the wheel.

Apart from changing the number of teeth on the gears—an expensive option—there is only one way to change the gearing on a rack-and-pinion system, and that is to vary the size of the steering wheel. Many modern boats have rack-and-pinion systems, but the pedestal is located just ahead of the rudderpost in a T-shape cockpit pur-

pose-built to allow a wheel of at least 30″ diameter. On the Pearson 30 and many other sailboats with trench cockpits, the size of the wheel is limited by the need for it to clear the seats. The smaller the wheel, the greater the effort required to turn the rudder. On *Secret Spirit,* where a 24″ wheel was about the biggest that could be used, the gearing would have been high enough to make steering the boat harder work than it ought to be. With a chain-and-wire system, the gearing can be changed by altering the size of the quadrant, sprocket, and pulleys, as well as by changing the diameter of the wheel. By juggling these factors, it's possible to determine the number of wheel turns required to get the rudder from lock to lock—anything from one to six or more, depending on the size and type of boat.

1 & 1a. Off comes the tiller, after 30 years. The first step in ordering the conversion kit is to drop the rudder and measure the diameter of the rudderstock with a micrometer. These are expensive, so Bill borrowed one from a friend. He sent the measurements to Edson so the quadrant and stuffing box could be machined to the right size.

2. The assorted components are spread out for inspection: quadrant, rudder stuffing box, sheaves, chain, and wire.

Other things to think about

The change from tiller to wheel affects more than just the boat's steering system. The cockpit ergonomics, designed around the tiller, will be entirely different when a wheel and its pedestal are plonked down right in the middle of things.

- Cockpits designed around a wheel are T-shaped, so there is a wide area where you can stand behind the wheel and brace yourself when the boat is heeled over; a trench cockpit won't have that luxury.

- The cockpit coamings on many tiller boats are designed to let you sit outboard with a tiller extension; you may not be able to reach a wheel from your customary perch.
- It's nice to be able to sit behind the wheel, but you'll almost certainly have to make your own helm seat.
- Your relationship with your sheet winches and mainsheet will change. Now that you are standing

If it is possible to use a radial-drive wheel instead of a quadrant, the number of moving parts in the steering system can be reduced.

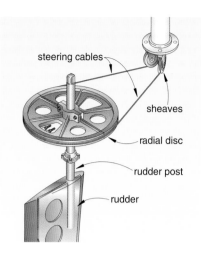

steering cables
sheaves
radial disc
rudder post
rudder

3. It's important to determine the optimum spot for the pedestal. There should be enough room behind it to stand comfortably. The manufacturer's recommend a minimum distance of 21 inches from the cockpit end.

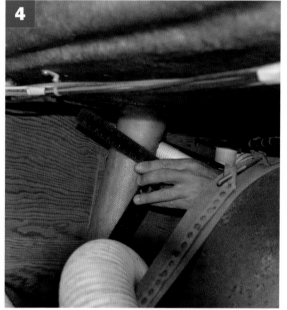

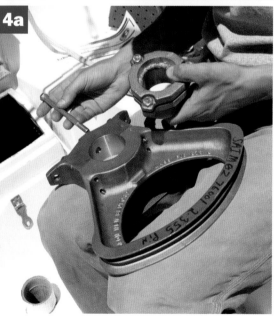

4. The first job is to cut through the rudder tube so that the stuffing box and quadrant (4a) can be mounted above it. Make very sure that you are cutting above the waterline.

behind a wheel, you may not be able to get to your primaries as quickly to trim the genoa, and the mainsheet traveler may need to be relocated. On some boats, the pedestal is fitted at the forward end of the cockpit so that the winches and mainsheet are closer to the helmsman; the downside is that this compromises access to the coveted space under the dodger.

- As much as anything, the location of the cockpit-locker lids will determine where the pedestal is positioned.

While you're at it, seize the opportunity to move your engine controls to the pedestal. The convenience (no more throttle levers up the pants leg) outweighs the slight extra expense.

Postscript

On paper, fitting pedestal steering to a Pearson 30 is a straightforward job. In practice, Bill and Tanya found that like

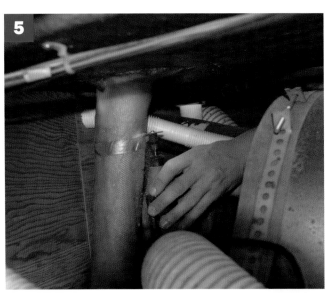

5. There was very little room to move in the confines of the Pearson's cockpit locker and quarterberth; Bill used a Dremel tool to make the cut.

6 & 6a. The stuffing box was pushed down over the top of the rudderstock and glassed in place with epoxy resin and overlapping strips of fiberglass mat, each layer a bit wider than the previous one. Now's when that helper you enlisted will start to earn his or her keep.

7 & 7a. Next it was time to fit the quadrant. This necessitated drilling a hole through the rudderstock, which was not easy given the limited room Bill had to work in. The bulkhead abaft the rudderstock had to be cut away to make room for the quadrant. The actual drilling of the hole took the better part of an hour, with a right-angle attachment on the drill and one person pushing and another pulling on the drill.

just about anything else to do with working on boats, the job swallowed all the time they'd allowed for it—and a lot more besides. If they had to do it over again, here's what they'd do differently.

- Liaise more closely with the manufacturer. Miscommunication led to several wasted days. "We found out only later just how much information Edson has on these boats."
- Match the instructions to the parts in front of you.
- Open every package and box, and fit all the components together for a dry run before starting the project. "If we'd done that, we would have saved several days that were spoiled because of missing or wrong parts."
- Check all the fasteners against their intended application. Bolts that were too short, too long, or simply missing also caused delays that could have been avoided.

8

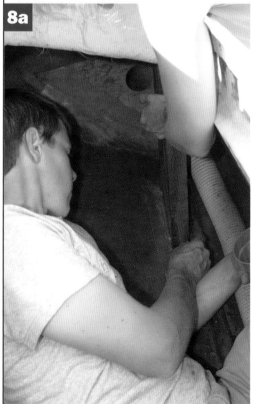

8a

8 & 8a. There was nowhere to mount the wire sheaves, so a length of hardwood was purchased and cut to size. Bill used African purpleheart, but any rot-resistant wood will do. The new uprights were glassed in place on either side of the cockpit trench.

9. Now it was time to fit the pedestal, and here's where Bill struck the first hitch. Measurements indicated that the idler wheels at the base of the pedestal would foul the top of the fuel tank beneath the cockpit sole. Edson makes a riser that fits under the pedestal to cure this problem, but valuable time was lost while it was ordered and delivered.

9

10

10a

10 & 10a. With the riser in hand, it was time to do some serious hole-cutting. Quite a large hole is required for the sheave plate, Bill traced around the inside of the riser before drilling the starter hole. Then it was time for the saber saw.

- Countless trips to hardware stores or chandlers for drill bits, tools, and other supplies wasted a lot of time. A well-stocked tool kit—before you start—is essential.
- This is not a project for those with minimal DIY skills.
- Patience is vital. Every little task takes at least twice as long as it ought to when you are stretched out in a tiny airless space, unable to move more than few inches in any direction.
- Even though the job proved more time-consuming than he'd anticipated—it took five days, counting all the wasted hours, delays while waiting for parts, and multiple trips to buy odds and ends—Bill is delighted with the end result. "The boat is so much more enjoyable to sail," he says. "It won't turn quite as tightly as before because of the rudder stops on the quadrant, but I can live with that. In terms of sailing pleasure, it's the best upgrade we've made."

11 & 11a. After cleaning up the edges of the cut and giving the exposed balsa core a good coat of epoxy to prevent moisture from getting into it, the riser is offered up.

12 & 12a. The sheave plate is bolted to the underside of the riser. Holes are drilled for the mounting bolts, and their sides are sealed with epoxy.

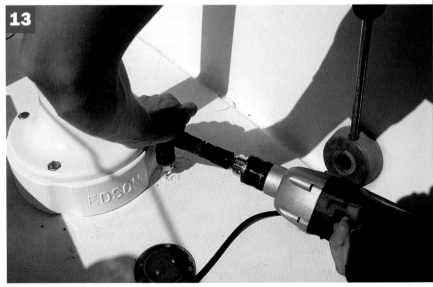

13. With the pedestal bolted in place, the holes are drilled for the grabrail. Here's another place where the right-angle drill attachment proved essential. Again, the exposed balsa core must be sealed with epoxy resin.

14

15

16

14. The next step is to locate the sheaves on their brackets so that there is a good lead to the quadrant. An Edson radial-drive wheel wouldn't have needed these sheaves. Bill fitted the chain and its wires over the sprocket in the pedestal and clamped the sheaves in various positions on their uprights while experimenting with the lead from idlers to quadrant. This sounds easy, but care is needed, for the angle between the sheaves and quadrant changes drastically as the rudder turns.

15. Once the sheaves are aligned correctly, they're bolted in place and the wires are connected to the quadrant with cable clamps. You can see how the location of the gas tank affected everything else. Bill rigged up the chain visible under the quadrant to act as a temporary steering stop. Proper fiberglass stops faced with rubber will soon be attached to the rudder tube.

16. Finished at last—well, almost. The new pedestal-mounted engine controls aren't connected yet, but that's a whole other story.

Installing a New Propeller

Mark Corke

replaced at the same time, but it wasn't. The owner at the time had probably blown his budget on the engine and thought the old prop would do for a while, but seven years later it was still there. The present owners reported there was some cavitation, which may been caused by the folding prop turning too fast because of its insufficient blade area and pitch. To address all these issues we chose a new, beautifully engineered two-blade folding propeller from Flex-O-Fold. Removing the old prop was the hardest part of the operation.

A folding prop like the Flex-O-Fold is a useful upgrade for almost any sailboat; it significantly reduces drag under water and thus increases boatspeed. The instructions that were included with the new propeller were easy to follow—and almost superfluous because there are so few parts. It is almost impossible to install this prop incorrectly.

You need to take a few precautions to make sure that the installation goes well and that the prop works as intended. Make sure you use a socket of the correct size when screwing on the shaft nut; a box wrench or crescent wrench will not do, for it might slip and round off the edges of the nut.

SYSTEMS

There were a couple of reasons why we wanted to change the prop on our *BoatWorks* Bailout boat, *Castaway*. First, the existing Martec folding prop was seriously undersized; second, the worn folding mechanism would need attention if the prop was retained.

The boat's original engine, a gasoline-powered Atomic 4, had been replaced with a more modern Yanmar 2GM diesel. The propeller should have been

Checklist

TOOLS
- ☑ Socket wrench
- ☑ Allen wrenches
- ☑ Wire brush
- ☑ Screwdriver
- ☑ File
- ☑ Blowtorch
- ☑ Prop puller (optional)

MATERIALS
- ☑ Propeller
- ☑ Loctite
- ☑ WD-40

1. We removed the old shaft anode, which was overdue for replacement. This gave us better access to the shaft and prop.

2. After removing the old blades and shaft nut from the Martec prop, we set about getting the old hub off. First we tried using WD-40 to break the bond between the hub and the shaft, but this wasn't enough.

3. We then applied a moderate amount of heat with a propane torch and knocked the hub off the shaft with a sharp whack from a 2 × 4.

4. With the old prop removed, we pried out the shaft key and gave the shaft a good cleaning with a wire brush.

5. Before installing the new hub we filed the bronze shaft key lightly to remove a slight burr that had formed over the years. If you do this, be careful not to remove any more metal than necessary.

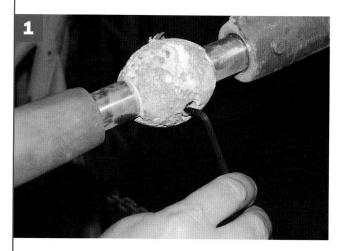

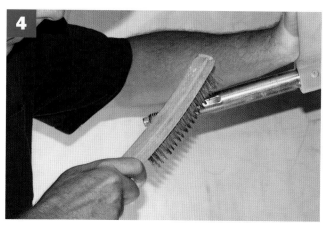

TOP TIP

Always select a propeller that matches your engine's horsepower and gear ratio. The boat's underwater profile is a factor in determining proper blade pitch and diameter, so don't be tempted to use any prop that happens to fit. All prop manufacturers can advise you on the correct unit for your boat and engine.

Installing a New Propeller

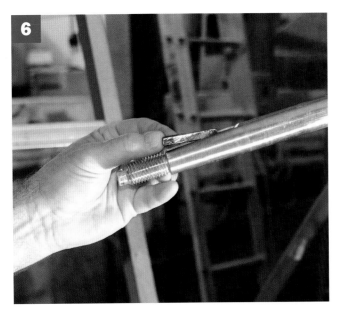

6. The key must fit snugly; it shouldn't have to be forced into its slot, nor should it move around.

7. Once the key is aligned with the corresponding slot in the propeller, the hub can be slid onto the shaft. It should slide on easily. Do not force it with a hammer. The retaining nut can now be placed on the end of the shaft.

8. We used a screwdriver to prevent the shaft from rotating and snugged the retaining nut with the correct-size socket. Wrapping tape around the screwdriver shaft prevents it from damaging the blade pinholes.

9 & 10. A small Allen-head grub screw threaded through the side of the hub boss prevents the retaining nut from undoing itself. Use a small dab of Loctite to make sure the grub screw stays put.

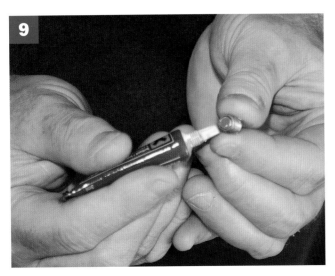

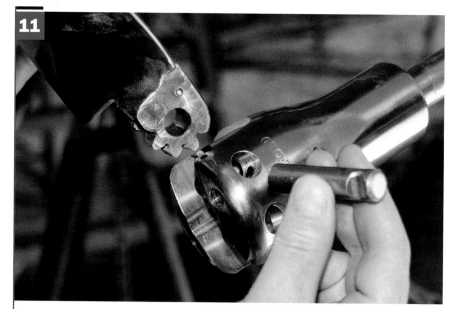

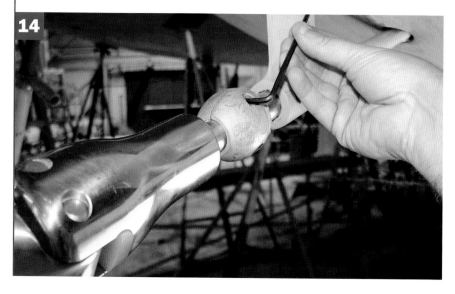

11. Now the blades can be installed. A stainless-steel pin acts as a hinge for each of the blades, which simply slide into place. Pay attention to the orientation of the semicircular cutout in the pin. It should be on the starboard side as the pin is inserted.

12. The second blade is installed in the same way as the first. Make sure that the teeth of the folding gear are aligned. In this photo you can see the cutout in the pin; note how it faces down.

13. Two Allen-head machine screws are threaded into the rear of the hub, passing through the semicircular cutouts in the pins they hold in place.

14. The installation is now almost complete. The last step is to install a new correctly sized shaft anode.

RESOURCES

Flex-O-Fold
www.flexofold.com
781-631-3190

Installing a New Propeller

Plumbing

A good water system adds to the boating experience.

tensive summer cruising, we wanted a bit more sophistication. But how much is too much? I initially planned a simple system, with a more powerful water pump supplying faucets in the galley and head as well as a transom shower—the latter a request from the children, who unaccountably like to swim in the frigid waters of New England. It's much better to wash the salt off on deck than down below.

A simple plan

Step one was to rough out the proposed system on a plan of the boat's interior (see figure page 189). Drawn to scale, this allowed me to calculate how much tubing I would need and where and how to make the connections. The tubing runs would include low points where I could tee in valves to let me drain the system in the fall so I could avoid winterizing it with antifreeze. I also decided to move the water pump out from under the galley sink and into a side locker where it would be easier to service. I would replace the galley faucet, add a freshwater manual pump in the galley, and install a new faucet in the head.

This simple plan soon morphed into something more complicated. Why not take advantage of the free energy provided by my diesel cooling system and install a water heater? The kids would be even more impressed with their transom shower. I could put a second shower in the head, and there'd be hot water for dishwashing too. I anticipated appreciative cheers from the whole family. So I decided to install a water heater. The resulting system is, I think, about as good as it gets for an elderly 34-foot coastal cruiser.

Photos by Peter Nielsen

O f all the upgrades you can lavish on an older boat, few will give you more bang for your buck than a complete overhaul of the freshwater plumbing system. An improvement in water quality should be immediately apparent; any of the new breed of water pumps will be quieter and less power-hungry than their predecessors, and with a little planning, you can make your boat much more user-friendly both for your family when cruising and for yourself at winterizing time.

The water system on *Ostara*, a 1973 Norlin 34, was about (or just below) average for a boat of its age. Two 20-

gallon fiberglass tanks of recent vintage were mounted under the port settee, feeding a faucet in the galley via an elderly Jabsco pump and another in the head via a Whale Gusher foot pump. Another Gusher pump in the galley supplied salt water, a great idea for offshore sailing, when fresh water needs to be conserved. On tracing the saltwater hose, I found it was connected to the intake line for the toilet. Call me old-fashioned, but I didn't like the thought of that.

This setup had obviously served the previous owner well enough, but he had done a lot more racing than cruising. With children aboard and plans for ex-

Checklist

TOOLS
- ☑ **Cordless drill**
- ☑ **Hole saw**
- ☑ **Screwdrivers**
- ☑ **Tube cutter**

MATERIALS
- ☑ **Semi-rigid tubing, ½" ID**
- ☑ **Reinforced PVC tubing, ½" ID**
- ☑ **Couplings**
- ☑ **Hose clamps**

Pipework

Item one on the gear list, obviously, is water hose. There are two realistic options—food-grade clear reinforced PVC hose or semirigid, solid-colored plastic tubing as made by Whale and Sea Tech. The former must be joined with nylon couplings and stainless-steel hose clamps; the latter use clever push-fit couplings, including simple straight and angled connectors to tees, valves, and adapters. I had replumbed my previous boat using Whale Quick Connect hose and couplings and did not hesitate to order it again.

With each connector coupling costing between $4 and $8, depending on type and where you buy it (as always, check around online for the best deal), semirigid tubing appears to be the more expensive option. But when you add up the cost of the nylon tees and stainless-steel hose clamps needed to make PVC

Whale's Quick Connect hose and couplings.

tubing connections, there's not a lot of difference. The semirigid tubing doesn't bend as much as PVC hose, so you may need to make a few more connections. On the other hand, the semirigid tubing is actually cheaper than PVC tubing.

Where the semirigid stuff really scores is in speed and convenience. The push-fit connectors couldn't be eas-

ier to install and remove, so you can make major changes to the pipe runs without much fuss. And if you have to make up a manifold, with multiple outlets from a single inlet, there is no better way than to use a semirigid system.

There are other advantages. Clear tubing that is exposed to light soon has a coating of algae growing inside it, but solid-colored semirigid tubing doesn't admit the light and thus the nasties don't flourish. Some people mix and match, using PVC tubing on long, hidden pipe runs and semirigid tubing where lots of connections need to be made. One of the semirigid tubing's few drawbacks is that the ends that fit into the connectors must be cut perfectly square and be scratch-free or they won't seal properly; you'd be foolish not to buy the proper cutting tool.

You may be tempted to use domestic copper tubing, with compression fittings, on your boat. You wouldn't be the first. I

TIP

I was advised by the Whale engineers to install a non-return valve directly downstream of the water tank. Sometimes water can leak back from a pump via a poorly sealed connection or failed seal, and, by maintaining pressure in the hose, the check valve prevents the pump from continually cycling on and off. They also suggested I run a separate cold-water line to the manual pumps in the head and galley, teed off upstream of the electric pump. This prevents the electric pump from forcing water through the manual pumps.

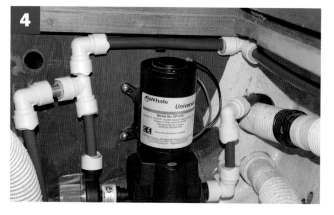

1. Sometimes you have to make the best out of a bad job. The Whale fittings were easy to connect to the existing tubing from the water tanks.

2. Some of the old PVC tubing. Eeeww, as my daughter said.

3. Push-fit connectors, like the ⅝" ID Whale Quick Connect system, are quick and easy to use.

4. The water pump was moved from under the galley sink to a more accessible location. Note the tee to the manual pumps is taken off upstream of the electric pump.

Plumbing

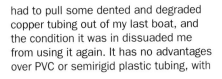

5. Where it was easier to use ½" ID PVC tubing, we did so.

6. Hot and cold pressure lines and the manual pump line to the head.

7. The cockpit shower is installed.

8. Sometimes it's not easy to do battle with tight old-boat spaces.

9. It works! Clear, clean water issues from the new galley mixer.

hoses so that they don't interfere with stowage under berths and can't be kinked or crushed by heavy gear. Try to keep the runs out of the bilge so they don't get scuffed and dirty. The semirigid tubing worked well when it came to feeding it under moldings and along the hull sides, but there were a few places where we could have gotten away with fewer connections had we used PVC tubing.

Pumps

If you're happy with a basic, stone-axe-reliable water system and don't need pressurized or hot water, just install manual pumps in the galley and head; good units are available from Fynspray/Imtra and Whale. The latter's foot-operated Gusher pump seems to be the most popular choice.

If you want a pressurized system, the pump should be sized according to the number of outlets it will have to service. Prices are linked to pumping capacity; you can get a low-powered, 2-gallon-per-minute pump for under $100, or spend as much as $550 for a hefty 10-gpm model. If you want to run a shower, you'll need a minimum of 3.5 gpm. Remember that a more powerful pump will consume more electricity. Big diaphragm

had to pull some dented and degraded copper tubing out of my last boat, and the condition it was in dissuaded me from using it again. It has no advantages over PVC or semirigid plastic tubing, with

the added disadvantage of being more likely to fracture from freezing. You could use domestic PVC pipe, but that's hardly worthwhile on a typical boat.

It takes a bit of planning to route

What We Didn't Use

1. An accumulator, or expansion tank, is a slightly pressurized metal or plastic tank with a water-filled bladder inside. If the water pressure drops—for instance, if a faucet is turned on momentarily—the water in the bladder flows back into the pipes. This keeps the pump from starting up immediately. If your system suffers from water hammer or knocking, an accumulator will cure it. We decided not to install one because, like many modern pumps, the 4.75 gpm Whale I used is extremely quiet, and because replacing the entire water system pretty much guaranteed there wouldn't be any leaks.

2. Many slip-domiciled boats have a shore-supply connection that allows a marina hose to be plugged into the ship's water system. This is often accomplished via a garden hose fitting linked to the tank, but that's not a good

idea; letting water pressurized at 100 psi into a system that's not designed to cope with more than 40 psi is asking for trouble. If you must do this, buy and install an inline pressure regulator. I decided I could live without plumbed-in shore water.

3. I debated whether to install an inline water filter, but so far I have not done so. The tanks are fairly new and the water does not taste bad. If I do eventually install a charcoal filter, it will go in the feed line to the two manual pumps.

4. I decided not to fit a saltwater pump at the galley. If I decide to install one in the future, I'll plumb it to a through-hull and seacock, which it will share with a deck wash pump.

pumps, like the belt-driven Jabscos, are also noisier than the new generation of low-power pumps.

On that note, I'd strongly advise you to also install manual pumps in the galley and in the head(s), and to urge guests to use them. This saves both energy and water; there's nothing that annoys me more than seeing someone brush his teeth with the water running. And you would be stupid indeed to rely solely on electric pumps for your water supply.

The best electric water pumps for pleasure-boat use operate automatically, with an integral sensor or switch that turns them on when a faucet is opened. These are now so common, and so reliable, that there is no reason to install a more complicated remote-switch pump with a switch built into the faucet. Diaphragm pumps are better for pressure water systems than impeller or centrifugal types, for good reason. They're self-priming, use less power, and can be run dry.

Faucets

It's perfectly feasible to use domestic faucets on your boat. An adapter with a barbed tailpiece will allow you to connect PVC tubing. I think most household faucets and mixers look clumsy and out of place on a boat, though. Marine/RV faucets are available in assorted styles and finishes, with prices ranging from affordable to excruciatingly expensive. Whichever type you choose, it pays to install a shower/mixer type with retractable hose in the head. Even if you don't shower on board, it comes in handy for rinsing salt out of your hair.

Conclusion

Don't be afraid to seek technical advice from manufacturers, and don't be afraid to tackle a job like this yourself. The hardest part is getting into the cramped spaces where builders usually hide the pumps and plumbing. If your boat didn't have pressure water, you'll have to run a new wire from the switch panel to the pump, and that'll be the hardest part of the installation.

Thanks to **Whale** for technical help and guidance.

RESOURCES

Attwood
www.attwoodmarine.com
616-897-2290

Defender
www.defender.com
800-628-8225

Groco
www.groco.net
410-712-4242

Imtra
www.imtra.com
508-995-7000

Jabsco
www.jabsco.com

Shurflo
www.shurflo.com
800-854-3218

Whale
www.whalepumps.com
978-531-0021

West Marine
www.westmarine.com
800-685-4838

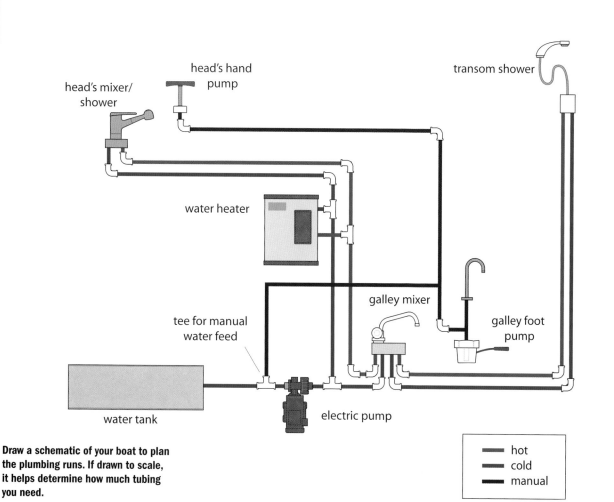

Draw a schematic of your boat to plan the plumbing runs. If drawn to scale, it helps determine how much tubing you need.

head's mixer/shower · head's hand pump · transom shower · water heater · galley mixer · tee for manual water feed · galley foot pump · water tank · electric pump

— hot
— cold
— manual

Illustration by Joseph Comeau

Plumbing

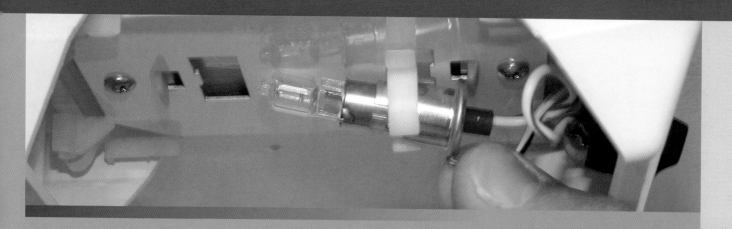

Electrics and Electronics

Many boaters will freely admit that they and their electrical systems are strangers to each other. Few things cause as much confusion as electrics. This is a shame, because a 12-volt electrical system is a pretty simple affair. Once you've learned the basics, you're set to take on projects like changing your lights and fitting extra electronics.

The group of electrical projects assembled here pretty much covers the spectrum, from how to make good connections (thus avoiding the single biggest cause of marine electrical problems) to troubleshooting common electrical malfunctions, to installing a shore-power system. (Note that while a competent amateur can easily install 120-volt AC shore power, AC power can kill; make sure all your work is to American Boat and Yacht Council standards.)

We also show you how to use a multimeter, and what's involved in rewiring a boat. To boost your confidence, Mark Corke talks you through a couple of easy projects that will be great building blocks.

I too was terrified of electrics until dwindling finances made me realize that I had no choice but to rewire my 48-foot cutter myself. A bit of reading gave me the confidence to tackle the job, and I was thrilled with the results and with my new skills. I hope this section does something similar for you.

Jim Haynie

Electrical Troubleshooting

When electrical equipment doesn't work, most people believe that it has a short circuit. Usually this is wrong. There are generally two types of electrical problems—a short and an open circuit (or open). Most problems involve an open, or a break, in a circuit that will not pass current. An open circuit can have either infinite resistance, because of loose or broken connections or damaged components, or excess resistance, because of corroded connections, undersized wire, or improper wiring. In both cases the symptom is the same—the unit in question stops working. This usually occurs when a switch is turned on. Sometimes an open circuit will operate intermittently for a while before it fails completely.

A short always leaves a much more observable, and often more dramatic,

calling card. With a short circuit, current goes through a path that has basically no resistance. In a 12-volt system this means that a great deal of current can be drawn from the battery. Normally the resistance, or load, in a properly operating circuit keeps excess current from leaving the source as it does its job. But when there is zero resistance a short will draw all the current that the battery can possibly deliver, often more current than the wires can safely handle.

That's why a short will probably produce one or more of the following symptoms: smoke, sparking, arcing, burning smells, fire, blown fuses, tripped circuit breakers, and, occasionally, loud noises. If a short occurs on a circuit without a fuse or breaker, it will very likely burn through a wire or even destroy a component. This will turn the short into an open circuit, and then it

won't work. So if you smell smoke or a pungent electrical odor, you can be reasonably certain that a short has occurred inside a device and the circuit is now open.

If this is the case, basic troubleshooting will usually pinpoint the problem. Most circuits on a boat have either

TOP TIP

Much of a boat's wiring is in dark and hard-to-reach places. Before you start trying to trace an electrical fault, have a few light sources ready to go. A regular flashlight is of little use when you need both hands free. A head flashlight is invaluable, as is one of those battery-powered portable fluorescent lights sold in camping and department stores.

one device in series with a switch or other control or several devices in parallel controlled by a single switch or breaker. A lighting circuit is a good example. Under a normal load, an open anywhere in a circuit will act like an infinite resistance in series; it will drop all the source voltage and prevent current from getting to a device.

Troubleshooting in practice

Suppose there is a problem in a 12-volt running-light circuit, and the light is not operating. Even though the test process does not involve AC or high-voltage circuits, make sure that all shore power is disconnected and turned off.

To determine what voltage is available and to see if the circuit is working properly, attach the black probe of a voltmeter to the ground side of the circuit (the negative battery terminal, or ground) and test each connection point with the red probe. A circuit's test points are shown below. With the black voltmeter lead on point B (the ground), begin to test the circuit by putting the red probe at point A. If you don't get a reading of 12 volts (minimum), you know there is a power-supply problem. Chances are good that nothing else in the boat is working either.

Then go to point C, the next positive connection point in the circuit. Less than 12 volts at point C means there is a bad connection or bad wiring between A and C. If you get 12 volts at point C but nothing at point D, you know that the switch is either turned off or is not working properly. If the switch is good, one of the two connections to the switch may be faulty. Less than 12 volts at point D means that a bad or corroded connection or switch is producing high, but not quite infinite, resistance and is dropping the voltage so much that the bulb isn't getting enough current to make it burn.

If you get 12 volts at point D, but the lights still won't work, moving the red probe to points E, G, and I will help locate the problem by showing which point is receiving 12 volts. If there is 12 volts at D and zero or less than 12 volts at any of the other points, you know that there is an open or bad connection in the circuit between point D and the point with the low reading.

Once you locate the defective section, use the ohms range of the meter to discover which connection or wire is open. Cut power to the circuit by disconnecting the positive battery terminal, and then test across each connection and wire for zero resistance. All wires,

connections, switches, fuses, breakers, and other conductors should have zero (or very nearly zero) ohms of resistance; those showing high resistance are likely open.

Here's how it works in practice. First take a measurement at points A and B (the positive and negative battery terminals). The meter shows 12.54 volts at point A (Photo 1); that is the source voltage from the battery.

If the circuit is working properly, all subsequent readings at points A, C, D, E, G, and I should indicate a little over 12 volts when the switch is turned on. The points on the ground side of the lights (B, F, H, and J) should read nearly zero.

These measurements are taken at the back of the electrical panel. Photo 2 shows a reading being taken at point C on the panel. This is actually a breaker (an automatically fused switch); all major circuits in recently built boats will have breakers.

Photo 3 shows the measurement at point C, where the battery wire connects to the switch. The black probe is clipped to the battery's negative terminal, and the red test probe is on the connection that carries current into the main breaker. This should be the same voltage that feeds into the breaker for the light circuit. The reading of 12.49 volts shows that the circuit is good up to this point. Photo 4 shows the red probe on point D, the other side of the running light circuit breaker. When the breaker is off there should be no voltage at this point; with the breaker on, a measurement of 12.44 volts means that the switch is working properly. The small drop of 0.1 volt is meaningless, but a drop of a full volt is a sign of a bad connection or a faulty breaker.

On smaller boats these measurements can sometimes be made by leaving the meter's black probe clipped to the negative battery terminal and then touching each test point with the red test probe. If not, you'll have to use a local ground point near the component being tested or extend the meter's negative test lead so that it can stay clipped to the negative battery terminal. I prefer the latter to avoid any chance of confusion if there are faults or opens on the ground side of the circuit.

If you've tested the breaker switch and points A, C, and D and find that all work properly, it's time to test the lamp fixtures. The first thing to do when testing an inoperable lamp (lamp L-2) is to open the fixture. When you touch points E, G, and I with the red probe, the voltmeter should show a little over 12 volts at each point. The voltage will vary slightly (no more than half a volt) because wire lengths from the panel to each light are different.

Look at the light fixture. The wire from the panel is first captured by a screw, and the current is carried through a spring connector to the bulb. Always test the screw first and then the metal base of the bulb. Photo 7 shows a reading of 12.36 volts at the screw with the switch on. This indicates that adequate current is reaching the fixture. Next put the red probe on the metal end (base) of the bulb. In this case it has only 10.94 volts (Photo 8). The significantly lower voltage indicates that the circuit is partially open, probably because of corrosion on the spring connector and on the bulb's metal base. Clean the bulb and the connector and retest. Clean the contacts with fine bronze wool and spray with electrical contact cleaner. There should be a full 12 volts running to the bulb.

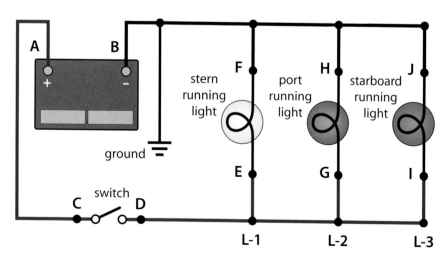

To test a circuit, attach the negative, or black, probe of a multimeter to the battery negative (B) and then move the positive (red) probe to the various points in the circuit. Photos 3, 4, 7, 9, and 10 refer to this figure.

Cleaning just the positive side can uncover another problem. Suppose the bulb remains unlit. You know you have a full 12 volts at point G; when you move the red probe to the connecting screw and the metal bulb base on the other side (point H and Photo 9), you would expect to see zero volts if the circuit was working and the switch was off. Since there is infinite resistance between the bulb and ground, a measurement of 12 volts at point H, the ground side of the bulb, indicates an open circuit. The way to fix it is to take out the bulb again and clean the upper, or ground, side of the bulb and the upper spring connector. When the bulb is replaced, the circuit will not be open and the bulb should burn brightly.

When the switch is on, a reading of 0.54 volt (nearly zero volts) on the ground side of the circuit (point H) is perfectly normal because a burning bulb requires 12 volts to work (its normal voltage drop). If all the lamps are burning properly, you should read almost zero volts when you put the red probe at any of the points (F, J, and B) on the ground side of the circuit.

To summarize

When you're troubleshooting a good circuit, all tests on the positive side should indicate 12 volts or more at points A, C, D, E, G, and I when the switch is turned on and nearly zero volts at points F, H, and J. If the lights still won't burn, put the red probe on points F, H, and J; the readings should be more than a volt.

Next, move the red probe to the connection points between these points and test them in sequence. Begin with the point that is farthest from the negative terminal and move toward it in sequence. At some point you will find that there is 12 volts on one side of a connector or wire (closest to the positive battery terminal) and zero volts on the other. If this happens you know that the circuit is open between those two points, because the resistance is dropping the voltage far more than any or all of the lights possibly could.

You can confirm this with a no-power resistance test, which involves disconnecting the power from the circuit and setting the meter to ohms. Place the meter's two probes on opposite sides of the item to be tested. If current is passing correctly, the meter will show zero or nearly zero ohms. A high reading indicates either an open or a connection that needs to be cleaned. Test the switch by turning it off and on during the test. The reading should be nearly zero ohms when the switch is on and infinite ohms when it is turned off.

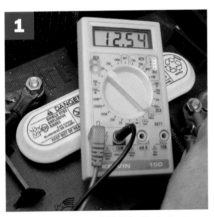

1. A meter reading of 12.54 volts indicates adequate supply.

2. The electrical panel. The second switch operates the running lights.

3. Point C has 12.49 volts; the wire to the panel is good.

4. Testing point D shows that the switch is good.

5. The white wire is an extension for the meter's black test lead made from regular lamp cord.

6. The author opens one of the light fixtures.

ELECTRICS AND ELECTRONICS

Photos by Jim Haynie

Extending the Multimeter Lead

You can buy a professionally made test lead to run back to the battery, but I find that an inexpensive 120-volt AC extension cord works just fine. I cut the ends off, pull the two wires completely apart, and strip off about ½" of insulation from all four ends. Then I splice the two lengths together and cover the splice with electrical tape. If you buy a 25' cord, you can make a 50' extension wire that should be long enough to troubleshoot a circuit on anything smaller than a megayacht.

A short length (about a foot) of wire with alligator clips on each end (available from an electronics store) makes it easy to clip the extension wire to the multimeter's test probe and then run the wire to the battery's negative terminal (see photo). Wrap the bare ends of the clip leads to keep them from touching grounded metal or other connection points.

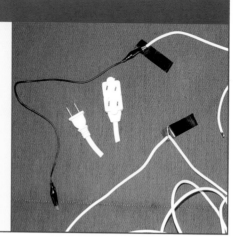

Use household extension cords to lengthen multimeter leads.

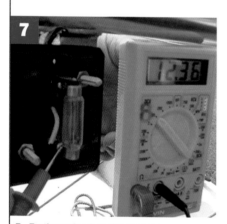

7. Testing point G at the connector screw.

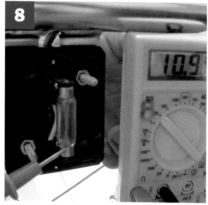

8. A reading of lower than 12 volts on the metal bulb base indicates a poor connection due to corrosion.

9. Testing point H. There should be nearly zero volts here.

10. Testing point H again when the circuit works properly shows nearly zero volts, as expected.

Mark Corke

Ted Hugger

Installing a Shore-Power System

It's beyond me why the first owner of my Pearson 323 didn't get the shore-power option when he purchased the boat back in 1979. We now keep the boat at a dock, and shore power is great for keeping the batteries fully charged, for powering the water heater (also plumbed through the trusty Atomic 4 engine, which means that we can also run the engine to heat water), and for using power tools or a vacuum cleaner. All this without running an extension cord down the dock.

The original owner wasn't alone; most small boats of this era didn't have shore-power systems. And many sys-tems that were installed may now be marginal at best, a safety hazard at worst, and certainly deserve to be rewired. Here is how I went about selecting and installing 30-amp shore-power service.

Unlike DC current, which is what powers your 12-volt system, AC current is inherently dangerous. If you have any doubt about your ability, hire a qualified marine electrician to do the job. Working on an AC system like the one I installed, however, is well within the reach of a boatowner with average mechanical skills and a willingness to carefully plan, research, and, most important, follow instructions. The American Boat & Yacht Council (ABYC) is an invaluable source for guidelines and specifications. Be sure to get a copy of *ABYC Standard E-11, AC & DC Electrical Systems on Boats*.

Equipment selection

There is a wide range of shore-power options now available, including 15-, 20-, and 30-amp 125-volt components, plus 50- and 100-amp 125/250-volt sys-tems. Most marinas in the United States provide specialized 30-amp three-blade twist-lock receptacles. Pre-assembled shore-power cables can be found most marine retail stores. The 30-amp yellow or white cables are made with #10 AWG three-conductor wire and come in standard lengths of 25 and 50 feet. Select the shortest cable that will meet your needs. Look for a cable set with a water-resistant molded vinyl cover that will help keep the elements out and protect the wire-to-plug connection points from being strained or twisted.

Shore-power inlets for a marine installation are designed to work with the unique three-pronged locking connectors found on standard 30-amp shore-power cables. These power inlets are permanently mounted on the exterior of the boat and are fitted with a hinged weather cover to protect the plug sockets from rain and salt spray when the cable is disconnected. These fittings are available in stainless steel or molded plastic. Buy only components that are UL Marine–listed, with the designation on the device itself.

IMPORTANT SAFETY NOTE

Before you work on a shore-power system, make sure to first disconnect the breaker on the dock, then shore-power cable, and finally any DC-to-AC inverter from its battery.

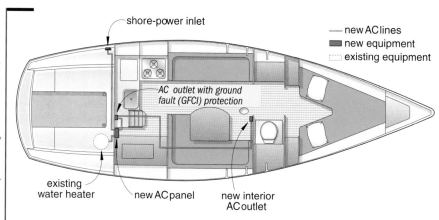

shore-power inlet

AC outlet with ground fault (GFCI) protection

existing water heater

new AC panel

new interior AC outlet

— new AC lines
■ new equipment
▯ existing equipment

Illustration by Kim Downing © 2004 Sail Publications

Making a detailed wiring diagram showing existing equipment and new components is an essential first step.

The three-conductor (triplex) wire used for marine AC applications consists of a hot (black) wire, a neutral (white) wire, and a grounding (green) wire in a white jacket. It should be tinned copper, Type 3 stranded wire that is least #16 AWG. The wiring from the 30-amp shore-power inlet to the panel must be at least #10 AWG.

AC distribution panel

The heart of the shore-power system is the AC distribution panel. A typical panel features a main shore-power disconnect breaker for turning the ship's AC system on and off, along with individual breakers for specific circuits. Panels are available in a variety of configurations and come with and without voltage and amperage meters. Nestor Quiros, sales engineer for Paneltronics, recommends selecting a panel with both voltage and amperage meters. "The voltage meter is useful in monitoring minimum system voltage, especially when motors are in the circuit, because a motor can be damaged in a low-voltage situation," he says. "And ammeters are helpful in monitoring system loads and ensuring that you do not exceed 30 amps."

Quiros also suggests allowing for future electrical needs when selecting a panel. If your present electrical system requires three breakers, which is what my boat needed (battery charger, water heater, and AC receptacle circuit), you should select a five- or six-breaker panel. The extra capacity gives you the ability to wire in additional circuits in the future without replacing or adding a panel.

Planning

First you must draw a basic wiring diagram of your boat, showing where each component will be placed and how the wires will be run. (Refer to the diagrams in ABYC Standard E-11 for guidance.) Carefully measure the length of the wire runs and note potential obstacles. Always lay out the system on paper first, before you buy any components or pick up a screwdriver.

Locate the shore-power inlet in a place where it won't foul sheets or dock lines. Also consider how the shore-power cable will run along the deck to the inlet when you are plugged in. Try to keep the cable out of high-traffic areas, and keep in mind that when it is plugged in the plug housing, the cable will extend outward several inches from the socket. I fitted mine on the outside forwardmost section of the cockpit coaming. This allows the cable to run along the cabintop, while keeping the side deck and cockpit clear.

Always keep the AC panel well separated from the DC system to avoid confusion. Most panels are not ignition-protected and should never be mounted in a machinery space where explosive fumes could collect. If the length of the wire running from the shore-power inlet to the AC panel is over 10 feet, an ap-

proved in-line fuse or breaker must be fitted as close as possible to the inlet.

Make a detailed diagram of how any old system is wired before removing it. Where possible, tie a messenger line to the end of each wire before you pull it out.

I installed my AC panel in the boat's saloon in a small vertical storage bin on the forward side of the engine-room bulkhead between the nav station and the galley. It is within 10 feet of the shore-power inlet on deck and provides easy access for the wire runs to the inlet, the battery charger, and the water heater. The panel controls are quite visible and are easy to reach and operate from this position, but are also protected and out of the way. The panel is mounted on the removable face of the bin, so that access is easy and simple.

When positioning my AC outlets, I carefully planned the wire runs, looking for a combination of the shortest distance and easiest installation access. Avoid placing outlets in areas subject to

Ted Hugger

The hole for the author's shore-power inlet has been cut into the coaming face, fastening holes have been drilled, and the power wire has been passed through the sealing gasket and connected to the inlet.

ABYC Standards

The American Boat & Yacht Council (ABYC) develops voluntary safety standards for the design, construction, equipage, maintenance, and repair of small craft. The guidelines laid out by ABYC are accepted by the industry as standards for safe applications in recreational boats. Rely on these standards when selecting equipment and installing electrical systems on your boat. American Boat & Yacht Council, 613 Third Street, Suite 10, Annapolis, MD 21403; 410-990-4460; www.abyc.com.

Other references

Boatowner's Mechanical and Electrical Manual, by Nigel Calder (International Marine/McGraw-Hill)

Sailboat Electrics Simplified, by Don Casey (International Marine/McGraw-Hill)

Installing a Shore-Power System

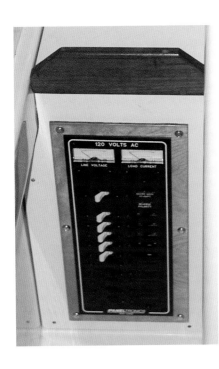

The author's AC distribution panel is mounted in a closed vertical bin on the engine-room bulkhead between the nav station and the galley. Never put panels that are not ignition-protected in machinery spaces.

water spills or splashes, or where appliance cords and plugs might become a safety hazard.

Because I use the DC system for general lighting, I did not rewire the boat with a full complement of AC lights and outlets. My plan called for installing one AC ground-fault circuit interrupter (GFCI) outlet in the galley and a second outlet on the aft side of the head bulkhead. Because the latter outlet is wired through the galley outlet and is protected by the galley outlet's GFCI circuitry, I can use a standard outlet here.

Panel installation

Using the template provided with the panel, mark off the area to be cut out of the surface where the panel will be mounted. Drill a hole in each corner of the area large enough to accommodate a saber-saw blade, then cut out the opening. Drill the pilot holes for the panel's mounting screws, but don't install it yet.

Shore-power inlet. Once you've chosen a location for the inlet, make sure you have adequate access behind the mounting surface and that there are no obstructions, such as wiring or plumbing in the immediate area. Refer to the inlet manufacturer's instructions for the correct hole diameter, and use a hole saw to cut the opening for the inlet.

Position the inlet in the hole, then mark and drill the four holes for the nuts and bolts that secure the inlet to the boat. Remove the inlet cover and—following the manufacturer's instructions—strip the end of each of the three connectors (black, white, and green) for the inlet wires. Slip the inlet's flexible gasket ring over the cable and attach each colored wire to the appropriate fittings on the inlet. Drop the wire through the hole into the boat, position the gasket and inlet, and insert the bolts from the outside. If your inlet has a backing cover (a good idea), slip the cover over the end of the wire from the inside of the boat and run it to the back of the inlet. Secure both the backing cover and the inlet with the bolts and nuts. Tighten the wire-retaining collar on the backing cover to secure the wire.

Run the wire to the AC panel, following the contours of the boat's interior; secure the wire at intervals no more than 18″ apart with nylon cable clamps or wire ties. Make sure the wire travels in straight runs with smart, tight curves. There should be no loose or hanging wiring. Wherever wire passes through a bulkhead, line the holes with rubber grommets or waterproof padding material to avoid chafe.

Attach the inlet wires to the AC panel by connecting the black (hot) wire to the hot terminal and the white (neutral) and green (safety ground) wires to the appropriate bus bars indicated in the panel manufacturer's instructions. Make all connections with ring terminals crimped to the wire ends. It's best to use waterproof ring terminals with adhesive shrink tubing attached to the connectors. If your ring connectors do not come with tubing, it can be purchased separately to seal connectors from the elements.

Branch circuits. Measure and cut each branch-circuit wire. Identify the

Powering Up a Pocket Inverter

Small pocket-size 50- to 300-watt inverters that convert 12-volt DC power to 120-volt AC power are typically used to power small AC appliances—computers, TV sets, VCRs, DVDs, cell-phone battery chargers, and the like. Even on large boats equipped with AC generator sets, a pocket inverter's relatively low cost and the fact that it makes almost no noise make it a useful option for powering modest short-duration AC loads.

But an inverter is unlikely to power a load much over 90 to 100 watts when using a standard cigarette-lighter plug. Any greater power demand causes the unit to shut down and sound its warning buzzer. In order to use the inverter's full output, it is necessary to cut the cigarette-lighter plug off the end of the power cord and connect it directly to a 12-volt source capable of supplying a current of 25 to 30 amps.

None of the ordinary two-pin low-voltage polarized plugs and sockets can deal with even a fraction of an inverter's current demand. Marinco's ConnectPro electric trolling-motor connector kit solves this problem.

The Marinco kit contains a three-prong plug, a bulkhead socket with a waterproof cover, and an adapter that allows #6 AWG wire to be connected to the socket in place of the #8 wire the socket normally requires. The plug is polarized and fits in the socket in only one position, ensuring that the

The Marinco plug (left) is ideally suited for connecting a small inverter to the boat's supply. The cigarette-lighter plug (center) and the low-voltage two-pin plug (right) are unable to deliver the full current to the unit.

correct DC polarity is always maintained when making the connection. The O-ring on the plug provides a water-resistant connection when inserted in the socket. The back end of the plug is enclosed in a soft molded-plastic jacket.

In my opinion, the ConnectPro is a superior connector for any plug-in 12-volt power requirements. Not only is the connector able to handle higher loads, but the connection itself is safer and more secure. Marinco/AFI; tel. 707-226-9600; www.marinco.com.
Chuck Husick

ends of each piece of wire with masking tape and a waterproof marker ("water heater" or "galley outlet"). You can also buy premarked adhesive wire markers from electrical supply stores. Leave 12" to 18" of extra wire at the panel to make it easier to remove the panel later for repairs or service. Run the wires from the AC panel to the outlet locations or appliances; secure all wires with nylon cable clamps or wire ties every 18" or less. Install outlet boxes and outlets following the instructions provided by the manufacturer, and make connections to any hard-wired appliances, such as a water heater. Be certain to provide chafe protection with a suitable clamp or bushing when wiring outlets or appliances.

Go back to the AC panel and connect each branch-circuit wire to the appropriate terminals on the panel using ring connectors and adhesive shrink tubing. Bundle the wires using nylon wire ties every few inches to organize the service area at the back of the panel. Finally, attach the descriptive labels for each circuit to the outside of the panel. Here's where you'll be glad you labeled each wire. Position the panel on the mounting surface with screws, taking care not to kink or bind the wiring behind the panel. Bear in mind that the ABYC requires that AC panels be installed in a suitable enclosure.

Interconnection to DC ground

The most important part of the installation will be the connection of the AC sys-

When working on electrical circuits, be methodical. Label each wire to make wiring and fault tracing easier and avoid mistakes. AC/DC circuits should be kept apart; use a separate distribution panel for each.

tem ground to the boat's DC system negative ground. Begin at the grounding bus bar that came with the AC panel and run a #8 or #10 AWG green wire to the DC negative ground connection on the engine (usually you'll find it on the starter). This wire, required under ABYC E-11, is there to ensure that a fault in the AC system that somehow gets into the DC system (such as a battery charger failure) cannot introduce hazardous levels of AC voltage into the water or create a shock hazard on board the boat.

Shore-power procedures

Once you've properly installed your shore-power system, maintaining and operating it is relatively simple. But be sure to connect and disconnect your shore-power cable in the proper sequence so as to avoid electrical shock and fire hazards.

- Turn off the main shore-power breaker on the boat's distribution panel.

Installing AC power on board makes it possible to use 110-volt appliances when your boat is connected to shore power (left). There are plenty of 110-volt power sockets in the saloon, allowing it to boast conveniences more akin to a house than a boat (right).

- Turn off the power breaker at the dockside receptacle.
- Connect the shore-power cable at the boat first, and then connect the cable to the dockside outlet. This way, if you accidentally drop the end of the cable into the water, the cable will not be carrying live current.
- Turn on the power breaker at the dockside receptacle.
- Turn on the main shore-power breaker on the boat's distribution panel.
- If the polarity-warning indicator is activated, immediately disconnect the cable. Because you've used the proper locking connector fittings in your shore-power system, the cause of any instance of reversed polarity will be in the marina's system. Contact the marina operator.
- To disconnect the shore power, reverse the procedure, and then close the shore-power inlet cover tightly.

If you do accidentally drop the shore-power cable into the water, turn off the power breaker at the dockside receptacle and disconnect the cable. Rinse the connector end of the cable in fresh water and allow it to dry thoroughly before reconnecting it to the shore-power system.

Once your shore power is plugged in and operational, monitor the voltage and amperage meters from time to time. Do not operate your AC system with current of less than 105 volts; appliances with motors can be damaged if operated below this level. Voltages above 125 to 130 volts can also cause damage to your system. Use the amperage meter to monitor your use of power. If you attempt to use more than 30 amps, the breaker should trip. By referring to your ammeter as you plug in or turn on AC appliances, you can be sure you're not inadvertently exceeding your system's capacity.

Nigel Calder

Troubleshooting Engine-Starting Problems

ELECTRICS AND ELECTRONICS

In a typical engine-starting circuit, a heavy cable runs from the battery's positive terminal through a battery isolation switch to the main terminal on a solenoid (see figure page 202). The solenoid is usually mounted on the engine's starter motor. A second large terminal on the solenoid is connected to the starter motor, which in turn is grounded to the engine block through its mount bolts. A heavy strap or cable connects the engine block to the battery's negative terminal. In rare instances an insulated ground is used on the starter motor, which then has its own ground cable.

Inside the solenoid are an electromagnet and a plunger. A separate circuit feeds positive battery current from the solenoid's main battery terminal through an ignition switch and back to the electromagnet. This circuit is grounded through the solenoid and starter-motor case or through its own ground wire. When the ignition switch is closed, the electromagnet is energized; it pulls down the plunger, which closes the main solenoid points, feeding power to the starter motor.

This basic circuit may be complicated by one or two refinements, such as a separate ignition switch and starter button, a neutral start switch to prevent engine cranking when in gear, and/or a second small solenoid-type switch (a relay) that is used to energize the main solenoid. The latter arrangement is common on large diesels where the current draw of the main solenoid is relatively high; it enables smaller wires to be used in the ignition circuit than would otherwise be needed.

Failure to crank

If the engine won't turn over, link a couple of cabin lights to the cranking battery (you may have to close an emergency paralleling switch and turn off the house battery isolation switch) and make a fresh attempt to crank the engine. The lights should dim, but stay lit. If the lights do not dim, no current is flowing through the starter. If the lights go out, the battery is dead or the starter is shorted. Check the battery first.

Assuming the battery is charged, two more quick tests will isolate problems in the starting circuit. Note that these will generate sparks; the engine room must be properly ventilated, especially if the boat has a gasoline engine. For the first test, use a screwdriver to jump out the main solenoid terminal and the smaller terminal, which has the wire coming from the ignition switch or relay. (If there are two small wires to the solenoid, one is likely to be a ground wire and it is the other one that goes back to the switch.) This will bypass the entire switch circuit, if the motor now cranks, the ignition switch or circuit is faulty (probably the

Starter-Motor Repairs

The most likely problem with a starter is a worn-out brush or one that is stuck in its holder. Remove the starter's rear housing to expose the brushes. If these have worn to the point where they are disappearing inside the brush holder, the brush spring may be hanging up on the brush holder, or not exerting pressure to maintain an effective brush contact with the commutator (the segmented copper bars on which the brushes ride).

In either case, if no spare brushes are available, you can slip a temporary spacer between the brush and its spring to increase spring pressure (the spacer need be no more than a piece of folded cardboard). You'll need to overhaul the starter as soon as possible.

If the brushes are in good shape, move the springs aside and slide the brushes in and out of their holders (by pulling gently on the attached wires) to make sure there is no binding. A tight brush can be sanded down by removing it and rubbing its sides across a piece of fine sandpaper (400-grit wet-and-dry) laid on a flat surface. Very little material will need to be removed.

If the brushes are fine, inspect for broken or burned wires and repair any you find. Polish an excessively dirty commutator with a piece of fine sandpaper, and clean the grooves between the copper bars by dragging the tip of a screwdriver across them (taking care not to scratch or burr the copper). Blow out accumulated carbon dust and/or spray the commutator with a proprietary electrical cleaner.

At the other end of the starter, inspect the pinion and its associated springs and clutch (if any) for mechanical damage or binding on the starter-motor shaft. Sometimes rusting will be interfering with the movement of the pinion; in this case a good shot of penetrating oil will free things up. Beyond this there isn't much that can be done while underway.

switch, especially if it operates with a key—in the marine environment these switches are often best replaced with a sturdy push-button switch).

If the starter has still not turned over, use the screwdriver to jump out the two main solenoid terminals (see photo). Hold the screwdriver firmly to the terminals. The full starting cur-

A beefy screwdriver blade shorted across the large contacts on the back of the starter solenoid will bypass the starter switch. Because the full current from the battery will flow through the blade, a firm grip is necessary to prevent arcing

rent will be flowing through its blade, so considerable arcing is likely. A big chunk may be melted out of the blade if it is not held firmly. Don't allow the screwdriver to touch the solenoid or starter-motor case, as this will create a dead short with considerable pyrotechnics.

If this test produces no arcing, there is no juice flowing to the solenoid. You need to check the battery isolation switch and all terminals. If arcing occurs but the starter doesn't spin, the starter is probably faulty. If the starter spins, the solenoid is defective.

In most circumstances, even if the starter spins it will still not crank the engine since the solenoid plunger must be operating to engage the starter-motor gear with the flywheel. However, if the problem is in the main solenoid points (the most likely bet), an engine can often be started by having one person hold the ignition switch on (this will engage the plunger) while another jumps out the main solenoid terminals (which will bypass the defective points). Jumping out the starting circuit at the solenoid at the same time as jumping the main solenoid terminals can produce the same effect.

Sluggish cranking

Assuming that the battery is well charged, if the starter attempts to spin but is sluggish, the problem is likely to be the result of voltage drop in the main starting circuit. Voltage drop occurs as a result of unwanted resistance. Even mi-

nuscule resistances that would cause no problems in other circuits can cause a major loss of performance. This is because of the high amperages needed to crank an engine; the greater the current flow through a circuit, the greater the impact of unwanted resistance. Resistance can arise as a result of undersized cables or poor connections. Both are easy to test for.

Try to crank for up to 10 seconds, but without starting the engine (to prevent this, simply close the throttle on a diesel; on a gasoline engine, disable the ignition). Immediately after this, feel all the terminals and cables in the primary starting circuit—the two battery terminals, the isolation-switch terminals, the two main solenoid terminals, the starter-motor terminals, the engine-ground strap terminal, and all intervening cables. Pay particular attention to the engine-ground strap and its terminals since this is a common source of problems. There is unwanted resistance at any point that is warm or hot to the touch. Terminals and connections need cleaning. Warm cables need to be replaced with larger cables.

Getting home

More-sophisticated tests can be made with a volt/ohm meter, but the above procedures will usually isolate a problem and you can frequently fix it on the spot.

If you can't, you should be able to jump out the offending circuit and get home to make repairs.

Mark Corke

Solenoid Repairs at Sea

If tests reveal faulty solenoid points, it is often possible to make at least a temporary repair. Most solenoids have a plastic cover held in place with a couple of screws. If the various cable attachment nuts and their cables are removed and the screws are undone, the cover can be pulled off. This needs to be done with care since there is likely to be a spring in here, which may fly out.

Removing the cover gives access to the contactor and points—the key pieces of metal that actually make the circuit to the starter motor. If these are pitted or burned, they can sometimes be reversed to expose a new surface. Otherwise, the contactor and points need to be sanded down to clean smooth metal. The unit is then reassembled.

Typical engine installation diagram.

Illustration by Jim Sollers/Don Casey's Complete Illustrated Sailboat Maintenance Manual

Charles J. Doane

A "No-Hole" Transducer

Most depthsounder transducers sold for use on sailboats these days are designed to be mounted through the hull. But some folks blanch at the idea of drilling huge holes in the bottoms of their boats. Others worry that the barely discernible bump on their hull will have barely discernible effects on their boatspeed. And if your hull has much deadrise, the transducer won't be pointing straight down. For in-hull installations, manufacturers usually recommend that the transducer be epoxied directly to the interior of the hull, but this does nothing to solve the deadrise problem, and you'll probably have to destroy the transducer if you want to remove it later.

Another option is to make an in-hull housing for the transducer. This will al-

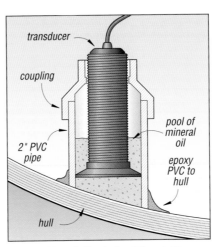

transducer

coupling

2" PVC pipe

pool of mineral oil

epoxy PVC to hull

hull

An in-hull installation is feasible only if your hull is solid laminate. Any voids or coring will interfere with the tranducer's signals.

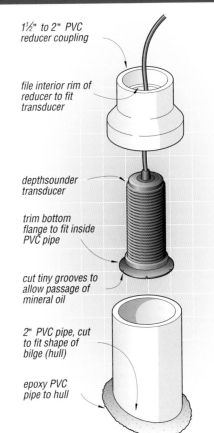

1½" to 2" PVC reducer coupling

file interior rim of reducer to fit transducer

depthsounder transducer

trim bottom flange to fit inside PVC pipe

cut tiny grooves to allow passage of mineral oil

2" PVC pipe, cut to fit shape of bilge (hull)

epoxy PVC pipe to hull

Illustrations by Kim Downing

low you to mount the transducer perpendicular to the ground, and you'll also be able to remove it easily for inspection or replacement. Building a housing is cheap and easy. All you need is a short length of 2″ PVC pipe and one 2″ × 1½″ PVC reducing coupling.

Step one is to trim the bottom flange of the transducer to fit inside the pipe. You want as close a fit as possible. Paint the rim of the pipe some bright color, then carefully center the face of the transducer flange over the pipe and press it against the wet paint. Let the paint dry, then grind the edge of the flange down to the circular line you've created. If you achieve a perfect fit, next use a hacksaw to cut three tiny grooves in the edge of the flange, equally spaced about its circumference. If the fit is less than perfect, you probably won't need the grooves.

Next cut an appropriate length of pipe at an angle that matches the deadrise angle in your bilge at the point where you want to mount the transducer. Then fit the transducer inside the reducing coupling. With most transducers you need only a bit of work with a file on the coupling's interior rim to get the transducer body to fit neatly into it. Assemble the three pieces—pipe, coupling, and transducer—as shown in the illustration, with the bottom face of the transducer just slightly above the angled bottom of the pipe. Once it is properly positioned, bond the transducer body to the coupling with plumber's epoxy putty.

Finally, mix up some epoxy filler and bond the pipe to the hull. Once the epoxy sets, pour in a little mineral oil—just enough to cover the transducer flange when it is inserted—and fit the transducer/coupling cap on the pipe.

As you push the transducer down into the pool of oil, the tiny grooves you cut will allow the excess oil to squeeze up above the flange. In a seaway this excess may slop around a bit, but the oil trapped below the flange will remain stable and bubble-free, providing a nice medium for the transducer's signals to travel through. The sounder's performance will be slightly impaired, but only in depths greater than 150 feet or so. Unless you are a dragger or an oceanographer, this shouldn't matter.

Mark Corke

Switching to LEDs

On the average small boat one of the largest, if not the largest, consumers of electrical power is lighting. Keeping all the lights on when you're tied up at the dock and connected to shore power is not a problem, but conserving power becomes a priority when you're sitting at anchor in some remote location. Preventing your batteries from going flat means either running the engine regularly or being stingy with the use of the interior lights.

The desire to conserve battery power while still making more-reasonable use of my lights prompted me to look at the alternatives to the standard incandescent bulbs. Not long ago, LEDs—light-emitting diodes—were very expensive and had a very low light output. This made them ideal for use as panel warning lights, but the amount of light they generated was unsuitable for general illumination.

LEDs are available in a variety of colors. Their low current draw makes them ideal for use on sailboats where there is a finite amount of battery power. Although they do get progressively weaker over time, their useful life span of 50,000 hours means they will never need replacing.

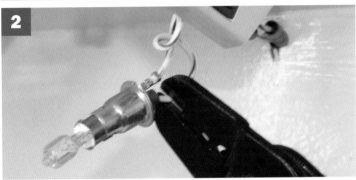

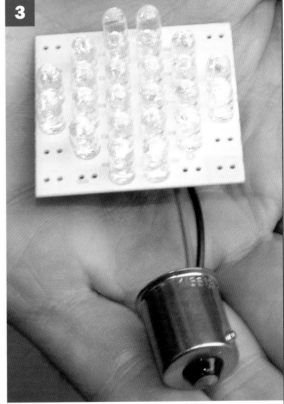

Recently, however, technology has advanced and prices have dropped. Second- and third-generation LEDs that have a very high light output and a cost that compares very favorably with that of a standard bulb are now available. Although still not suitable for every application, LEDs have distinct advantages over standard bulbs: they generate little or no heat, have an almost indefinite life span of about 50,000 hours, and—important for the average boatowner—use a tiny fraction of the power needed for a standard bulb.

A standard 10-watt bulb consumes almost 1 amp, and a 25-watt bulb consumes almost 2.5 amps. Thus, if you have several lights on in the cabin, the power drain is significant. The most frequently used lights on my boat are those on either side of the companionway, the one over the chart table, and the one above the stove. These lights had been fitted with 10-watt bulbs, and I changed them for a printed circuit board containing 24 super-bright LEDs. These yield a similar amount of light but use only 85 milliamps—about a tenth of the power consumption of the original bulbs. Each 24-LED array cost $15 plus shipping.

Changing the lights was easy. I did it using crimped connections. You can read about this in more detail on page 206.

1. Remove the cover of the light and pull out the existing bulb, noting which wire is the positive (normally red) and which is the ground (normally black).

2. Cut off the existing lamp holder, and then strip back the insulation on each of the wires about ⅜".

3. The LEDs came with a bayonet connector, so I cut this off and stripped back the insulation on the wires.

4. Make sure the wires are connected the right way round before you crimp the wires to the lighting fixture.

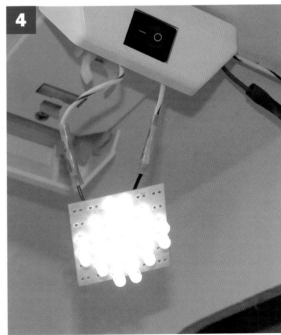

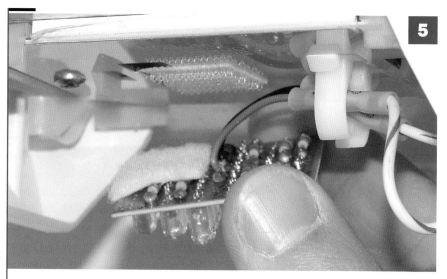

5. Use double-sided tape or Velcro to hold the printed circuit board in place. The heat output is so low that this is quite safe.

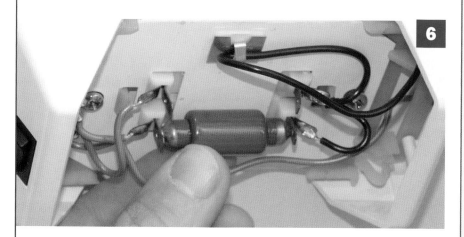

6

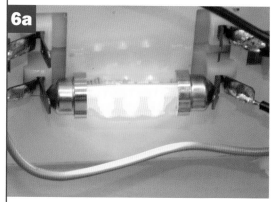

6a

6 & 6a. The light above the chart table also incorporates a red light for night use. I swapped the incandescent bulb for a bulb of similar overall dimensions containing six red LEDs (6a).

Other Options

Battery-powered lights

These battery-powered LED navigation lights could be used as a backup to the main lights or on a dinghy. Powered by four AA batteries, they meet all Coast Guard requirements for small boats less than 36 feet in length.

Bayonet

The simplest of all replacements is with this type of bayonet bulb; simply screw out the original and install this in its place. Although the initial cost of around $6 may seem high, it is a fit-and-forget item and, like the other LEDs, should never need replacing.

I picked up these LED lights in an automotive parts store. Meant for use on a trailer, they make an easy-to-install and high-output red light for chart table illumination.

RESOURCES

Super Bright LEDs
www.Superbrightleds.com
314-972-6200

West Marine
www.westmarine.com
800-262-8464

Switching to LEDs

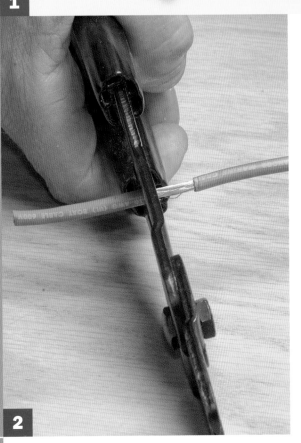

1

2

ELECTRICS AND ELECTRONICS

Mark Corke

Crimping Terminals

Electrical failures have got to be among the major headaches facing any boatowner. Unless you have a rowing vessel, chances are your boat will have some form of an electrical system. How complex it is depends on its size and systems. But one thing is certain: Unless the wiring is in tiptop condition, some part of it will fail, probably sooner rather than later.

Wiring on a boat leads a hard life; corrosion, vibration, and chafe all conspire to degrade an electrical system. Bad connections are to blame for many problems, and knowing how to make proper crimped terminals will avoid many of them. Simply twisting wires together or wrapping them around a terminal screw will not do. Proper crimped terminals are neat, allow the free movement of electricity, and prevent short circuits. Practice on some spare bits of cable until you are able to make perfect joints every time. Tug the connector to test the integrity of the completed joint; if there is any movement or if the terminal comes off, you need to cut back the cable and start over.

Terminals and wire come in a variety of sizes described as gauge; the smaller the number, the larger the cross-sectional gauge of the conductor and the greater its ability to carry electrical loads. Always use wire that is sized for the maximum amount of current it will have to handle. Use only tinned marine wire on a boat. Untinned wire is cheaper, but it is very susceptible to corrosion.

1. Cut back any suspect and ragged ends using either a pair of side cutters or the cutters built into the crimping tool. This is especially important if the wire is at all corroded. You can skip this step if you are using new wire from a drum.

2. Strip off the insulation from the wire, being careful to cut only the sheathing and not into the actual wire. Remove only sufficient insulation to allow the wire to be entered fully into the terminal with no bare wire visible.

✂ Tools you will need

- wire
- crimping terminals
- heat-shrink tubing the same color as the wire
- crimping pliers
- wire strippers
- heat gun

Photos by Mark Corke

3. If you have stripped back too much insulation, you'll have to cut the wire to correct length. The cutters in the ends of the crimping tool do work, but proper side cutters will avoid spreading the strands like this.

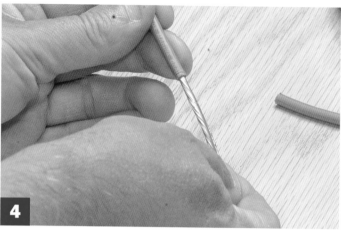

4. Grasp the wire in one hand, and with the other twist the strands together between thumb and forefinger. This binds the strands tightly, making it easier to push the end of the wire into the terminal.

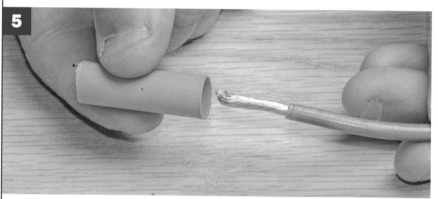

5. Cut a 1" length of heat-shrink tubing the same color as the wire's insulation and slip it onto the wire.

6. Slide a terminal connector onto the end of the wire. Ensure that it is pushed fully home, and then use the crimping pliers to squeeze it onto the wire. Note that the crimping jaws are color-coded. The colored dot on the jaws of the pliers must correspond to the color of the terminal.

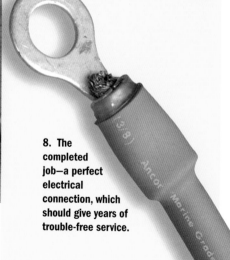

8. The completed job—a perfect electrical connection, which should give years of trouble-free service.

7. Slide the heat-shrink tubing up the wire so that it covers the crimp completely; use a hot-air gun or a match to shrink it in place. Do not apply too much heat; warm it just enough so it shrinks around the connector and wire.

Crimping Terminals

AC Power from an Inverter

Plug-in inverters are a cheap method of running a laptop on board.

Photos by Mark Corke

Inverters change the DC voltage available from a boat's battery into domestic 110-volt/60-Hz AC power. Modern inverters do this efficiently and almost silently. Over the past decade they have become much cheaper and more compact and the available power range has expanded.

Why have an inverter?

Small- to medium-sized inverters are usually purchased to power ordinary domestic tools and appliances, such as drills, small food processors, sewing machines, TVs, and AC rechargers for notebook computers—the sorts of devices that make life away from the marina easier or more enjoyable for the crew. Medium-sized inverters may also power small microwave ovens, breadmakers, and hair dryers. Inverters allow you to avoid the often high price and restricted selection of 12-volt equipment and to use gear that cannot run on 12-volt power.

As an alternative to a portable gasoline generator, an inverter has the attraction of being quiet, and can be activated at the flick of a switch. A larger inverter may serve as a cheap alternative to a genset, provided the main engine is running simultaneously.

Larger inverters may be professionally installed to complement gensets and shore power in sophisticated AC systems, providing flexibility and increased dependability. Larger inverters often have remote controls and graphic displays, and some can be monitored and controlled via a network. But the topic here is stand-alone 12-volt inverters.

Ratings

Equipment ratings. Inverters are rated by their ability to produce AC power, usually measured in watts (note that 1 horsepower equals 746 watts, and conversely 1 kilowatt equals 1.34 horse-

power). Before choosing an inverter you should read the specifications for the equipment you want to run from it. This is usually printed on the appliance in watts or possibly kilowatts (1 kW = 1,000 W). If just the current is specified, the nominal power (in watts) is current (in amps) × 110 (the voltage). If several appliances are to run simultaneously, their power draw can be added together but there are pitfalls to be aware of.

Inverter ratings. Inverters suitable for running a laptop or recharging a NiCad, NiMH, or LiIon battery pack may be rated at 100 watts or less; inverters with outputs above 2 kilowatts are powerful enough to run most domestic appliances or several smaller ones simultaneously. Even greater outputs are possible with 24-volt DC systems. Unless an engine is running, larger systems need big battery banks and powerful recharging capacity. Inverters in the 500–1,000-watt range are more easily supported, with and without the assistance of the engine.

Manufacturers usually publish a "continuous" power rating at a specified ambient temperature (it may be less in the tropics), plus a "maximum" or "pulse" rating, and perhaps also a "30-minute" or other medium-term rating. The continuous rating must safely exceed any long running requirements—say, for a computer or TV—but (unless a medium-term rating is also given) should

not be exceeded even by equipment that runs for only a few minutes at a time—food processors, microwave ovens, power tools, and the like.

Starting power

Peak, pulse, or maximum ratings are intended to cover only brief surges, but are important because many types of equipment need a lot more power to start than to run. An appliance's rating ignores the extra power needed to start it. There is usually no problem powering up electronics, but rotating machinery is a different matter. Even unloaded drills and vacuum cleaners may draw three times their "rated" current during startup. Motors that start under load, such as fridge compressors and watermakers, may draw eight times as much.

Even a laptop can be problematic—check its AC adapter rating, which includes battery recharging, and not the computer's own rating. Another example where a simple rating can be misleading is with microwave ovens, which tend to quote averaged power. It doesn't matter to a shore supply but may overload an inverter that, on face value, seems to be adequate.

A further complication is that many motors start with a high "lagging power factor," which means maximum current flows slightly after each alternating voltage peak. A high power factor may double the power drawn to provide the already high starting current; that's why some inverters incorporate automatic "power factor correction" circuits. The power drawn starting a nominal 300-watt drill may mean the inverter has to momentarily provide the equivalent of nearly a kilowatt—something many 400-watt continuous-rated inverters are unable to do. Overloading may trigger an inverter's thermal or current self-protection circuits. If these are inadequate, the inverter might pack up permanently.

Either way, failure to take starting loads into account is likely to result in disappointment, and since your equipments' real starting requirements are probably unknown, trying before you buy

is a prudent precaution. If this isn't practical, consult potential suppliers via e-mail with your list of equipment types and ratings and be guided by their opinions. Some inverters have maximum ratings three or more times their continuous rating; others may be only 30 percent higher. This difference tends to be associated with waveform.

Output waveform

If you looked at domestic AC electricity using an oscilloscope, you'd see something like (a) in the illustration. This sine-wave oscillation, repeated 60 times each second, is what AC equipment is designed to work with. Some inverters do produce sine-wave outputs, but for reasons of efficiency, overload capacity, and cost, many produce more angular waveforms. Most modern inverter outputs have compromise shapes that are referred to as trapezoidal, modified square, or modified sine waves.

Compatibility. Nearly all appliances will run on most "modified" waveforms, although microwave ovens, for example, may need longer cooking times. Some motors and transformers run a bit hotter, but most motor problems have to do with starting power, not waveform. Timers on washing machines and some appliances such as breadmakers may not work, but this is usually because they draw so little power that the inverter automatically switches to standby mode. Running a small light bulb simultaneously may prevent this.

It's a bit of a Catch-22 situation, because the sine wave certainly suits some equipment better. But for a given continuous rating, modified waveform inverters tend to be cheaper and lighter, providing much higher surge capacities for starting motors, acceptable voltage regulation (often using what is termed pulse-width modulation), and better efficiency.

Efficiency. Depending on the usage pattern and battery-recharging options, efficiency may be an important consideration. Modified-waveform inverters often reach peak efficiencies near 95 percent at fairly low loads and remain above 80 percent up to full load. Sine-wave outputs may peak at 90+ percent efficiency, but their efficiency tends to steadily decline above and below some optimum power output. All inverters are inefficient at very low loads, so if you run a laptop or fluorescent lighting for many hours, it makes sense to buy a small inverter specifically for such uses and get a bigger one for when more output is needed.

Interference. Modern lightweight inverters use high-frequency switch-mode

technology—the output waveform envelope is 60 Hz, but the DC is chopped and transformed at tens or even hundreds of kHz, rather than the 60 Hz of conventional line-frequency inverters. This allows the use of much smaller transformers and for the shape and power content of the waveform to be better regulated. A minor drawback is that smaller transformers contain less stored energy to help with motor starting. But a potentially more serious problem is that switch-mode inverters can generate strong electromagnetic interference (EMI). EMI causes problems with radios in particular, but may "get into" other onboard equipment. Susceptibility varies with brands and models, and a lot of modern equipment is fairly immune. But radio and TV receivers, by their very nature, cannot completely protect themselves from radiated EMI.

After installing any inverter, it is prudent to systematically check whether switching the inverter on and off affects the operation of other critical gear—especially autopilots. The check should be done with the inverter under load, but if interference is found, also check that it isn't the load source itself that's causing the interference.

Regulation

Inverter output voltage and frequency may vary with the load and state of battery charge, although most have crystal-oscillator frequency control and some claim better voltage regulation than the domestic supply. In practice, most marine gear is pretty tolerant of frequency variations and momentary low voltages. Overvoltage is more important because it may cause sudden failure or lead to progressive damage. Ordinary domestic surge or spike arresters are a worthwhile precaution with any AC-powered electronic equipment.

Isolation. Inverters used on boats should be isolated types, which means their transformer(s) isolate both AC output wires from the DC supply. This is for safety and helps to avoid electrolysis, but you must still treat inverter power with all the caution you would domestic AC. If you don't know whether an inverter is isolated or not, have it tested and consider installing an electrocution safety relay if it isn't isolated. It's worth noting that the test facility on these safety devices may not function unless the inverter is running with a load because, as an energy-saving feature, many inverters power down when unloaded.

Protection and monitoring. Switch-mode inverters are often soft-start (this avoids high starting currents) and may

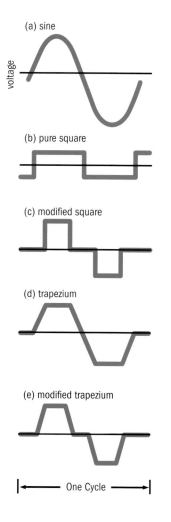

The waveform depends on the type of inverter. A is a pure sine wave from mains power. B–E are modified artificial sine waves from inverter power.

(a) sine

voltage

(b) pure square

(c) modified square

(d) trapezium

(e) modified trapezium

|← One Cycle →|

have various self-test features and protections. Power-on-demand and automatic-standby modes save some power when an appliance is being used only intermittently, but it's still worth switching the inverter off if it won't be needed soon. Other useful features are low-battery cutouts or warnings, high-input and/or -output voltage cutouts, reverse-polarity protection, and temperature- and/or current-overload cutouts. These features are usually microprocessor controlled, sometimes with remote control panels.

Feeding buzz

Running an engine simultaneously may be quite acceptable for uncommon or relatively brief loads, such as using a drill for repairs or running a microwave for 20 minutes. Provided the engine can generate enough 12-volt power to keep the battery up, there is no need to invest in batteries that are large enough to meet the associated inverter demand. But no one wants to run the main engine while watching a video, or to find the batteries flat afterward. So routine inverter use may require additional investment in batteries and perhaps in extra charging capacity, too.

Warren Miller

Troubleshooting with a Multimeter

When the galley dome lamp doesn't light, you check the obvious culprits. Is the battery switch energized? Is the circuit breaker on (or has a fuse blown)? You might try changing the light bulb. If there is still no light, what's the next step? Before you start tearing down the headliner, some simple troubleshooting tricks can help you isolate failures quickly.

Many electrical failures are the result of a short list of problems. The most common is an open circuit—that is, a circuit that is incomplete. Another cause can be a circuit with excessively high resistance created by a faulty or corroded connection. A short circuit is complete, but it bypasses the appliance and creates a potentially hazardous situation. Finally, individual components (switches, breakers, fuses, and so on) or even the appliance itself can be the culprits.

The multimeter

A good multimeter can be one of the most powerful and useful implements in your tool bag. Combined with a basic grasp of certain concepts and procedures, it is all you need for simple electrical trouble-shooting.

Let's start with the meter. There are two basic types of multimeters, analog and digital. While high-quality analog units can be found, digital models are easier to use and vastly more accurate than an inexpensive (and lesser-quality) analog meter. You can

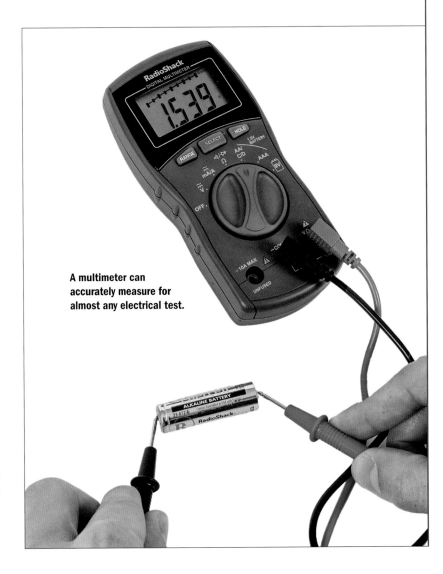

A multimeter can accurately measure for almost any electrical test.

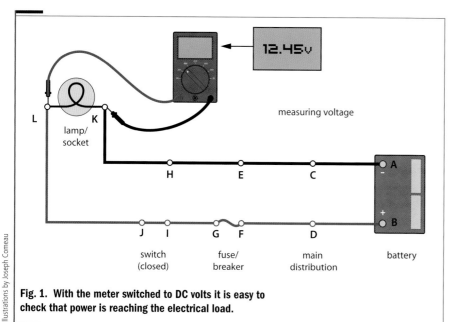

12.45v

measuring voltage

L — lamp/socket — K

H   E   C

A −

J   I   G   F   D

B +

switch (closed)   fuse/breaker   main distribution   battery

Fig. 1. With the meter switched to DC volts it is easy to check that power is reaching the electrical load.

expect to spend $50–$100 for an adequate digital unit. Avoid $15 specials. You will lose accuracy and protection circuitry. If you pride yourself on having high-quality tools, you can spend up to $300 on a meter.

Basic definitions

Voltage (volts) is the measurement of electrical potential. In the popular flowing-water analogy, voltage is akin to water pressure. If the voltage is too low, equipment will not work properly.

Resistance (ohms) is the measurement of obstruction of flow. In a water system, resistance varies with the size of the pipes. In an electrical system, likewise, the longer or smaller the wire, the greater the resistance. A poor or faulty connection will also increase resistance.

Amperage (amps) is the measurement of the rate of flow in an electrical circuit. With water, it's often measured in gallons or liters per hour or minute. A properly working electrical circuit with flowing current (amps) requires adequate potential (volts) and not too much resistance (ohms). This relationship is represented by Ohm's law: I (current) = V (voltage) divided by R (resistance in ohms). In other words, if you know any two variables, you can deduce the third.

Making measurements

This article covers simple low-voltage and resistance measurements. AC circuits and high-amperage DC appliances (like windlasses, inverters, alternators, and starters) require special testing pro-

cedures and equipment and are not covered in this discussion.

Since many boats have an electrical panel that handles both DC and AC distribution, it is imperative that you remove the AC shore-power cord from the boat inlet plug and turn off or isolate any onboard inverter before you begin. AC circuits can be lethal!

Before you start making measurements, you need to prepare an extended test lead. I like to use about 40′ of 12- or 10-AWG white wire. I choose white to avoid confusion when this lead is sometimes used as a positive or neg-

ative extension. You will also need an alligator-type clip for one end and a banana clip (mini plug or whatever your meter requires) at the other end.

Voltage is measured by making good contact between a ground and an uninsulated wire or connection. You will usually set your meter in the 20-volt-scale range. Resistance is measured by isolating (disconnecting) a section of wire or circuit and making good contact with both ends. Failure to completely isolate a circuit can damage your multimeter. Power should be off when checking resistance.

Amperage, or current strength, is measured by inserting the meter in series into a circuit. This requires breaking the circuit, connecting the meter to each broken end, and allowing the current to flow through the meter. Most small multimeters are either incapable of making current measurements or are limited to measuring less than 10 amps. Thus, for basic troubleshooting purposes, amperage measurements will not be discussed. Often amperage values are not needed or can be derived by Ohm's law or obtained from specifications.

Simple testing (voltage)

The most basic voltage test (and a useful baseline) is simply a measurement across the two posts of your battery. Usually this is 12.7 volts for a fully charged battery; remember the actual value for comparative purposes. Now return to the original example of the galley dome lamp. You are sure that the

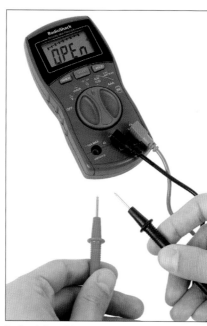

A circuit is said to be "open" when there is a break in the wiring.

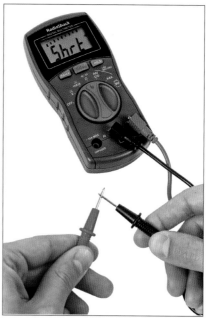

Some meters make it easy to tell when there is a short circuit.

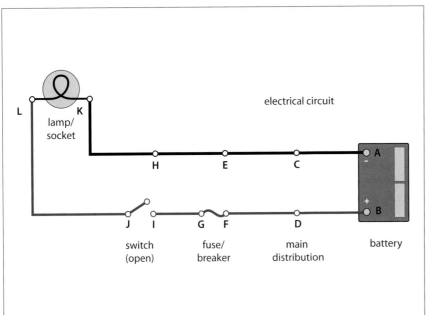

Fig. 2. An open circuit. With the switch open, the bulb will not light as the circuit is broken.

tioning), a voltage loss can be traced with the original tests.

Simple testing (resistance)

You can use the ohmmeter function on your multimeter for more detailed confirmation of the implications of your voltage measurements. When measuring the resistance of an actual portion of a circuit, and not the appliance itself, there are three possible scenarios. A specific resistance measurement usually indicates a point of unwanted resistance in the circuit (think of a blockage in a pipe). Zero (or very near zero) resistance indicates that the portion of the circuit is viable, and that current will flow when it is reconnected. Infinite resistance indicates that no current can flow, which implies an open circuit. To confirm an open circuit, first isolate the suspected section of circuit (disconnect both ends).

Let's take the positive leg of the circuit as an example. Disconnect at points B and L (Fig. 2). Using your extended lead, measure at each end of the partial circuit. A reading of infinite ohms confirms the open circuit. A specific ohm reading indicates a point of excessive resistance. A zero (or very near zero) reading implies a resistance-free portion of the circuit. Repeat this procedure on the negative leg, if necessary, and then gradually isolate individual portions of the circuit, down to the compo-

battery switch is on, the fuse or breaker is operational, the lamp switch is in the on position, and a good bulb is installed.

Start your troubleshooting routine by measuring the voltage at the bulb's wire connections (Fig. 1, points K and L). Any value near ship's voltage (perhaps 12.7 volts) indicates that the socket (or fixture) is faulty. Let's assume your voltage reading is zero. Plug your extended lead pin into the meter's negative receptacle. Attach the alligator clip to the negative battery post. Now probe the positive side of the lamp (points B to L). A zero volt reading indicates an open circuit on the positive side of the circuit.

If you measured something close to ship's voltage, now move your leads to the meter's positive receptacle and positive battery post and probe the negative side. Again, a zero volt reading indicates a problem on the negative side of the circuit. Now you can trace back down the suspect side (A to J, A to I, A to G, A to F, and A to D). The point at which you find full voltage is just before the point of failure.

Limitations of voltage measurements

Consider these measurements as a go/no-go test where you are looking for an open circuit (a broken wire, a faulty switch, or some other open connection). What happens when there is a partial connection, excessive corrosion, or some other point of high resistance? When no current is flowing, there will be

times when the modest current load imposed by a multimeter can't reveal a high-resistance fault downstream of the point in question.

Repeating these tests with a simple test light can quickly isolate the problem. The small load of the lamp can trip a point of resistance (the lamp glows dimly, showing partial ship's voltage). For example, if the galley lamp is glowing very dimly (as opposed to not func-

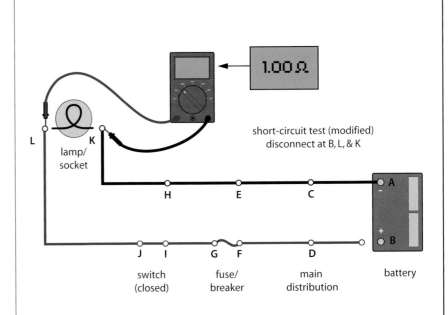

short-circuit test (modified)
disconnect at B, L, & K

Fig. 3. With the meter set to ohms track your way back down the circuit. Make sure that the power is off or you will blow the fuse in the multimeter.

nent level (switches, fuse holders, and breakers). Always remember to disconnect each portion before measuring.

Equipment checks

Let's say you have exonerated the entire circuit and the appliance in question still does not function. A resistance measurement across the input leads can reveal an internal failure in the equipment itself. Since some resistance is to be expected, depending on the appliance, consider this another go/no-go test. Infinite resistance indicates an internal open circuit. Zero resistance (in many but not all cases) implies an internal dead short.

Short circuits

A short is a portion of a circuit in which a hot lead (or connection) is directly connected to the ground return, thereby bypassing the load itself. Although a short circuit can manifest itself as a minor current leak, the most dangerous are dead-shorts. In a dead-short, extremely high current can flow through the circuit with disastrous results if the circuit has no breaker or fuse. This is the primary cause of catastrophic boat fires.

Note that "evidence" of a short circuit (a blown fuse or a melted wire) is rarely the point of the actual short. In the case of the blown fuse, a fire was prevented. In the case of a melted wire, the circuit was not adequately protected, and the short overloaded the point of highest resistance.

To test for dead-shorts, use the ohmmeter function on your multimeter. Physically disconnect the power lead from the circuit to be tested (Fig. 3, point B). Now disconnect the appliance and probe with the meter at both ends (K to L). Since the circuit is broken at point B, you should read infinite ohms (no short). A reading of zero ohms indicates a dead-short.

Once a dead-short has been confirmed, start breaking and then reconnecting connections farther from the meter, while noting the readings (leave the power and appliance disconnected). For instance, turn off the switch (I to J). If the zero ohms reading remains unchanged, then the short exists between J and L. If the reading increases to infinity, close the switch, and break the next connection (in this case, the fuse). If you get zero ohms, then the short is between I and G. If it still reads infinity, repeat the test until you find the culprit.

Your trusty multimeter, together with these simple tests, should make troubleshooting your electrical circuits an easy proposition.

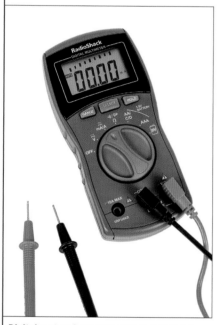

Digital meters have now almost completely replaced earlier analog types. Costing a few dollars, they are a useful addition to any toolkit.

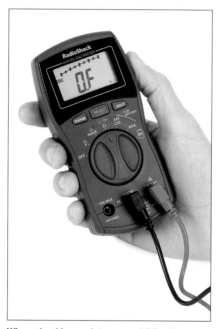

When checking resistance and DC voltage, make certain that the red lead is connected to the correct terminal on the meter.

Troubleshooting with a Multimeter

213

Installing Cockpit Speakers

Photos by Mark Corke

⏱ Approx. job time: 4 hours

📖 Skill level: Easy to moderate

✂ Tools you will need

- Sandpaper
- Compasses
- Ruler and pencil
- Jigsaw or RotoZip tool
- Drill
- Screwdriver
- Cable crimpers

Materials

- Speakers
- 16-gauge speaker wire
- Crimps
- Heat-shrink
- Small cable clips
- Epoxy

ELECTRICS AND ELECTRONICS

The sound of the sea swishing past the hull is often all the music you need when sailing, but there are times when being able to listen to your favorite tunes is a joy. Of course, I wouldn't think of playing loud music in a quiet anchorage; not all boatowners share my penchant for Puccini. But when the time is right and I'm alone at sea, I do want to be able to listen to some tunes.

I already had a stereo installed in the cabin, but the speakers were down below. If I turned up the volume so I could hear the music in the cockpit, there was a strong chance of deafening anyone belowdecks. The solution was to install a set of dedicated waterproof speakers in the cockpit. I had been thinking of this for some time, but couldn't decide on the best place for them. In the end, I opted to mount the speakers below the seats to port and starboard of the footwell.

1

2

214

3

1. Choose locations for the speakers. There will undoubtedly be some conflict between where you would like to site them and where you can actually put them. Remember that speakers contain high-powered magnets, so keep them well away from the compass and anything else that might be affected by a magnetic field.

2. Once you've chosen the locations, check and double-check your measurements—not only for symmetry port and starboard, but also to make sure nothing will foul any part of the installation after the holes are cut.

3. Speakers should come with a mounting template or at least a set of dimensions for the cutout, as mine did. After marking the center of the hole, I drew in the circle with a compass. Any errors in your siting should be apparent at this stage, so this is your last chance to correct matters.

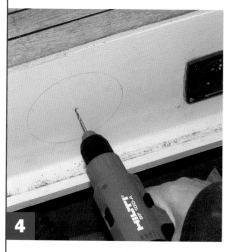

4

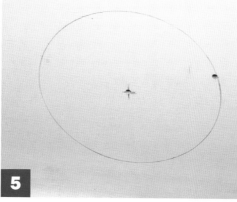

5

4. I wanted to use a RotoZip to cut out the speaker aperture, so first I drilled a $\frac{1}{16}$" hole for the trammel point in the center. If you're cutting the hole with a jigsaw or by hand, this step will not be necessary.

5. I also drilled a starting hole for the cut at a convenient point on the circumference of the circle. Drill this hole at a spot that will work best for you. Of course, you can always drill more than one hole if you need to.

6. After setting the correct radius on the trammel point, I inserted the cutter into the starter hole and moved the RotoZip gently around to cut out the hole. If you use a jigsaw, you'll have to follow the line by eye. Be careful and neat, but don't fuss too much; the speaker mounting flange will cover the hole.

6

Installing Cockpit Speakers

7

8

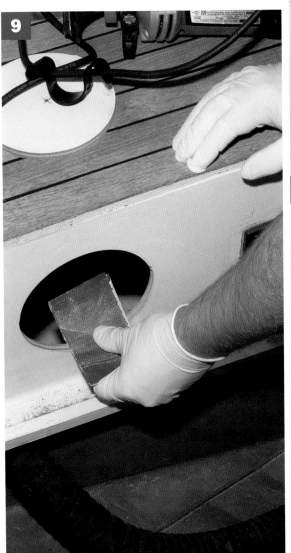

9

10

11

credit

7. Voilà. A perfect hole with a nice smooth cutout.

8. Now is a good time to get rid of the filings and dirt that have fallen into the cockpit and lockers. I like to keep things tidy as I go in order to avoid a major cleanup later.

9. Sand or file away any rough edges in the cutout. You can pat yourself on the back for taking care with the initial marking and cutting.

10. Seal the edges of the cutout with epoxy to keep moisture out. This is especially important if the structure you cut into is a cored laminate. If this is the case, cut back the core about 3/4" from the edge of the cutout and fill the void with thickened epoxy. This will not only preserve the integrity of the core, but will also provide something solid for the speaker mounting screws to bite into.

11. Allow at least 24 hours for the epoxy to cure. Then place the speaker in the cutout and drill holes for the mounting screws or bolts. My speakers came with self-tapping screws, but I discarded them and instead used small bolts and nuts, which are more secure.

12. Run the speaker wires back to the stereo unit, supporting them as necessary with suitable wire clips and ties. I used self-adhesive pads, which are easy to apply and do not require drilling and screwing. If you have to splice on more wire, use 16-gauge speaker wire and connect it with crimp connectors covered with heat-shrink to keep out moisture.

13. The completed job with the speakers permanently mounted in place and the covers snapped on. Note that all parts of these outdoor speakers are plastic and are water and UV resistant. Speakers intended for indoor use have paper parts that would be ruined if they got wet.

TOP TIP

Speakers normally use two-part red-and-black wiring. Pay careful attention to which wire connects to which connection, both on the speaker and on the back of the stereo unit. Most speaker wire has a tracer color on one line to make identification easier. If you connect the wires the wrong way around, the speaker will still work but will be out of phase; the sound will not be as good as it should be.

Mark Corke

Photo by Mark Corke

Rewiring Your Boat

Although our *BoatWorks* Bailout project boat, *Castaway*, is generally in good shape, it soon became apparent that the electrical system was one of the things in need of an upgrade. Wires seemed to run everywhere like spaghetti, and trying to figure out what switch powered which circuit was strictly a hit-or-miss affair. When the boat was built, in the 1970s, electrical systems were simpler. There was much less electronic equipment available, and onboard power demands were much lower. As often happens in these cases, as equipment was slowly added over the years, new electrical connections were more or less improvised. Also, the existing wiring on *Castaway* was not up to current ABYC standards and did not look especially safe. We didn't check it, but my guess is that there was an awful lot of stray current and power leakage.

Because we planned to install some new electronics as well as a power-hungry windlass, it made sense to completely replace all the wiring in the boat. With time at a premium, we called in the experts from Jack Rabbit Marine. It took Peter James and Kim Wicker four full days to strip out and rewire the boat. This may seem like a long time, but these days, even on a modest 34-foot

boat like *Castaway*, there is normally a lot of wiring to contend with. This is not to say that rewiring a boat is out of the question for a competent DIY owner. I, for one, am not the most conversant with electrics, but I have wired up several boats, and it is true that confidence increases with experience. At first glance the job can seem overwhelming, but once you're over the initial shock, the waters start to clear. If you focus on wiring up each circuit one by one, it soon starts to look more manageable.

Getting started

The first thing to do before breaking out the wire cutters and soldering iron is to sit down with a pencil and paper and draw a rough outline of your boat, including bulkheads and other immovable structural parts. Make the drawing large enough so it won't get cluttered as you add things to it. Next, sketch in the approximate locations of the various electronics and electrical components you have onboard. When you are finished, the sketch should look something like the one shown in Figure 1. Then you need to refine each circuit diagram. Draw each individual circuit neatly, and carefully label the wires from the panel to each component and back to the panel.

You can see how this is done in Figure 2. I like to create separate drawings for all but the simplest of circuits and the store the lot in a dedicated folder for later reference. This comes in handy should I later need to do some fault tracing or want to add more equipment.

Once you've identified each circuit, what needs to be connected to it, and where it is going to run, work can start in earnest. It is very tempting to just rip out all the old wiring, but I would caution against this unless you're certain of your capabilities. I prefer to rewire a boat in stages. For example, first remove all the wiring for the forward cabin and replace it, then do the main cabin, then the nav station, and so on. Again, the job will seem more manageable if you do it in small chunks rather than all in one go.

Most, if not all, of the wiring will likely terminate at the distribution panel, so this is where things normally start to get confusing. It is imperative that you mark each end of every cable, not only to help with the wiring, but also to make fault tracing easier should it be necessary later. The best way to do this is with shrink-on wire numbering rings. Work out some numeric identification code, then use this code to label the wiring diagrams you drew up earlier.

Distribution

As we did on *Castaway*, it is quite likely you will want to install a new DC distribution panel. On older boats you'll usually find there are insufficient circuits on the old panel to properly power all the equipment onboard. This was certainly the case with *Castaway*. The panel had too many cables tacked onto the back of it, so replacing it was an easy decision. In its place we installed a new panel from Blue Sea that has room for all current and future circuits and also includes an ammeter and voltmeter for monitoring battery condition.

Unlike *Castaway*'s old panel, which had old-fashioned fuses, the new Blue Sea panel has more-modern circuit breakers. You must keep in mind that any fuse or circuit breaker on a panel is there to protect the circuit and not the equipment it is powering. For example, though a distribution panel may have a 5-amp breaker on each circuit, each individual piece of equipment will likely draw much less power than this and therefore must be protected by its own fuse or breaker (although in practice this is seldom done); you'll find the recommended size either on the equipment itself or in the owner's manual that came with it. (Note, too, that we also installed a new AC distribution panel on *Castaway*.)

A major part of any rewiring job is actually running all the wires. If some of the existing wiring still looks good, it is tempting to reuse it, but this is a bad idea. Wires on boats live in a harsh environment; salt, moisture, and vibration all conspire to break down even the best installation over time. Wires used on boats should be UL 1426, as speci-

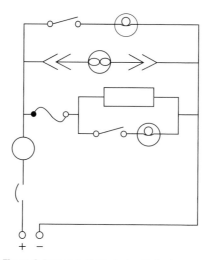

Figure 2. Typical individual circuit diagram.

fied by Underwriters Laboratories, and each separate strand of wiring should be individually tinned to prevent corrosion.

As mentioned, when running wires you should label each one to show what it connects to. It is also a good idea to use color coding. See the table for the ABYC's recommendations.

Another important thing to consider, is, of course, the size of the wire. Wire is measured in cross section—the greater the wire diameter, the more able it is to carry a given load. Wire that is too thin will get hot and overheat, which could easily lead to a fire onboard. Even if it doesn't overheat, undersized wire creates unwanted resistance that will lead to a voltage drop in the circuit. The length of the wiring run also has a bearing on voltage drop; the longer the round trip from the power source to the component and back again, the thicker

the wire needs to be. There is a formula for determining this, but I prefer the table shown on the next page. Of course, the crew from Jack Rabbit Marine have done so much of this before they can pick up the correct-size wire almost by instinct.

COLOR	USE
Red	General DC positive conductor
Yellow	Preferred DC negative conductor
Black	Alternative DC negative conductor
Green	General DC grounding conductor
Dark blue	Cabin and instrument lights
Dark gray	Navigation lights
Brown	Bilgepumps
Brown/ yellow stripe	Bilge blower
Orange	Accessory feed
Purple	Ignition
Yellow/ red stripe	Starting circuit
Light blue	Oil pressure
Tan	Water temp
Pink	Fuel gauge

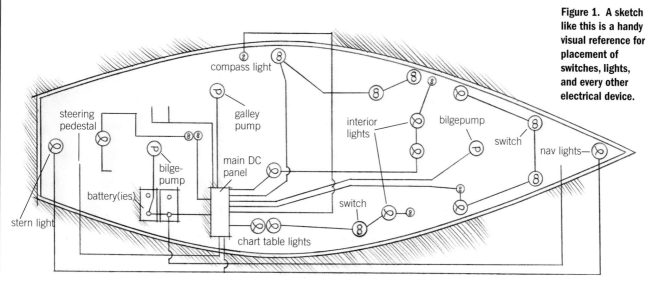

Figure 1. A sketch like this is a handy visual reference for placement of switches, lights, and every other electrical device.

compass light

steering pedestal

galley pump

interior lights

bilgepump

switch

nav lights

main DC panel

bilge-pump

switch

battery(ies)

switch

stern light

chart table lights

Illustrations by Rachel French (top); Steve Sanford (bottom)

Sizing Wires

MINIMUM AWG WIRE SIZE

CURRENT DRAW IN AMPS	10	20	30	40	60	80	100
1	16	16	16	16	16	14	14
2	16	16	16	14	14	12	10
5	16	14	12	10	10	8	6
10	14	10	10	8	6	6	4
15	12	10	8	6	6	4	2
20	10	8	6	6	4	2	2
25	10	6	6	4	2	2	1

ROUND-TRIP LENGTH OF CONDUCTOR IN FEET

The numbers in the table refer to the minimum AWG (American Wire Gauge) wire size; if in doubt, always go one size larger. Note that the smaller the number, the larger the cross-sectional dimension.

1. A complete rewiring job requires some serious wire. Kim Wicker and Peter James prepare to start rewiring *Castaway*. The heavy-duty cables in the foreground are for the batteries and windlass connections, which in this case are 4AWG. Note, too, that ABYC now recommends the use of yellow for DC negative returns to differentiate them from AC negative circuits.

2. The back of the original DC distribution panel was not as neat as it could be, but more important, there was insufficient capacity for all the new electrical demands.

3. The back of the new Blue Sea panel is much larger than the original and can accommodate all of *Castaway*'s equipment without having too many items connected to each breaker. To the left of each bank of breakers are the bus bars for connecting the negative returns.

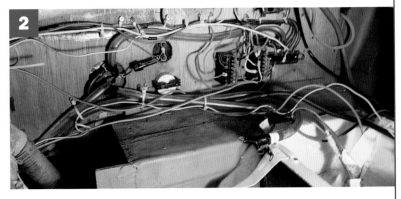

ELECTRICS AND ELECTRONICS

4. With the new panel installed, work can start on connecting up the new wires as they are pulled through their runs. These are later clipped back to the woodwork with cable ties to tidy them up and to ensure that no undue strain is placed on the connections themselves.

5. Terminate each cable with a ring terminal; wrapping bare wire around a screw is just asking for trouble. A set of ratcheting crimpers makes for perfect connections. Note the markings on the jaws denote the wire gauge, which in this case is 10AWG.

6. In the old days all you needed were a few circuits for nav lights and little else.

7. The new panels. The lower, larger DC panel replaces the old fused panel and has room for three more breakers, should they ever be required. It also incorporates an ammeter and voltmeter for monitoring battery condition. The smaller panel at the top is the new AC panel.

8. Experts always make lists! Making a note of which circuits are which avoids confusion and ensures things go smoothly. Number tags on the cables make identification and fault finding easier.

FURTHER READING

Sailboat Electrics Simplified
by Don Casey (International Marine/McGraw-Hill)

The 12-Volt Bible for Boats
by Miner Brotherton (International Marine/McGraw-Hill)

More Improvement Projects

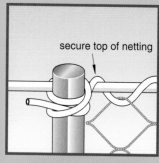

secure top of netting

Repairs and maintenance—that's the stuff you *have* to do. Improvement projects are altogether much more fun, in part because they are purely optional and in part because they will either increase your enjoyment of your boat or improve the way it functions. Usually, these two go hand in hand.

There is, literally, almost no end to the number and variety of such projects. They don't need to be as ambitious as replacing a hatch. I had fun thinking up the ideal lifeline system and then installing it on our project boat. One of our readers worked out the best way to place safety netting around her boat to keep her toddlers on board. Another got a great deal of satisfaction from making some organizers for the cabin of his boat.

Being clear about what you're going to do and what skills, resources, and time you will need to do it is the key to success in any project. The ones we've included here have all been carried out by enthusiastic amateurs, usually on their own boats, and are well within the capability of any reasonably handy boatowner.

Lifeline Replacement

Photos by Peter Nielsen

Right up to the moment my friend fell overboard, I'd never thought about lifelines much. They were just there, a fact of onboard life, like the grabrails on the coachroof or the mooring cleats or the alloy toerail, and certainly worthy of no more thought than those other taken-for-granted items.

We all saw it happen. JJ was leaning outboard, knees braced against the top lifeline, arms outstretched as he guided the dinghy along the topsides. Without warning the wire gave way and he was gone, one deck shoe flying off as he somersaulted toward the frigid water. Instead of the expected splash, though, there was a thud followed by a string of curses. He'd landed headfirst in the dinghy.

We were still laughing about it ten minutes later as we examined the broken lifeline. It had snapped where it passed through one of the stanchions. Rust bleeding from cracks in the plastic sheathing told the story; under its pro-

tective covering, the stainless-steel wire had slowly corroded until only a few bright strands remained in the center. It could have gone at any time. Had it happened at sea during the rough passage we'd just completed, it would have been no laughing matter.

The boat was 12 years old, and the lifelines were obviously original. It was ironic that she had recently been equipped with state-of-the-art safety equipment—brand-new liferaft, new life rings and lights, man-overboard retrieval gear—but that no thought (let alone money) had been expended on something that could prevent the need to use this expensive MOB gear.

When we bought our "new" boat last year, I saw at a glance that the plastic-sheathed lifelines were junk. Not only were they too thin—she had been used only for racing, so I guess the wire was underspecified to save a few pounds—but they were all-too-obviously old and dangerously corroded.

Replacing them was but one item in

a long list of jobs that needed doing, and since they didn't interfere with the actual sailing of the boat, I just warned anyone who came on board not to trust them and left the project for autumn.

You can either have new lifelines made by a rigger or you can do it yourself. Alongside the machine-swage fittings designed for professional use, Johnson Marine and Hayn Marine offer

---

🕑 **Approx. job time: 8 hours**

📖 **Skill level: Easy**

✂ **Tools you will need**

- Cable cutter
- Sharp utility knife
- Pencil
- Tape measure
- Bolt-type or lever-type lifeline tool

Note: Swage-It tools must not be used.

fittings with hand-crimp terminals suitable for the do-it-yourselfer. How hard could it be? I decided to find out.

First I measured the lifelines to work out how much wire to order. Then I had to decide what kind of wire I wanted. PVC-coated 7 × 7 stainless-steel wire is by the far the most popular choice. You can get it in ⅛″ or 3⁄16″ thicknesses—with the coating the 3⁄16″ wire actually measures 5⁄16″. It looks good, and it's easy on hands and ropes. The drawback is, of course, the potential for invisible corrosion if water finds its way under the sheathing—as it inevitably will.

Uncoated 1 × 19 wire—like that used on shrouds—is increasingly seen on new boats and older ones that have been imported from Europe. It has a nice clean look and is much less likely to corrode than coated wire. On the minus side, it is harder on hands, fingers, and ropes. Uncoated 7 × 7 wire would be even worse, and its rough finish would attract dirt.

A third option, in increasingly common use on high-end racing boats, is to use low-stretch ¼″ braided rope instead of wire. Modern high-end rope can easily match and in some cases exceed the breaking strength of coated wire, and the finished job would look good, too. However, it is more expensive than wire, I doubt it would last as long, and the ends would need to be spliced. Since Ostara's new lifelines ended up with 24 terminations instead of the original 12, this would have entailed either a solid weekend of splicing at home or paying someone to do it for me.

In the end I chose covered 3⁄16″ 7 × 7 wire for its user-friendliness. If I'd been off to the tropics or on the high seas, I'd have chosen uncovered 1 × 19, purely for peace of mind. Even though the covered wire won't last as long, it will be good for at least five years and maybe as long as ten.

The job was spread out over a couple of weekends, as winter weather allowed, but I estimate it took me a leisurely 8 hours in total, including installing the stanchions and braces. It was time well spent—the new lifelines and stanchions look great and have greatly improved my peace of mind.

Rethinking the System

The need to replace the lifeline wires turned into an opportunity to upgrade the entire system. Ostara is a Norlin 34, built to the IOR rule in 1973 as a racer/cruiser. She has four stanchions on each side and was not intended to have lifeline gates. Since we often sail with small children and elderly relatives, we wanted to be able to drop part of the lifelines in order to get guests on and off the boat more easily. There was also a safety aspect; it would be useful to be able to clear a section of lifeline out of the way in a man-overboard situation, rather than trying to lift a casualty over the lifelines.

The previous owner had split the starboard lifelines and added a pair of pelican hooks at the third stanchion, thereby fashioning a rather crude gate. When the hooks were released, the lifelines went slack all the way to the bow. This was obviously a safety hazard in itself.

Installing a standard 2'-wide lifeline gate on each side would have meant adding new stanchion bases between the existing third and fourth stanchions. This would have looked odd and have involved a great deal more work than the solution we eventually adopted—adding bolt-on braces to the third and fourth stanchions on each side. These added strength and provided resistance to the pull of tensioned lifelines from the bow and stern pulpits. We then added pelican hooks and proper lifeline gate fittings. These gates are much wider than is usual, but they let us transfer sails and other awkward loads (like in-laws!) to and from the launch or dinghy very easily.

Ostara's hull was molded in two pieces and has a hefty inward-turned flange at the sheerline to which a solid fiberglass lip at the deck edge is secured. The outer 4" of the deck edge have no core material, so there was no need to

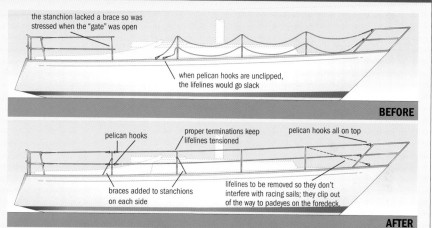

the stanchion lacked a brace so was stressed when the "gate" was open

when pelican hooks are unclipped, the lifelines would go slack

BEFORE

pelican hooks

proper terminations keep lifelines tensioned

pelican hooks all on top

braces added to stanchions on each side

lifelines to be removed so they don't interfere with racing sails; they clip out of the way to padeyes on the foredeck

AFTER

Illustration by Kim Downing

I replaced the old tapered stanchions with straight ones—they hurt less when you fall on them.

seal off the edges of the holes that I drilled for the stanchion braces. On many other boats this part of the process will take longer as it's imperative to ensure that water can't find its way into the core.

The four stanchions to which the braces would bolt were all bent, scuffed, and rusty to varying degrees, so I installed new ones. The contrast between the shiny new stanchions and the remaining old ones was so great that I had no alternative but to replace them as well.

Finally, I harbor delusions of doing some PHRF racing—well, the boat came with a set of good racing sails, so it would be a shame not to use them—so when it was suggested that fitting pelican hooks to the upper lifelines at the pulpit would allow me to clip them out of the way to allow a big genoa to set better, I thought, Why not? If nothing else, it should psych out the opposition. The racing #1 genoa's sheeting point is far enough aft that its sheet rubs on the top lifeline when it is eased, so I'll place clear plastic tubing over the wires to protect them. I'll also be able to unclip the top lifeline at the gate if the need arises.

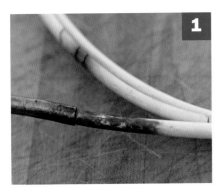

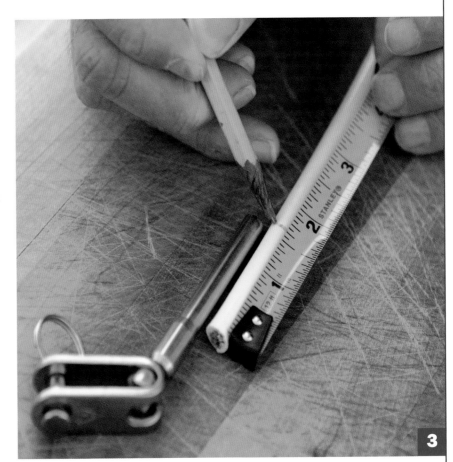

1. Remove the old lifelines. You can see how rusty the old ⅛" wire has become.

2. Johnson Marine sells two types of hand-crimping tools. The small bolt-type tool was $35, while the big lever-action tool was $215.

3. Time to fit the first terminal. Hold the wire against the terminal and mark the cover at 1¾".

4. Cut the cover carefully and peel it off. This is the most tedious part of the exercise. By the time I'd done this 24 times, I was regretting not having chosen uncovered wire.

5. Place the terminal into the proper die for the cable thickness and tighten the bolt just enough to grip the fitting. Insert the bare wire, making sure the cover is snug against the end of the terminal.

6. Tighten the bolts alternately until the die blocks are hard up against each other.

7. Loosen the bolts and move the terminal ⅛" for the next crimp. Repeat step 6 until you have a total of five crimps.

A Question of Strength

Johnson Marine says a properly installed ³⁄₁₆" hand-crimp terminal will handle a straight-line pull of 2,500 pounds—that's around 65 percent of the wire's breaking strain. This drops to 1,200 pounds for a ⅛" terminal. The company stresses that you shouldn't use hand-crimped fittings for standing rigging.

It is rare for a lifeline terminal or the wire itself to fail, unless the wire has corroded. When a person falls to leeward and is caught by the lifelines, the stanchions are far more likely to bend than the wire is to break. A heavy weight coming suddenly onto the lifelines is also going to place a lot of stress on the lifeline gate fittings and on the bow and stern pulpits, so it is not wise to skimp on the hardware you buy.

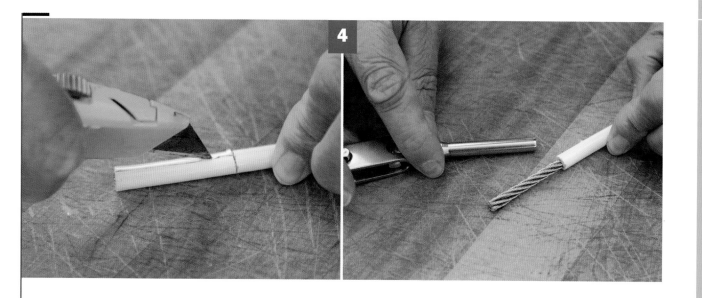

Inspecting Lifelines

Just as a missing 50-cent cotter pin can bring down a mast, an insignificant fitting in a lifeline system could lead to a tragedy. You should inspect your lifelines regularly. Ensure that all circular pins are in place and that the lock nuts on turnbuckles haven't come loose and allowed the barrel to unwind itself. Use a magnifying glass to check for cracks in the swage or crimp terminals. Inspect covered wire closely for cracks in the coating that may have let salt water in. Usually these occur where the cable passes through a stanchion. Rust marks where the wire enters the terminal are a sure sign of trouble.

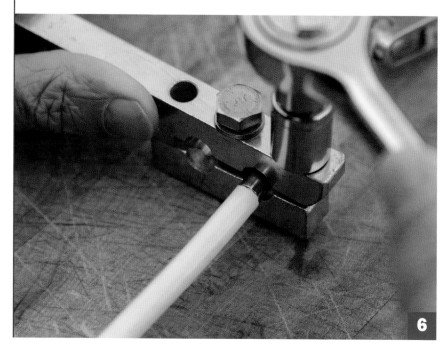

8. Adjust the terminal so it is two-thirds fully extended before you attach it to the pulpit (or whatever fitting you want to start with). Do the same with the terminal that will be at the other end of the wire. Then thread the cable through the eyes of the intervening stanchions and pull it and the fitting toward each other. This is a good time to have a helper. Only when the cable is taut should you mark it for the cuts. It is almost inevitable that you will make at least one mistake; luckily, you can buy new threaded studs rather than having to replace the entire terminal.

9. I bought a $20 bolt cutter that snipped through the coated wire with ease. Bare stainless wire would have been harder to cut.

Repeat steps 3 through 9 as required.

10. The bolt-action tool works well, but it would have taken forever to complete 24 terminations, so I borrowed a Johnson lever-action tool. You need only three crimps with one of these; it takes about a minute to do each terminal.

11. I used a Johnson caliper tool to measure each crimp, as shown.

12. Look at the contrast between the new gate fittings (left) and the old ones (right).

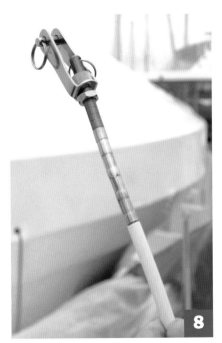

8

9

10

What It Costs

Coated ³⁄₁₆" cable ⁵⁄₁₆" (diameter) costs between $1 and $1.90 a foot; shop around for the best deal. The same goes for uncoated 1 × 19 cable. I needed 140' of coated ³⁄₁₆" cable for *Ostara*.

You may well be able to reuse the fittings from your old lifelines and simply replace the crimp terminals at a cost of around $10 each. For a basic system that just has four terminals on each side, this will let you get away with spending under $80 on hardware plus the cost of the cable—say, less than $200 for a 34-footer. If you had a rigger replace the cables using machine-swage fittings—which cost about the same to buy—he'd charge you up to $8-to-10 per swage.

Since I took this opportunity to seriously upgrade the system and couldn't reuse any of the old fittings, the cost of upgrading *Ostara*'s lifelines was much higher. Here's what I used. All fittings were top-of-the-line from Johnson Marine.

Prices quoted are full retail—you would be able to shave a few bucks off each fitting by shopping around and by choosing less-expensive pelican hooks and adjusters. If I had not opted to install gates and new stanchions, the cost of this project would have been well under $300. As well as increasing deck safety, the new lifelines and shiny new stanchions have really improved the appearance of the boat.

6 over-center gate or Pelican hooks	$289
4 interlocking gate eyes	$145
4 eye-to-eye fittings	$101
6 short adjusters	$150
Tools	$55
Cable	$130
Stanchions and braces	$340
TOTAL	**$1,210**

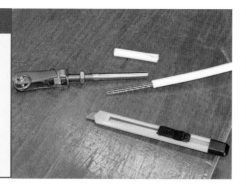

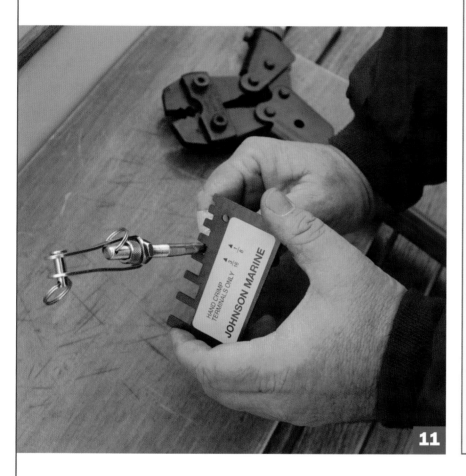

11

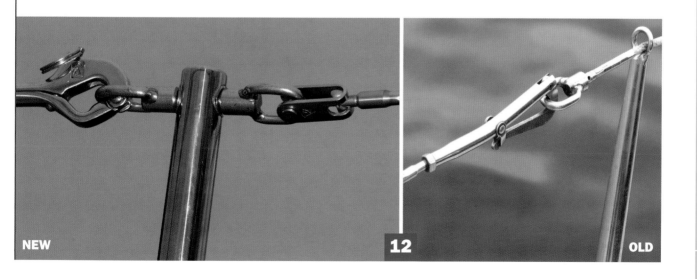

NEW

12

OLD

BEFORE The old hatch looks the worse for wear and was overdue for replacement.

AFTER

The new hatch not only looks cool but allows much needed light and air belowdecks.

Installing a Forehatch

Although I built my boat carefully, one thing that wasn't a success was the hatch over the head. It looked great, all varnished mahogany and brass hardware, and fit perfectly aboard my classic gaff cutter, but it leaked. The slow dripping made itself felt belowdecks. After putting up with the situation for seven years, I finally decided it was high time to install a better hatch.

I had several options. I could make a new wooden hatch, but there was no reason to believe it wouldn't leak like the old one. Moreover, the flat hatch always suffered in the sun, and I had to revarnish frequently to keep up its appearance. In the end I opted to put in a stainless-steel hatch with a Plexiglas panel to let in light and large neoprene gaskets to keep water out. I wanted a hatch that would not stick out like the proverbial sore thumb on *Mallard*'s deck, so bright polished stainless wouldn't work. Mariner's Hardware made a custom hatch for me and powder-coated the metal parts in a tasteful off-white paint that was better-suited to my boat's appearance.

In truth, choosing the new hatch took almost as much time as installing it. Here's how the installation went.

⏱ **Approx. job time: 5 hours**

📖 **Skill level: Moderate/easy**

✂ **Tools you will need**

- Japanese saw
- Chisel
- Square
- Tape measure
- Jigsaw or band saw
- Plane
- Sander

Materials

- Epoxy
- Teak
- Sealant
- Stainless-steel screws
- Sandpaper

1. After measuring the original hatch so I could order a replacement, I removed it carefully to avoid damaging the surrounding deck. Unscrewing the hatch cover was the first step.

2. I needed a variety of tools to separate the old wood frame from the deck. I used a flexible Japanese saw to remove most of the wood and a sharp chisel on the rest.

3. After removing the majority of the wood, I trimmed the deck back to its original profile with a small plane and an electric sander.

4. The new hatch could not be simply bolted to the deck; a subframe was needed to allow for the deck camber. I made it from teak to match the rest of the woodwork. After rough-cutting the teak, I placed it on the deck and wedged it level. Then I used a set of compasses to mark the scribe to the deck curvature.

RESOURCES

Mariner's Hardware
www.marinershardware.com
877-765-0880

3M
www.3m.com
888-364-3577

Interlux (epoxy)
www.yachtpaint.com
800-468-7589

Installing a Forehatch

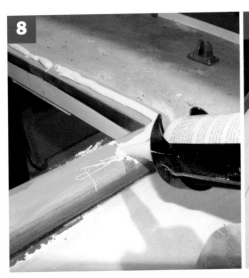

5. I joined the corners with miters cut on a chop saw, but I could have cut them by hand using a tenon saw and a miter box. I then cut the frame to fit the deck camber.

6. When I was sure everything fit properly, I glued the teak to the deck with thickened epoxy and let it cure overnight. Clamps prevented it from moving.

7. After removing the clamps and cleaning up the wood with sandpaper, I set the new hatch in place to check that all was well. I also predrilled the mounting holes.

8. To ensure that the hatch would be watertight, I laid down a good bead of sealant before bedding in the frame and inserting the screws. I cleaned off the excess sealant before it cured.

9. Unlike the original, the new hatch has no leaks and allows a good deal of light into the previously dark head compartment.

TOP TIP

Teak is expensive, so it may pay to do a trial run and make the trim pieces from cheap softwood first. If these are a good fit, use them as patterns for the more expensive hardwood.

MORE IMPROVEMENT PROJECTS

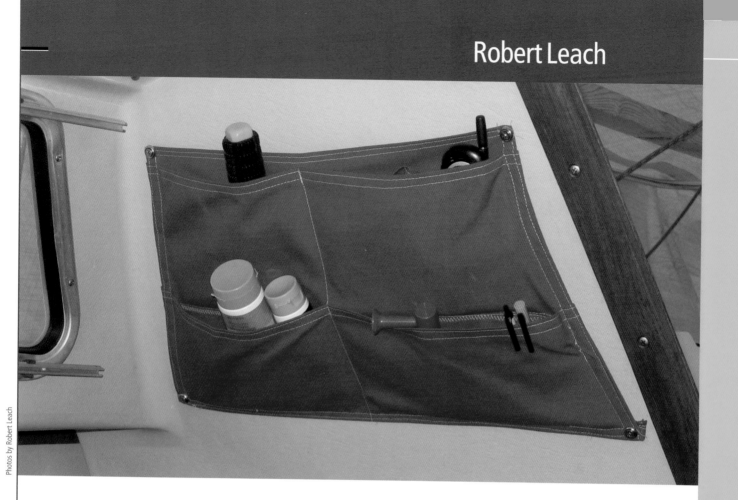

Making Stowage Pockets

Two things prompted me to make a cabin-wall organizer for my Catalina 22, *Time Out*. The first is that my boat, like most, is short of stowage. The second is that our youngest child, whom we affectionately call Dr. Destructo, likes to tear the cabin apart on a regular basis. To date, he has attacked the boat with paint thinner, bug spray, wheel-bearing grease, deodorant, and other things I can't mention here, for fear of provoking the wrath of the Child Protective Services. Don't get me started on the things he has thrown overboard. For his safety and ours, we decided we needed to be able to stow things out of his reach. The companionway bulkhead of our cabin was a perfect place to mount some storage pockets that would keep knick-knacks away from our child. Its location just inside the cabin makes it a great place for keys, the air horn, flares, the cell phone, and so on.

Cheap & cheerful

For this project I used some red Sunbrella fabric left over from making a mainsail cover (about 1 square yard). It is heavy acrylic canvas, easy to sew and extremely durable. Many people sell Sunbrella remnants on eBay, and if you're as cheap as I am and not too picky about the color, this is a great place to buy it. If you're color blind, you might want to consult the "other" boat-owner in your household to see if she thinks the organizer will complement the settee. After conferring with my fashion consultant, I fired up my mom's old sewing machine with some V69 UV-protected thread and #16 needles and got to work.

First I nabbed some black construction paper from my kids and used it to create a template for my organizer. This is about the most creative step in the process. Imagine how you would like the

---

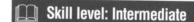

⏱ **Approx. job time: 6 hours**

📖 **Skill level: Intermediate**

✂ **Tools you will need**

- home sewing machine that can straight- and zigzag stitch
- V69 UV thread
- #16 needles for your machine
- marine canvas fabric
- sharp scissors
- construction paper and tape
- office stapler
- mounting hardware

organizer to look in your boat. Cut and tape the construction paper together to create an exact pattern. Remember that some items, like binoculars or a VHF handheld, need headroom to get in and out of their pockets. Gather together all the items you think you will store—suntan lotion, radio, sunglasses, keys, playing cards, hand-bearing compass, and so on—and design pockets for them.

Measure twice, cut once

Spread out the fabric on the floor or a large table. Place the template on top and lightly trace the outline on the fabric with a pencil. Since the template is the finished size of the organizer, you need to add a seam allowance of 1″ around the perimeter, so draw a second set of lines 1″ from the first lines.

So far so good. Now lay out fabric for the pockets. If your organizer is, say, about 10″ high, you can have two rows of pockets, each 5″ high. On a separate section of fabric measure out two strips for the pockets. Add ¾″ for the top and bottom seams; the strips need to be cut 6¾″. Cut them about 6″ longer than the width of the organizer and trim them to fit later.

Sunbrella will fray, so set your sewing machine for zigzag stitching and sew all the edges. Then use a warm iron (not hot) to press the perimeter edge of all the pieces on the seam line. This makes it much easier to sew. Now switch your machine to the single-stitch setting and sew the top seam of the organizer and the top seam of each of the strips for the pockets.

Stitch that

Next place the top pocket over the back fabric precisely where you want it. Make sure the fabric is centered, with the extra cloth hanging over. Use an office stapler, seam tape, or pins to secure the pocket in place. Run a row of stitching along the bottom, and then repeat the step with the bottom pocket. You are sewing just the bottom of the pocket, leaving the top open, of course.

It's simplest to make four equal pockets. Make a light vertical pencil mark on the center of the organizer and then single-stitch it.

Sewing the remaining sides is probably the trickiest part of the project. If you sewed the sides even with the back, you wouldn't have room in the pockets to store stuff like your wallet. So, to create volume in the pockets, you must pull the pocket strip out from the back. In essence, the top of the pocket must be longer than the bottom. (For my or-

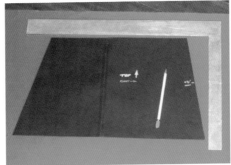

Above left: A big builder's square and a smooth flat surface make laying out the organizer easier.
Right: Iron the seams with a warm—not hot—iron.

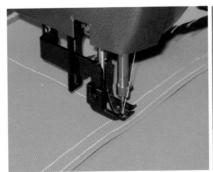

Above left: Use UV-protected thread and #16 needles when sewing Sunbrella.
Right: Trim the edges after sewing to keep fraying to a minimum.

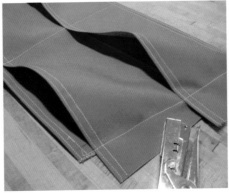

Above left: The pockets are wider at the top than at the bottom to enable easy access.
Right: Zigzag stitching on the edges prevents fraying.

ganizer, it was about 2″ longer.) Use your stapler to pucker the top of each pocket and hold the corner. Then single-stitch the side of each pocket to the back to secure it.

Once that is done, carefully trim the excess fabric to match the back. You can also zigzag stitch the cut edges to prevent fraying.

To complete the project, simply fold over the sides and bottom of the organizer to create a neat hem. I secured my organizer to the rear cabin wall with #10 stainless-steel screws and finish washers.

Lisa Suhay

Installing Lifeline Netting

Klas Juter

Keeping kids safe aboard is priority number one. Netting the lifelines on your boat is a good first step.

lifeline netting is a smart addition to your boat if you have small children, pets, or even a flaked jib to worry about. While the actual installation of the netting is simple, making it safe and presentable can be fairly tricky. Here's a step-by-step guide to netting installation, from conception to completion, for practically any sailboat.

The biggest question raised by most sailors about safety netting isn't price or difficulty of installation, but its effect on boathandling. If your boat is a relatively new design with all lines and sails running inside the lifeline area, the netting won't be a problem. Older and narrower boats, however, tend to have running rigging led outside the lifelines. This complicates things a little, but we found a way to lead our running rigging under the netting.

Materials

Standard lifeline netting is usually sold in 24″ widths, which is perfect for most installations. To figure out how much netting you'll need for your boat, multiply the length of rail you want to cover by 1.33. This formula was suggested by the sales staff at a local chandlery and worked very well aboard our Columbia 38, *Afrita*. The additional netting is required because of vertical stretch, which decreases the overall length of the netting as it's installed.

When you're shopping for netting, ask the dealer if the net's diamonds are individually knotted. If they aren't, don't buy it. Pressure on an unknotted net, whether from a falling toddler or the movement of a heavy sail, could part it unexpectedly.

Planning

You'll need to decide how much of the deck area should be netted. Running lifeline netting from the bow to the stern makes especially good sense if you have toddlers and/or pets on board. Don't cut corners by skimping on the netting length when you place the order.

Once you've purchased the netting, decide which method of installation suits you and your boat. The top of the net can be run in one of two ways. One is to weave the wire lifeline in and out of the top "diamonds" of the lifeline net. Unhook the lifeline, remove it from the stanchions, and weave it back through the netting and stanchions.

The other involves lashing the netting to the lifeline with a single length of ⅛″ nylon braid, a method I recommend (Fig. 1). When my husband, Robert, and I

netted our boat, we found it difficult to gauge exactly how taut the netting should be—in other words, how many diamonds to leave between stanchions. The second way is more forgiving and allowed us to leave our lifelines in place during installation (Fig. 2).

The most versatile way to secure the foot of the netting is to weave a length of ¼″ three-strand nylon through the diamonds at the foot of the netting and to use a clove hitch at each stanchion to secure the line and maintain tension (Fig. 3).

Installation

While one person can complete this project, we found that two is better. We worked aft to fore; I wove the top line

through the netting and around the lifeline; Robert wove the bottom line through the foot of the netting and tied the clove hitches. We were careful not to stretch the netting too much or place too much initial strain on it. Be sure to avoid overstretching. If you see a pronounced bow develop along the foot of the netting as tension is applied to the bottom nylon line, the netting has been stretched too tight between the stanchions. We stopped at each stanchion and inspected the shape of the nylon diamonds. If they appear to run evenly from top to bottom, the tension is correct; slanted diamonds mean that one end of the netting is too tight, so start again and leave more slack. We first tried securing the top of the netting from stern to bow and then weaving the bottom. However, this made it too difficult to regulate the tension on the top and bottom of netting, and we couldn't get it to hang correctly.

At the last stanchions, usually located at the bow and stern, secure the net by lashing it with nylon cord wrapped along the length of the stanchion, candy cane–style, through the end diamonds (Fig. 4).

Once you've finished stringing the netting, you must secure the foot so it won't ride up between the stanchions and create a gap above the toerail. If your boat has a slotted toerail, weave a nylon line through the foot of the netting, and tie it to the rail at the slots. For solid rails (like ours), you'll need to in-

Little crewmembers still need supervision in their "floating playpen."

Peter Nielsen

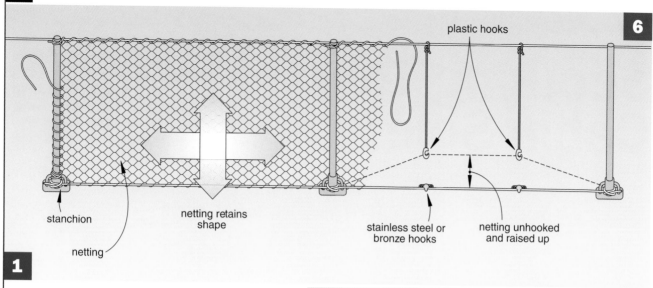

6

plastic hooks

stanchion

netting

netting retains
shape

stainless steel or
bronze hooks

netting unhooked
and raised up

1

1. When installing the netting, do not stretch it too far out of its original shape horizontally or vertically.

2. Secure the top of the netting with ⅛" nylon line threaded through the netting and wrapped around the lifeline. Secure the nylon line at the top of each stanchion with a clove hitch.

3. Secure the bottom of the netting using ¼" three-strand nylon line threaded through the netting. Secure the nylon line at the bottom of each stanchion with a clove hitch.

4. At the end of the stanchions, thread ⅛" line through the netting and around the stanchion. Secure the end with a clove hitch.

5. Install stainless-steel or bronze hooks, spaced every 2', to hold down the ¼" line and netting along the deck.

6. Tie plastic hooks on a short line to the top lifeline between the stanchions. If clearance is needed to run sheets or dock lines, you can unhook the netting at the deck and raise it up on the hooks.

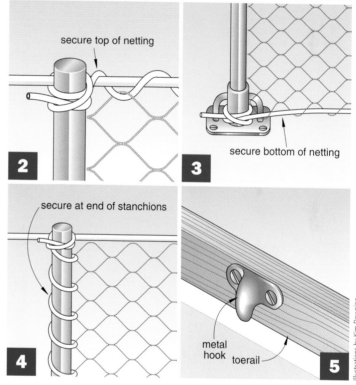

secure top of netting

2

3

secure bottom of netting

secure at end of stanchions

4

metal
hook   toerail

5

stall small stainless-steel hooks on the inside of the rail between stanchions to anchor the netting's foot. We placed the hooks about every 2' along our rail with good results (Fig. 5). Some dealers recommend drilling through a solid toerail to receive the lacing, but we couldn't bring ourselves to drill holes in the mahogany toerail that we had cut and installed ourselves. If you use hooks, make sure they're corrosion-resistant and beefy enough to withstand stresses on the netting.

Hooks are versatile on older boat designs, because the foot of the netting can be unhooked and pulled up between stanchions to run outboard genoa or

spinnaker sheets. To make this easier we tied two short lines with hooks installed on the ends (sail ties are an option) to the top lifeline between stanchions (Fig. 6). When we want to hold the netting above the toerail to run a sheet, we remove the foot of the netting from the hooks along the rail and rehook it to the hanging lines.

You also need to consider how to create a break in the netting so you can get on and off the boat. We found it's best to break the net at the clasp(s) in the lifelines. You can weave a temporary line to secure the gap while the boat is under way and remove it in port to assure that the netting isn't in the way

when you unclip the lifeline to disembark or load supplies.

Keep in mind that the sun can break down even the best netting in two years or less. It pays to check the condition of the netting and the lines that secure it every six months and then replace any parts that have deteriorated.

While your newly netted craft may bear a striking resemblance to a floating playpen, topside is still a dangerous place for little crewmembers. As with any other safety device, netting is obviously not a replacement for supervision where children and pets are concerned. Children should always wear life jackets and safety harnesses.

Installing Lifeline Netting

Securing Your Cabin Sole

⏱ **Approx. job time: 3 hours**

📖 **Skill level: Easy/moderate**

✂ **Tools you will need**

- **10-mm and 13-mm drill bits (included in the starter kit)**
- **Large countersink**
- **Pencils**
- **Tape measure**
- **Electric drill**
- **Wrench**
- **Screwdriver**

Materials

- **Floor Anchors**
- **Q-tips**
- **5-minute epoxy**
- **Masking tape**
- **Thin hatch tape**

Ever since I built my boat, the floorboards in the saloon have squeaked. The sole was one of my last projects, and I was anxious at the time to get the boat afloat. Then, at a boat show, I talked with a reader who had the same problem. That inspired me to finally sort out the squeaks.

Floorboards in boats pose something of a conundrum. On the one hand, you want to be able to get them up in a hurry if there's a leak; on the other hand, you want the boards secure when the boat is sailing. Screwing them down certainly holds them in place, but it precludes any rapid access into the bilge. Then I came across PYI's Floor Anchors. They secure the boards underfoot, but with only a half-turn of a screw they can be released.

Fred Hutchinson from PYI suggested that I make a trial run to get the hang of how the Floor Anchors work. The step-by-step photos show how this went before I tackled the larger task of securing the floorboards in my boat.

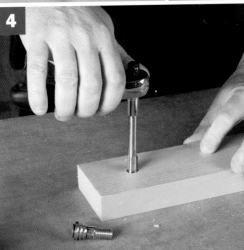

1. The Floor Anchor starter pack contains four anchors, a couple of drill bits, a tap, and a countersink (tapercutter), which you need to make a neat job of the project. Once you have these tools in hand, you can buy additional anchors as you need them.

2. Mark out the center of the spot where you want the finished Floor Anchor to sit. Don't put it too close to the edge of the sole panel, and make sure it is no closer than about 1/2" from the edge of the underlying support structure. I am using a piece of soft plywood here for my trial run.

3. With the floor panel held or clamped firmly onto the support, drill through the panel until you reach the predetermined depth you have marked on the drill bit with masking tape. Ensure that the drill is perpendicular to the panel. The required depth is given in the instructions and varies depending on panel thickness.

4. Remove the floor panel and set it aside; then tap the hole in the floor timber or support. I did not have a tap wrench of the correct size, so I used a small socket and a ratchet handle.

5. The next step is to open out the holes in the floor panel with the 13-mm drill. I used a drill press, which kept the hole absolutely plumb. A handheld drill works fine, but make sure to keep the drill upright.

6. Using a countersink ensures that the anchor sits flush with the top surface of the floor panel. You will need to apply a fair amount of pressure, as this cuts with a reaming action. You can't drill too far, though, because the collar keeps the bit from going any deeper than is necessary.

7. Apply thin hatch tape as required to the underlying surface of the floor panel. It provides cushioning and silences any creaks and groans.

8. After blowing out any dust from the tapped hole, smear in a little epoxy with the end of a Q-tip or other small stick. Don't use too much; this is simply to make sure that the bottom half of the anchor stays put. If you use too much epoxy, it could squeeze out and glue the floor panel in place. I used a 5-minute epoxy to speed things up; if you use regular epoxy, let it cure overnight.

9. Spread a little epoxy on the countersunk ridges on the top anchor section.

10. While the epoxy is still wet, use a large screwdriver to thread the complete anchor through the top panel and screw it into the tapped hole beneath.

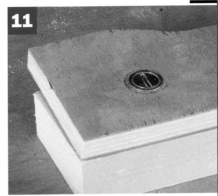

11. Screw the anchor down until the countersink is flush with the surface of the floor panel, as shown. Wipe up any epoxy that squeezes out, and allow it to cure. The job is now complete.

12. You can now release the panel with a half-turn of the screw. You can see here how the Floor Anchor works: a bayonet-type connector engages into the permanently fitted female receptacle.

13. With the trial run a complete success, I installed Floor Anchors in the main section of my saloon floor. No more creaks and moans from this floor.

RESOURCES

PYI Inc.
www.pyiinc.com
800-523-7558
$90 for the starter kit shown

TOP TIP

When you tape the drill bit to mark hole depth, leave a tag of tape sticking out from the side like a small flag (see photos below). This will whirl around, sweeping away the sawdust when it reaches the correct depth.

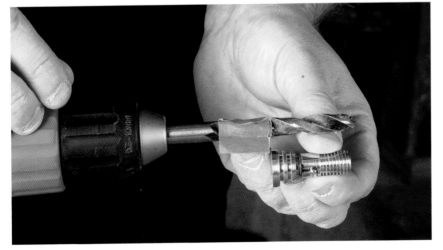

Contributors

John Arrufat sails a trailer sailer in the Pacific Northwest on which he has carried out numerous improvements over the years including fitting a flexible fuel tank.

Don Casey is the author of several books on upgrading old boats. He is now on an extended cruise of the Caribbean aboard his Allied Seawind 30.

Dave Baldwin is an associate editor at *BoatWorks* and *SAIL*. When not evaluating and reviewing new gear for the magazine, Dave can be found sailing on the Charles River.

Mark Corke is a *SAIL* senior editor who sails the Maine shore aboard his homebuilt gaffer.

Bluewater cruiser **Aussie Bray** circumnavigated the world aboard his homebuilt 44-foot cutter, *Starship*.

Charles J. Doane is *SAIL*'s editor-at-large. When not cruising in his Golden Hind, *Sophie*, Doane can often be seen hiding in boatyards with a list of jobs yet to be completed.

Nigel Calder is a *SAIL* contributing editor and has written numerous technical articles and books.

Paul Esterle currently repairs and restores sailboats from his base on Chesapeake Bay. When not working on a boat, he writes how-to articles and gives seminars on boat-repair topics.

Peter Caplen, a marine engineer, has renovated and run various wood and fiberglass vessels. His boat of the past 18 years is *Pershilla*, a 40-foot steel cruiser that he and his father built from a set of steel plates.

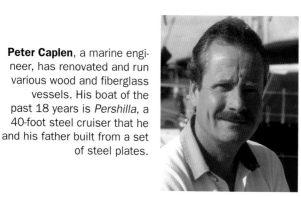

Jim Haynie teaches electronics; he has written a high-school electronics textbook as well as an electrical service manual for technicians. He sails his Hunter Legend, *Serene Zelda*, on Chesapeake Bay.

Ted Hugger sails his Pearson 323, *Chantilly*, out of Portland, Maine, where he also bases his marine-industry marketing business.

Clarence Jones is a writer and news media consultant who has owned trailerable sailboats for 30 years. His current boat is a Precision 21, which he and his wife sail from their home on Anna Maria Island at the mouth of Tampa Bay.

Quentin Kinderman has owned a variety of boats and is now refitting his Pearson 424 for family cruising.

Robert Leach is pastor of Ogden Dunes Community Church in Indiana. He and his family love to sail Lake Michigan and local inland lakes on their Catalina 22, *Time Out*.

Charles Mason is a lifelong sailor who has cruised the entire New England coast, sailed transatlantic, and transited the Intracoastal Waterway. He is the executive editor of *SAIL*.

Sailor and cruiser **Warren Miller** is an electrical systems technical adviser for West Marine.

Peter Nielsen is *SAIL*'s editor. He's constantly working on *Ostara*, a 1973 Norlin 34, which he and his family sail out of Marblehead, Massachusetts.

James D. Phyfe lives aboard his Contessa 35 in Padanaram, Massachusetts, and works as a mate on commercial tugboats.

When not looking after one or other of her boats, **Virginia Schultz** enjoys single-handed sailing and traveling to foreign destinations.

Bill Springer loves tinkering with his Cape Dory Typhoon and is a senior editor of *SAIL*.

Lisa Suhay lived aboard a 37-foot Columbia yawl, *Afrita*, with her husband and sons and later aboard the Jim Brown–designed trimaran *Gypsy Wind* for 5 years. She and her husband just bought a Bristol 26, which they are netting for 18-month-old Quinten.

Louk Marinus Wijsen is a re-tired attorney and former merchant marine officer. He sails his Bruce Bingham–designed Fantasia 35, *Noordzee*, in the San Francisco Bay area.